DAVID LAMB

THE
ARABS

David Lamb has reported for the *Los Angeles Times* from more than a hundred countries on all seven continents. An eight-time Pulitzer Prize nominee, he is the author of six books and has been a Nieman Fellow at Harvard, an Alicia Patterson Fellow, a writer-in-residence at the University of Southern California's school of journalism and a Pew Fellow. At present he works out of the *Times*'s Washington, D.C., bureau.

THE
ARABS

THE ARABS

JOURNEYS
BEYOND
THE
MIRAGE

DAVID LAMB

VINTAGE BOOKS

A DIVISION OF RANDOM HOUSE, INC.

NEW YORK

Second Vintage Books Edition, March 2002

Copyright © 1987, 2002 by David Lamb
Map copyright © 1987 by Anita Karl and Jim Kemp

All rights reserved under International and
Pan-American Copyright Conventions. Published in
the United States by Random House, Inc., New York,
and simultaneously in Canada by Random House of
Canada Limited, Toronto. Originally published in
hardcover by Random House, Inc., in 1987 and in
paperback by Vintage Books, a division of
Random House, Inc., in 1988, both in different form.

Grateful acknowledgment is made to Lowery Music
Co., Inc. for permission to reprint excerpts from the
lyrics to "Ahab the Arab," written by Ray Stevens.
Copyright © 1962 by Lowery Music Co., Inc., Atlanta Ga.
International Copyright secured.
All rights reserved. Used by permission.

Library of Congress Cataloging-in-Publication Data
Lamb, David.
The Arabs: journeys beyond the mirage.
Bibliography:
Includes index.
1. Arab countries.   I. Title.
DS36.7.L35   1987b   909'.0974927   87-45914
ISBN 1-4000-3041-2 (pbk.)

Author photo © Sandy Northrop

Manufactured in the United States of America
10 9 8 7 6

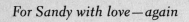

For Sandy with love—again

CONTENTS

MY INTRODUCTION to the Arab world came in Washington, D.C. I had only recently returned to the United States after four years in sub-Sahara Africa and thought I was going to stay put for a while. Not having to catch midnight flights to cover coups d'état in sad little countries was a pleasant respite in a journalist's life. Being an American among Americans offered a nice comfort level. My restless feet stopped itching. Briefly. Then, about the time I started planning imaginary itineraries and reminiscing a bit too often with friends about past travels to distant cubbyholes of the world—a sure sign the wanderlust was getting the best of me again—the *Los Angeles Times* needed a correspondent in Cairo and my editors asked if I wanted to pack up and cover the Middle East. I knew little about the Arab world, having been there only twice as a tourist, and even less about Islam. I accepted the offer on the spot.

There was a subculture of analysts in Washington who had built their careers around the Middle East, and I started making the rounds. My crash course took me to the shabby office the Palestinians had set up. I made an appointment to see the head of the delegation the next Tuesday. I showed up at the appointed hour but he did not, and his assistant dodged the one question I put to him: "With so much money in the Arab world, why are so many Palestinians still living in refugee camps?" He promised to reschedule the meeting with his boss, but my subsequent phone calls went unanswered. I drove across town to the new Israeli embassy, where the ambassador, military attaché and political counselor spent three hours briefing me and only let me go when I ran out of questions. Public relations, I was to learn, was a concept the Israelis understood and the Arabs didn't, and during my tour in the Middle East I was constantly struck by the Arabs' inability to present to the world a favorable or accurate image of either themselves or their causes. As the sultan of Oman would tell me, "In many ways we are our own worst enemy."

At each luncheon and interview, talking to Arabs and Americans, I always asked, "If I want to understand the Arabs, not just their politics, where do I go—the universities, the coffeehouses, the refugee camps, the government offices?" The question seemed to take everyone by surprise, and I never did get a satisfactory answer. For them, as for most Americans, the Middle East is an area of high-stakes diplomacy, a breeding ground of terrorism, a place of conflict between Arab and Jew. Undeniably, it is all those things, but what of the people, the 243 million Arabs whose homeland stretches from the sands of Arabia on the east to the Atlantic shores of Morocco on the west? Who are they?

This is the question I set out to answer in this book. Although I deal in considerable detail with the history and issues of the Middle East, *The Arabs* is intended to be neither a concise history nor a political analysis. Rather it is a book of images, of sights and sounds and moods, of people both royal and common—a montage that will, I hope, present a fair portrait of the Arab world and strip away some of the stereotypes that have led to so many misconceptions about its people, its religion, its great wealth.

It may be useful at the outset to say what I am *not*. I am not an Arabist, a political scientist or a religious scholar. I am a journalist. The grist of my craft is instant history, the medley of past and present that, at its best, brings insights into what was and what will be. The foreign correspondents whose work I have most admired over the years seem to share three qualities: an intellectual curiosity, a sense of humor and a concern for the people into whose lives they delve. I hope these attributes do not desert me as I sit here in Virginia, my computer filling the long moments of inaction with a demanding hum, and sift through the kernels of myth and fact from my encounters with the Arab world.

Those unfamiliar with the Middle East may be surprised to know that the majority of Arabs are poor, not rich; that Arabs as a group are capitalistic and politically moderate; that Islam—when not perverted by misanthropes who carry out murder and mayhem in the name of God—is a tolerant, compassionate religion, not a radical one; that rather than being gunmen and refugees, most Palestinians are educated, middle-class, economically successful; that Israel, the only democracy in the Middle East and the fulcrum of Washington's regional policies, shares with the Arabs the blame for creating turmoil and making peace impossible.

During my four years in Cairo, and in subsequent trips to the Middle East, my travels took me just about everywhere: from the Sinai peninsula, where I covered the Israeli withdrawal, to Lebanon for the Israeli invasion; from Beirut's Sabra and Chatilla refugee settlements, where I walked among the corpses of eight hundred Palestinian women and children, to Egypt's Valley of the Kings, where one of the world's first great civilizations was born five thousand years ago; from the space-age cities along the Persian Gulf—where poverty is unknown and free land, education and medical care are the rights of every man—to the slums of teeming Cairo, where peasants pay hundreds of dollars for the privilege of establishing residency in a tomb; from the start of a new day as the sun reached across the deserts of the Western Sahara to the long, dark nights of the Persian Gulf War.

Coming to grips with the Middle East was not easy. The Arab world is full of contradictions that seem to defy a Westerner's logic. It is a separate entity in the global community of nations, and simple categorization is difficult. What was I to make of the Saudi prince who took over the top three floors of the Hyatt Regency in Morocco for three months and walked the streets of Casablanca handing out free plane tickets to Mecca? How could I make sense of the Arab regimes that condemned the September 11, 2001, terrorist attacks on the United States, but were too timid to join the international campaign to wipe out Osama bin Laden's al-Qaeda network? Was I to believe Colonel Moammar Kadafi's insistence that the sacking of the American embassy in Tripoli was a spontaneous mob protest executed without government planning—especially when the Tripoli Fire Department got its signals crossed and showed up precisely twenty-four hours early to put out the flames that had not yet started? At every turn, the game rules were different. In the Arab world it is understood that hospitality is given freely to friend and foe alike, that the blessings of family and religion are to be cherished above all else, except possibly money, that what is said is not necessarily what is meant at all because, in the richness and imagery of the Arabic language, style counts more than substance.

On a flight from Cairo to the Persian Gulf I once shared generous quantities of whiskey with a young Arab businessman attired in a Western suit. When I met him for dinner the next evening in Bahrain, he wore a flowing robe and lectured me politely about the evils of alcohol. "At home I do things differently," he said. In Beirut I was denounced by Yasser Arafat's longtime spokesman for writing, in a relatively flattering profile of Arafat, that the Palestine Liberation Organization chairman looked like someone in need of a bath and a shave. "You have demeaned your profession with yellow journalism," said Mahmoud Labadi, a dark and brooding man I had talked to many times without ever understanding what he *really* felt or thought about anything. A year went by before I heard of Labadi again. By then he was the spokesman for Syrian-backed rebels who considered Arafat a traitor and were blasting his headquarters in Tripoli, Lebanon, with artillery. And from a thousand mosques, I have heard the call to prayer—not soft and pleading, as I would expect from a house of worship, but harsh and demanding—roll out into the desert darkness, and wondered what black void is filled by any organized religion that commands such unquestioned obedience.

But it is the contradictions and inexplicable mystery of the place that makes the Arab world so fascinating; few Westerners have ever visited it without initially being perplexed by the uniqueness of its character, and in the end, overwhelmed. Lowell Thomas went there in 1917 to travel with T. E. Lawrence—the uncrowned prince of Arabia—and wrote: "Arabia is indeed a topsy-turvy land. Where we measure most of our liquids and weigh most of our solids, they weigh their liquids and measure their solids. Where we use knives and forks and spoons, they use their hands. Where we use tables and chairs, they recline on the floor. Where we mount from the left, they mount their camels and horses from the right. We read left to right, while they read from right to left. The desert-dweller keeps his head covered in the summer and winter alike, and his feet usually unprotected. Where we take off our hats in entering a friend's house, they take off their shoes."

Unfortunately, the West, including many policy-makers in Washington, is as befuddled by Arab ways as Thomas was. We understand little about the Arabs and almost nothing about Islam, and our ignorance has put the West on a collision course with the Arab psyche, as though terrorists were born instead of made, thus conveniently ignoring Arab grievances rooted in a century of being deceived and humiliated by Western powers. We view Arabs as a threat and dismiss them as violent by nature without asking why, if that is so, Arab societies are among the most crime-free on earth. We feel shaken by the Islamic revival roiling Asia without realizing that it is a protest movement, against the failure of the people's own leaders and societies, against those who promised so much and delivered so little in the exhilarating Nasser era of the 1950s and 1960s, against those who followed Nasser and denied their people democracy and an outlet to vent their grievances.

If there is a discernible trend in the Middle East, it is toward sectarianism, often accompanied by religious extremism, for in the absence of democracy, the mosque becomes the sanctuary where ideas can be exchanged and the pressures of life reduced to manageable levels. The fundamentalism breeding there gives voice to the dissatisfied. The Arabs are a tradition-minded people, and much of their dissatisfaction stems from pressures that seem dumbfounding—the pressures of change wrought by a 1,500 percent increase in the price of oil in a decade's time, then the sudden collapse of the oil market, by the dashed promises of a political illusion called Arab unity, by the realization that Islamic extremism is a greater threat to moderate Arab regimes than to the West itself and thus has replaced Israel as the prime enemy for many governments.

Nothing has gone quite as the Arabs had hoped. Oil money did not bring political power. Confrontation with Israel brought neither peace nor victory. A crotchety old man in Iran (a non-Arab country) named Khomeini did not bring serenity or beauty to the dream of an Islamic republic. Time and again, the Arabs rejected what was offered at the negotiating table, fought losing wars, then decided to accept yesterday's peace plan. By then it was too late. So, always a step behind the times, not truly a member of the Third World or the First World, mistrustful of the West and modernity, the Arabs have withdrawn deeper into what does not threaten: family and religion. In doing so, they have become politically alienated from both their own rulers and the outside world.

The Arabs was published by Random House in 1987 after I returned to the United States from Cairo. Great changes, some of them unimaginable when I wrote the book, have swept the Middle East since then: Iran and Iraq accepted a U.N. resolution and fell into an uneasy peace; the Soviet Union collapsed and the Cold War died; North and South Yemen merged into a single country, which fought a civil war; Israel and the Palestinians signed the Oslo Accords, but despite some promising moments, neither the hatred nor the bloodshed between the two "cousins" of the Middle East ended; Iraq invaded Kuwait and the United States led an international coalition of Western and Arab countries that drove Iraq out of Kuwait in a ground war lasting one hundred hours.

So many changes, yet so little is changed. The Palestinian "problem" continues as the main irritant in the Middle East, influencing the growth of terrorism, Arab perceptions of the United States and the hope of stability. The Israelis can't bring themselves to surrender land they took from others, and the Palestinians can't figure out how to make their voices heard except through violence. Arab governments remain fragile, Arab leadership weak. In rereading *The Arabs*, I was sometimes relieved, sometimes saddened, to discover how much is as it was. The themes and the issues—and often conclusions one can draw—are virtually unchanged over the passage of fifteen years' time.

I have updated facts, statistics and events in the pages that follow. But I have left many sections as they were originally written, because even if names have changed, the themes and most of the points I hoped to make remain valid. For instance, two heads of state I wrote about in detail—King Hassan II of Morocco and President Hafez al-Assad of Syria—have died, but they are still discussed here. Power merely passed to their sons, and at this point I think it is more instructive to consider the long political careers of the fathers rather than the brief ones of the sons. What I look for now is what I looked for then: the history, culture and character that makes sense of the Arabs. I searched for the common denominators, the threads that wove a larger pattern and the parts that spoke for the whole. The intended goal is to make *The Arabs* a current book, not a historical one.

It is not my intent to be an advocate of or an apologist for the Arabs. Nor have I set out to build a case for either Israel or the Arab nations. Both are so certain of the righteousness of their cause, so sure that they are God's chosen children, that that task is best left for God, or others. Let this be a personal encounter with an alien culture, sketches of the Arab people and the forces that shape their lives—Islam, war and peace, poverty and wealth. It is the story of a volatile, unpredictable region where the sound of laughter is too seldom heard, where leaders are survivors, not innovators, where one meets countless sophisticated and gracious people who are not at all like the Arabs so often portrayed in Western stereotypes.

To a large extent the Arabs are misjudged in the West—and caricatured in the media in a manner once reserved for blacks and other minorities—for the simple reason that they *are* different. Their language, dress, prayers, behavior and thoughts don't fit into any neat package easily grasped by Westerners. Yet in hardly more than three decades, moving from illiteracy to video in a single step, they have become an important new global force, if not power. Today their children are enrolled in the best universities of Europe and North America. Arabs by the tens of thousands have become productive and loyal citizens of European and American countries. Arab money is invested in Western institutions, foundations and industries. Arab policies are felt everywhere from London to Washington. Arab human and natural resources have only recently begun to be fully tapped. One oil boom has come and gone; another almost certainly awaits us down the road.

While many Third World people languish in despair and poverty, the Arabs view their future with hope. Time, they believe, is on their side. Though many obstacles could derail their dreams of achieving economic and political power, of finding social justice at home and respect abroad, there is one thing of which I am certain: We need to get to know each other better, because in the end, the destiny of the Arabs will affect the destiny of us all.

THE
ARABS

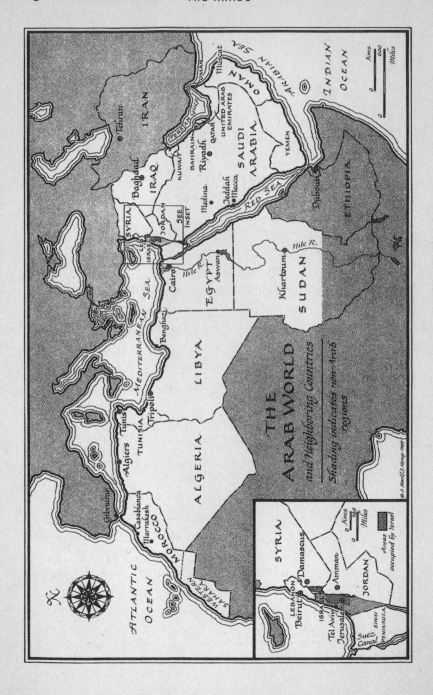

THE ARAB WORLD
and neighboring Countries

Shading indicates non-Arab regions

Areas occupied by Israel

ONE

A COLLISION OF CULTURES

GAMAL RASMI slumped into his chair and glanced about the dance floor, his fingers tapping a nervous beat on the tabletop. The Playboy Disco was nearly full, but he recognized not a soul. "I used to know everyone here, absolutely everyone," he said with a sigh, signaling the waiter for a German beer. The waiter didn't see him and hurried by to fill another order. The music grew louder. Gamal's fingers moved faster. "This getting married in Cairo, it may be a very stupid thing I am about to do," he said. "I may never be able to dance again."

Until recently Gamal had come to the Playboy almost every evening to dance and drink a beer or two, acting out his fantasy that he was John Travolta in the movie *Saturday Night Fever*. Then trauma entered his life: he got engaged. His fiancée, Manal, was a plump, silent woman who spent her time watching television and would not get into Gamal's car until he had plugged his portable TV into the cigarette lighter on the dashboard. Having only recently become conspicuously pious, Manal did not dance and did not condone the consumption of anything stronger than fruit juice. She also had started veiling—covering her hair and shoulders, but not her face, with a scarf—thus tacitly announcing that she had made her peace with God and would display her religion as a badge, which said, Look! This is who *I* am! This did not greatly please Gamal, but I noticed that he soon stopped drinking beer and started observing noontime prayers, bowing toward Mecca on the floor of our dining room, which we had turned into an office. "This makes me feel better inside," he said.

Gamal, who earned $175 a month as my *Los Angeles Times* Cairo bureau manager, was twenty-eight years old. He had a university degree in business, although he had never attended any classes. (College students are taught to memorize, not reason, in Egypt, and class attendance is not mandatory, so he crammed until dawn with the help of tutors before each exam period.) He had fulfilled his two-year military obligation, although I don't think he ever actually put on an army uniform—he had an influential friend in the army who had made some arrangement on his behalf. At heart Gamal was a rug merchant, always trying to cut a corner and turn a profit by swapping cars or investing in a boutique or cooking up some business deal. He was also an engaging young man totally devoid of spite or malice. He was impeccably honest and considered his job with me to be a contract of friendship. I would have trusted him with my life.

What most worried Gamal about getting married was the cost. First, he could not marry, or even spend time alone with Manal, until he had a fully furnished condominium. Then he would have to make a substantial dowry payment to his bride's parents. And finally, there was the lesson of his father, who divided his time between Egypt and Saudi Arabia as a used-car salesman and was supporting four wives, an acceptable arrangement in Islam as long as he remained financially responsible for them all. Gamal swore that he intended to have only one wife, but just to cover himself, he had written into his marriage contract that if he ever divorced Manal, he would owe her only twenty cents.·

Gamal, still wanting his beer, signaled for the waiter again. The club was dark, and the light of candles on each small table bounced off the faces of young Egyptian couples. They wore smart Western attire, and their conversations slipped easily in and out of Arabic, English and French. The disco music had reached torture levels of intensity, and Gamal could stand it no more. "Do you want to see me dance?" he asked, and without waiting for a reply, he was up and strutting across the dance floor, alone, arms pumping, head back, lost in the flashing lights and memories of his fading bachelor days. He was a man torn, like the Arab world itself, between two forces—the traditional, conservative Islamic values passed down through the centuries and the modern, liberal temptations of Western ways imported from alien cultures thousands of miles away.

The resultant clash of cultures is hardly a new phenomenon in the developing world, yet few people have found it more unsettling than the Arabs. For them, far more than for most, the future is rooted in the past—in their own unique and rich heritage, in their belief that what Mohammed the Prophet taught thirteen centuries ago is a precise guide for today's life—and when their sons would rather watch *Chicago Hope* than go to the mosque, when Nike sneakers and a greed for material things replace prayer beads and the need for spiritual fulfillment, then the very foundation of their Arabness is challenged and shaken.

"Nobody was ready for all the money that descended on us during the oil boom of the seventies," Bahrain's minister of development, Youssef Shirawi, told me one day as we sipped sweet tea in his office. "In having to choose, we accepted the manifestations of a modern, Western civilization, but refused its rulings. We accepted technology, for instance, but not science. People became confused, and they ran away to find comfort in Islam."

What the Arabs wanted to do with their petrodollars was to import Western technology without sacrificing their Eastern culture. Cars were necessary for transportation, but should not be employed for death-defying racing events. Chemistry was fine in itself, though it became evil when used to produce whiskey. As Lebanon's Sheik Abdulaziz Salameh put it: "Television is a useful invention of the industrialized West. But Westerners have turned it into the home of the devil with all those films of crime, sex and immorality. We have mimicked the West in many ways. I insist that television be used for purposes more in keeping with Islamic tradition." Western technology, however, cannot be isolated. With it come Western culture and Western financial values, and the accumulation of wealth can become a religion as powerful as Islam or Christianity. The Arabs saw their world changing, and it scared them. They responded as so many others have in times of crisis: they turned to religion, heeding the muezzins' call that, like the bells of Christianity and the horn of Judaism, summoned the multitudes to prayer with promises of hope.

> *God is most great.*
> *I testify that there is no god but God.*
> *I testify that Mohammed is the Prophet of God.*
> *Come to prayer.*
> *Come to success.*
> *God is most great.*
> *There is no god but God.*

The call to prayer offered a return to simpler, less threatening times. Those who abided strictly by the revelations Mohammed received while in a trance from the angel Gabriel would be rewarded with a "perfect" life. There would be no need to question. Every event, every turn of fortune, would be determined by God. *Inshallah* (If Allah wills it).[1] Tell an Arab friend that you will see him tomorrow or wish him a safe journey or say that you hope his

[1] *Allah* is the Arabic translation of "God." Although the words are interchangeable, I generally have used the latter in this book. Since Muslims, Jews and Christians worship the same God—and Arab Christians use the word *Allah* when they refer to the God of Christians—many Arabs believe that "God," not *Allah*, should be used in English texts for the same reason that an author would write the word "car" and not translate it as *sayyara*. To do otherwise, they say, is to convey incorrectly the impression that Allah is an alien and separate god.

business meeting goes well, and the reply is always the same—
"*Inshallah.*"

"Never," warns the Koran, "say of anything, 'I shall do that
tomorrow,' without adding, 'If God pleases.' Invoke thy Lord, if thou
hast forgotten and say, 'Perhaps my Lord will lead me to do a more
reasonable thing.'"

IN MANY ways, the Arab world today is a religious empire. It encom-
passes eighteen countries and 4.6 million square miles, an area 25
percent larger than the United States.[2] The largest country, Sudan,
is more than three times the size of Texas; the smallest, Bahrain,
would fit neatly inside the boundaries of New York City. Except for
a small, aged generation of Jews and a relative handful of Christians—religious minorities have not fared well in the Middle
East—94 percent of the people are Muslim.

Outsiders tend to think of the Arab world as a cohesive unit. Lin-
guistically, culturally and religiously, it is to a large extent. Yet in
political and human terms, this empire is fractured and diverse.
The Saudis and Moroccans, for instance, are separated at the
extreme by forty-five hundred miles and speak dialects that are
mutually incomprehensible. The Tunisians eat *couscous* (steamed
semolina with meat and vegetables); the Egyptians prefer *ful*
(cooked beans served with a variety of foods). In Iraq 58 percent of
the people are literate; in Yemen 57 percent are illiterate. A Yemeni
has a per capita income of $740 a year; a Kuwaiti, $22,700. A
Libyan lives in Africa, an Omani in Asia.

[2] Several countries in sub-Sahara Africa have large Muslim populations, and
one of them, Somalia, is a member of the Arab League. But there are only
eighteen countries that are Arabic-speaking and are members of the Arab
League: Algeria, Bahrain, Egypt, Iraq, Jordan, Kuwait, Lebanon, Libya,
Morocco, Oman, Qatar, Saudi Arabia, Sudan (which has a black non-Arabic-
speaking minority), Syria, Tunisia, the United Arab Emirates, and Yemen.

But until the mid-1960s, these were superficial differences to the Arab. He viewed the rivalries that divided the Arab nations as merely a temporary obstacle on the road to eventual Arab unity. Culture is a greater force than politics, he believed, and the strength of being Arab is in the heart. It is a sense of oneness among brethren, a bond born in the sharing of a history that goes back to the earliest days of mankind.

TWENTY THOUSAND years ago an ice cap covered much of Europe. The ice generated masses of cold air, which created a blockade that prevented rainstorms from drifting across the Atlantic. Unable to move west, the storms swung down across North Africa and the Middle East, and transformed the region into a land as green as the English countryside. It teemed with wildlife and was crisscrossed by great river systems. Olive groves covered what is now the Libyan desert, forests and grasslands stretched for hundreds of miles across the now-sandy wastelands of Egypt, through which the river Nile flows without a single tributary.

Later the ice cap melted, and the Atlantic rains moved northward again. Gradually the grasslands and forests of the Middle East turned into desert and steppe. Dry wadis reached through the Sahara and the Arabian Peninsula, and in his search for food and game, man was forced out of the highlands and into the valleys of the Nile, the Jordan River, and the Tigris and Euphrates rivers of Mesopotamia (now Iraq). In these valleys, some eight thousand years ago, Neolithic man settled and became the world's first farmers.

Some anthropologists say man himself originated in the Nile and the Tigris-Euphrates valleys. Others believe the first inhabitants of the Middle East were the black-skinned Nubians who emigrated northward up the Nile Valley and across the Red Sea. What seems most likely is that life evolved in different places at about the same time and that at some point the Arabian Peninsula—an area one third the size of Europe—became a junction of migrating populations. The nomads of the peninsula were to become known as Bedouin, a term Westerners incorrectly used for a long time as a synonym for Arab.[3] Their society was based on the clan, a group of united families in which individual rights were subordinate to those of the majority, blood ties were through the male line, and story-telling provided the only entertainment for the adults and the pri-mary source of education for the young.

For the clan—or for the collection of clans that joined to become tribes—survival was a daily challenge. One needed to be tough to endure the desert and both strong and cunning to hold off raiding parties from other clans that preyed on the weak. Unity was essen-tial, and so was the concept of strength in numbers. Conformity counted more than individuality. The desert and the men who wandered there were both feared and respected, and from the Bedouin came the roots of today's Arab hospitality: any man, friend or foe, who had the courage and strength to cross the desert and appear at another's tent was embraced as a brother for three days and given water, food, lodging. On the fourth day he was on his own. The kiss could become a sword, and the visitor might be hunted once more as the enemy.

"I shall always remember how I was humbled by those illiterate herdsmen who possessed, in so much greater measure than I, generosity and courage, endurance, patience and lighthearted gallantry," wrote Wilfred Thesiger after journeying across Saudi Arabia's Empty Quarter in the 1940s. "Among no other people have I felt the same sense of personal inferiority."

The migrant populations that had married and mixed in Arabia left the peninsula in successive waves as a new race—the Arabs—starting in about 3500 B.C., a thousand years before the Great Pyra-mids of Giza were built in Egypt. They settled in the arc-shaped

[3] "Bedouin" comes from the French version of the Arab word *badwai*, mean-ing desert dweller.

region now known as the Fertile Crescent.⁴ There in the river-fed valleys of Syria and Mesopotamia they gave birth to the first known civilizations.

While Europe was populated by nomadic tribes who lived in mud huts, the Egyptians were recording their history in a written language. They invented surveying to lay out canals and ditches for irrigation. They developed engineering to build the pyramids. As the world's first astrologers, they established a 365-day calendar and divided the day into twenty-four hours. From the papyrus reeds by the Nile they produced the first paper. From grain they made the first beer, from grapes the first wine, which they sealed in jars with mud stoppers. Men shaved, cut their hair and wore wigs. Women used perfume and cosmetics.

To survive the Nile's annual flooding and to utilize the silt that made their crops grow, the Egyptians had to cooperate and organize. For that, they created government and levied taxes according to the depth of the river's flood waters. The deeper they were, the greater the amount of silt left behind, thus the more plentiful the harvest and the higher the taxes. An elaborate bureaucracy evolved to keep records, and a great emphasis was placed on literacy. "Behold," schoolmasters told their students, "there is no scribe who lacks for food." (Egypt's painfully cumbersome bureaucracy is scornfully referred to by Egyptians today as "the curse of the pharaohs.")

The Arabs believed the world was round when the Europeans thought it was flat. They devised algebra, invented the universal astrolabe—a forerunner of the sextant—and discovered and named chemical substances such as alkaline. Fifteen hundred years ago, while Attila the Hun was raiding Gaul, Italy and the Balkans, Arab

---

⁴ The Fertile Crescent is vaguely shaped like an arc. It starts in the eastern Mediterranean, in what are now Israel, Jordan, Lebanon and Syria, then swings back to the southeast into Iraq's Tigris and Euphrates river valleys, ending near the Persian Gulf.

tribes were gathering annually in Arabia for week-long poetry festivals; in order to make the arduous journey to the celebration safely and on time, the tribes often declared truces in their constant warfare. Their poems spoke of survival and conquest and the challenges of the desert.

> I was far ahead of misfortune before, but now
> it tramples upon me with its shod hooves.
> I used to wear a badge of distinction and led
> the troops astride a noble steed.
> When enemy horsemen attacked, I was the
> first to meet them and cover the retreat of my men.
> But today, I have no mount on which to carry my baggage.
> Oh, how shameful! I have been humbled and subdued.

Later, after the birth of Islam in the seventh century, the great Arab cities—Cairo, Damascus, Baghdad and Córdoba in Spain— became the intellectual centers of the world, nurturing the foremost philosophers and scientists as well as the finest libraries and universities to be found anywhere. Arab doctors and scientists found answers to questions that Europe had hardly begun to ask. Many of the world's great scholars—among them Plato, Pythagoras and Archimedes—traveled to Egypt to study the advancement of a culture.

For seven hundred years, the writings of Ibn Sina (980–1037), or Avicenna, as he was known in the West, remained the basic text for European medical students, and the ninth-century "philosopher of the Arabs," Al-Kindi, eloquently argued that the search for truth was the most exalted of human endeavors. In mathematics, the Arab *sifr*, or zero, provided new solutions for complicated equations. In medicine, Al-Razi was the first to diagnose smallpox and measles and to use animal gut for sutures, and Ibn al-Nafis, a Syrian, discovered the fundamental principles of pulmonary circulation. In agriculture, the Arabs learned how to graft a single vine so that it would bear grapes of different colors, thus laying the foundation for Europe's future wine industries. Arab shepherds made the bagpipe that one day would return to Palestine with the British army, and an Arab author, Ibn-Tufail, wrote what many consider to be the first real novel, *Hayy ibn Yagzan* (Alive, Son of Awake). The Arabs brought the techniques of irrigation, navigation and geography to western Europe, and Arab architects, using horseshoe-shaped arches and cubical supports, redesigned Spain with airy, mosaic-tiled buildings that had graceful patios and a feeling of openness. The missionaries carried the basis of that style to Mexico, then to Southern California, where it remains today as a mark of affluence in many contemporary homes.

AT THE core of being Arab is the language itself. Indeed, the most accepted definition of *Arab* today is one who speaks Arabic. None other seems to work. The real Arab comes from one of the thirteen tribes of the Arabian Peninsula, but what of the millions who don't? Most Arabs are Muslim, but what of the six million Egyptian Coptic Christians? A European lives in Europe, an Asian in Asia, but does an Arab live in Arabia? So after decades of fruitless debate among the Arabs themselves, Middle East scholars generally agree that an Arab is one who speaks Arabic, a Semitic language related to Hebrew.

Unlike the Romance languages, there is for speakers of English a lack of cognates, or words derived from recognizable roots, in Arabic. The sounds, script, numerals, twenty-eight-consonant alphabet and vowel system are different, the tenses imprecise. Although more than six hundred English words—including alfalfa, algebra, admiral (from *amir al bahr*, or prince of the sea), alcohol, assassin, cotton, magazine, sugar, traffic, tariff, zenith—have Arabic derivations, Westerners usually have a frightful time mastering the language.

Consider the trouble Westerners have in just agreeing on spelling the name of the Libyan leader, Moammar Kadafi.[5] The *Los Angeles Times* spells it Kadafi; *Newsweek* doubles the *d* to spell Kaddafi; the *New York Times* and the *Christian Science Monitor* substitute *Q* for *K* to make it Qaddafi; the U.S. government exchanges a *d* for an *h* and slips in another *a* to get Qadhaafi; the *Washington Post* prefers Gadhafi, and the Associated Press, Khadafy. To set the record straight, an accurate transliteration would be Qathafi, with the *th* pronounced as in *the*.

Classical Arabic is the language of the Koran, the Muslim Holy Book, and is the word of God. And because it is divine, it cannot change. It is already perfect, just as Shakespearean English is to the English scholars. Every thought and every word man needs to deal with the twentieth century are already there, recorded from God's revelations to the illiterate merchant Mohammed beginning around A.D. 610.

The French notwithstanding, no one attaches more importance to his language than the Arab. For him Arabic is more than a medium of conversation. It is an object of worship, an almost metaphysical force that draws man closer to God. In many schools children are taught not to reason and question but only to memorize, to file away the Koran verse by verse as though the mind were a computer floppy disc. At Cairo's religious university, Al Azhar, students are not accepted for enrollment until they have memorized all 77,934 words of the Koran. "Master Arabic," they are told, "and the wisdom of the Koran is unlocked." It is the language of the angels, of heaven. Protect the purity of Arabic and God's word remains forever unsullied. But if Arabic is allowed to develop, to become more contemporary, religious scholars fear that the Koran's

[5] Throughout this book, I have used the *Los Angeles Times*'s style for spelling most Arabic names and words. Kadafi is a Bedouin tribal family name meaning "one who throws."

meaning will become blurred, that into the black-and-white Koranic interpretation of life will seep some gray.

Today these scholars are worried. The pressures of modernity, of scientific discoveries and of Western culture are confronting Arabic's ability to absorb and grow as a living language. How, for instance, should Arabic accommodate the word "sandwich," something that wasn't around in Mohammed's time? How about "television," "automobile" and the thousands of scientific, military and mathematical terms that have crept into contemporary vocabularies of every language? Libya's Kadafi has confronted the problem by phasing out the English and French departments at Al Fatah University and by banning all words that do not have an Arabic derivation. No one, for example, calls a Peugeot a Peugeot in Libya anymore; they call the French-made car a *hamam*, the Arabic word for pigeon.

In colloquial Arabic, which the classical purists dismiss as a low-level spoken language without fixed rules, the media and the public have adopted foreign words. "Sandwich" is *sandawitsh*, "television" is *tilivizyoon*, "bus" is *autubiis*, "radio" is *radio*. To the purists this is another nettlesome encroachment of Western culture, and the fifty-four scholars at the Egyptian Language Academy have worked long hours in recent years to find words in the Koran that describe all that has changed in thirteen hundred years.[6] For "sandwich," they came up with a term that translates as "a divider and a divided thing together with something fresh inside." For "automobile," their alternative was "that which goes by itself," because self-propelled is a construction that does not exist in Arabic.

Predictably, no one says that he is getting into his "that which goes by itself" to find a cheese "divider and a divided thing together

[6] Similar language institutes operate in Syria, Iraq, Jordan and Morocco. (The Moroccan institute is run by the Arab League.) But there is little coordination between them, and many of their decisions conflict.

with something fresh inside." He gets into his *sayyara* and buys a cheese *sandawitsh*. The offerings of the academy, which at first were ridiculed, are now simply ignored. Its members are making such slow progress that only now are they searching for words to define medical and scientific discoveries and innovations made by the West decades ago.

No one suggests that classical Arabic, so rich in vocabulary, will join Latin in the graveyard of dead languages—the importance of the Koran in daily life negates that possibility—but the pace of the academy's work does seem to indicate that classical Arabic, like the heart of Arabia, will remain married to the past, as is Shakespeare's English. Its usefulness will be as a medium for religious and intellectual discussions.

Today few Arabs outside religious circles speak—or are capable of speaking—classical Arabic in informal conversations. Colloquial dialects have taken its place, but they vary so much from region to region that Arabs often cannot understand each other without modifying their language. (To say "I want," a Moroccan would use *brit*; a Saudi might use *uriid* or *uhib*.) This is a troubling portent: if language is the great unifier of the Arab world, the hallmark of identity, then how solid will the foundation of oneness be once the Arabs lose their mastery of it in its diverse forms?

THE PREVAILING Western perception of the Arab was captured nicely during the 1980s in a political cartoon in a Boston newspaper. It showed a robed and bearded figure kneeling in prayer, and over his head, in heavy black letters, was a single word: HATE! Once Jews, blacks and other minorities were subjected to similar degradation; today hardly anyone but Arabs is still fair game for media bashing. The Arabs, I think, are singled out primarily because, unlike most other peoples of the developing world, they have resisted assimilating Western ways or capitulating to Western values. Thus they are seen as a threat and, armed with oil and the ability to make war or peace with Israel, are thought to be in a position to translate that threat into actions that affect the industrialized world. The West feels comfortable with Israel because Israelis are perceived to be Europeans; it accepts the African or Indian who dresses, thinks and acts like a Westerner; it considered Japan civilized only after Japanese businessmen put on a necktie and began speaking English. But the Arab remains always the Arab, a man held hostage by religion and culturally obsessed with identity.

For an Arab Muslim of pious persuasion, his faith is more than a religion; it is a complete way of life, because Islam and the forces of society are in constant interplay. Islam is politics, law, social behavior, and is so exacting in detail that the Koran even prescribes procedures for divorce, loans and wills. God is reached through knowledge and faith, intellect and will, and every man communicates directly with his God, rather than using priests as intermediaries. Says Libya's Kadafi, "The solution to all human problems is Islam."

Taken to the extreme—as almost everything seems to be in the Middle East—I found this widely shared sentiment troublesome. It is a detriment to progress because for the orthodox, coping with modernity does not require intellectual analysis, much less a search for deduction from fixed principles. Only faith is necessary. Inshallah. Indeed, in Islamic institutions, the very word "innovation" is heresy, because nothing can be new; all knowledge is already in the Koran. To follow the familiar path is best. (The practices of Mohammed are known as the Sunna, meaning "the trodden path.") Even science is viewed as something of an atheistic tool, which perhaps helps explain why the Saudi Arabian sheik Abdullah Aziz ben Baz has dismissed the work of both early Arab scholars and modern scientists, and was insisting in the 1980s that the world was flat and that the United States' moon landings were a hoax.

"The theory of knowledge for Arab Muslims is different than that in the West," Hussein Amin, an Egyptian writer on Islamic affairs, told me. "With you, knowledge is the means to conquer the unknown. With us, it is a collection of material embodied in books which you can possess by reading—and the older the books, the better. True Muslims believe that what Mohammed left is perfect for all countries and all times, so developing Islam is out of the question."

WHILE IN the Arab world, I sometimes felt I was in a time capsule, yet I never had to look far to find the forces of change at work. Oil had jarred the pillars of everything that was sedentary, and on the eastern rim of Arabia I found a country whose transformation stirred the imagination. There, in a once-forgotten corner of the world, a young sultan had led his people out of the Dark Ages and onto the threshold of the twenty-first century. The journey had taken but a second on the clock of history, yet in that flash Oman had moved to challenge the notion that oil-induced modernity was incompatible with traditional Arab values.

Oman, about the size of Kansas, is situated on the southeastern tip of the Arabian Peninsula. It overlooks the narrow Strait of Hormuz, the passageway for one fifth of the world's daily oil production, and stretches inland through mountain gorges, rocky plains and searing-hot plateaus. The region is so rugged that less than 0.2 percent of the land is farmed, and is so rooted in conflict that the borders with Saudi Arabia and the United Arab Emirates are still undefined and the border with Yemen is in dispute. For centuries, anarchy, insurrections, invasions, civil wars and tribal fighting racked this starkly beautiful country whose name translates in a tribal dialect as the "peaceful land."

I arrived in Muscat, the capital, at night. The outline of fifteenth-century Portuguese forts cast long, soft shadows over the desert, and the moon was almost bright enough to read by. On the four-lane road from the airport to my hotel, Buick limousines and Datsun 280-Zs roared by my Mercedes-Benz taxi at breakneck speed, weaving past motor scooters whose drivers had rifles—old British

Enfields or the prized Russian Kalashnikov—slung over their backs as a symbolic mark of manhood. Reaching up the hillside were clusters of modern, spacious homes, air conditioners humming, lights ablaze, and in the gully below them, as though they were a permanent part of the landscape, a dozen tents with TV antennae protruding. Outside each was parked a Toyota pickup truck. Donkeys and camels grew fat and lazy grazing nearby.

Twenty minutes from the airport was the Intercontinental, a wonderful hotel, where an Omani attendant greeted arriving guests with Arab coffee heated over open coals in the lobby and poured from a brass urn. He was the last Omani employee I saw in the hotel; the rest of the staff was composed of foreign contract workers, mostly Thais and Pakistanis, for aside from driving taxis—cars remain a status symbol in the Arab world—citizens of the oil-producing countries aren't much interested in jobs below the level of executive director. In the lower level of the hotel, near an indoor garden of flowers and hanging vines, was an English pub, whose British bartender poured liquor for foreigners but served certain Omanis only after cautious scrutiny on the premise that Arabs don't (or, at least, shouldn't) drink. I fell into conversation there with a group of young American Navy airmen, based at Diego Garcia, who flew P-3s over the Arabian Sea, patrolling for Russian submarines. Their missions were highly classified, and their presence in Oman was supposed to be a secret.

"We don't exist, so I hope you won't write anything about us being here," the pilot said, reaching for another Wm. Younger's Tartan on tap.

His crewmen had to change into civilian clothes before leaving their plane during overnight stops at Oman and were permitted to visit only the luxury hotels that cater to foreigners. Out of sight, out of mind, the government reasoned. An American military presence was welcomed in the region as long as it was figuratively just over the horizon.

Unlike the other oil-producing sheikdoms and kingdoms on the peninsula and around the Persian Gulf, Oman has a history of contact with the outside world, a history that went beyond the confines of the desert. Its people were great seafarers whose trade routes carried them to India and China more than a thousand years ago and whose seventeenth-century empire included most of the southern Arabian Peninsula as well as Zanzibar and Mombasa on the East African coast. Except for a brief period of Persian rule, the Omanis have remained independent since expelling the Portuguese in 1650, and their history seems to have made the Omanis more worldly in outlook and less fearful of change than many of their neighbors.

Oman did not start producing oil until 1964, and its reserves are modest compared with those of three superrich nearby friends, Saudi Arabia, Kuwait and the United Arab Emirates. But to appreciate how Sultan Kaboos ibn Said has used his resources to develop the sultanate, it is worth opening the time capsule that, just a tick ago on history's clock, had made Oman as paranoid and isolated as Albania is today. Oman's age of darkness began in 1938, when Kaboos's grandfather abdicated in favor of Kaboos's father, Sultan Said ibn Taimur. Suddenly the present was gone, and for the next thirty-two years, until 1970, the future was to become something best ignored. The new sultan closed Oman's doors to the world, and with a handful of trusted British advisers ran the place like a penal colony. Oman was now secure; it was going back into the past.

Apprehensive of any outside influences that would corrupt Islamic and Arab traditions, Sultan Said made it illegal to wear glasses, ride a bicycle or own a radio. Western clothes, dancing and smoking were forbidden, and the ban was enforced with public floggings. Women were not permitted to attend school or appear in public unless cloaked head to toe in a black *abeyas*, a shapeless, sexless garment that gives the wearer a distinct resemblance to a penguin. Oman's missions abroad were closed; virtually no foreigners were allowed into the country, and the few students who had gone abroad to study were denied the reentry visas needed to come home.

As recently as 1970, the year after Neil Armstrong walked on the moon, the wooden gates to Muscat swung shut each evening at dusk. Those walking the streets after dark had to carry a lantern at arm's length and continually announce themselves to avoid the risk of being shot as strangers. In the entire country there were only three miles of paved roads, twelve doctors, fifteen telephones and three religious schools, which Sultan Said grudgingly allowed to function despite his opposition to education. Living in a mud palace in Salalah, the sultan kept the national treasury under his bed and communicated with the capital, five hundred miles north, via shortwave radio. His people eked out a meager living through subsistence farming and fishing. Their per capita income was one hundred dollars.

To this day no one can fully explain what motivated Sultan Said. Probably it was nothing more than fear—of change, of the unknown, of new ideas—the same fear that grips so much of the Arab population today as it struggles to keep the past secure. But new ideas were spreading, particularly among the young, and they were coming from an unlikely place, Saudi Arabia. By then, in the late 1960s, Said had made two mistakes that ensured Oman could not forever remain immune to the forces of change: he had granted an oil concession to the Iraq Petroleum Company, owned jointly by several of the largest international oil firms, and he had sent his only son, Kaboos ibn Said, off to Britain to be educated at Sandhurst, the military academy.

Kaboos, a teetotaler and something of a moralist, returned home after graduating from Sandhurst and spending a year with a British regiment in West Germany. He had discovered the world. His new passion was light opera, and he would lie on the bedroom floor for hours listening to Gilbert and Sullivan. His affinity for Western culture so infuriated the sultan that he smashed Kaboos's favorite album, *The Pirates of Penzance*, over his knee. Kaboos protested and was placed under house arrest for three years.

But desert justice was to prevail. On July 23, 1970, Kaboos and several of his father's British advisers appeared at the palace with an ultimatum that the sultan abdicate. Sultan Said fired a few harmless shots into the ceiling, then meekly boarded a waiting Royal Air Force plane bound for London. He was installed in a suite at Claridge's Hotel, where he died two years later at the age of fifty-eight.

I met Sultan Kaboos during one of my last swings through the Middle East in 1985. He was a strikingly handsome, gracious man, fortyish and soft-spoken. His clipped beard was turning from gray to white, his eyes were sharp and dark like those of a falcon. In the belt of his ankle-length *dishdasha* was stuck an ornate silver *khunjar* (dagger). He had divorced his wife because she bore him no son and had remained a bachelor, which had led to much speculation, particularly over who would eventually ascend to the throne. I had been warned beforehand that he would not talk about the coup — "When you overthrow your father, you have some painful memories," the sultan's British adviser had said — so we talked about Oman's rapid development since 1970, and I asked if perhaps he, like the Shah Mohammed Reza Pahlavi of Iran before him, wasn't moving his nine hundred eighty thousand subjects faster than they were prepared to go.

"If you had asked me that nine or ten years ago," he said, choosing his words carefully, "I'd have replied, 'Well, hopefully we will do all right,' but within myself I'd be asking, Are we really ready for this? Now I can honestly say, yes, I think we can progress without destroying ourselves, our culture, our way of life. We are enjoying modern ways but we are not losing ourselves in them."

Per capita income had soared to one thousand dollars in the years since his father's exile; thirteen hundred miles of superhighways stretched throughout the country; the fifteen telephones had grown to thirty thousand; a $400 million university, Oman's first, was under construction. "It's hard to believe that so recently this was a poor country with no progress at all—we were just at a stand-still," said the university's elderly director, Amor ibn Ali. There is one hospital bed for every five hundred people, a ratio that com-pares favorably with that of Western countries, and the 490 schools have an enrollment of 168,000—girls as well as boys. Kaboos was particularly upbeat the day I talked to him: he had just announced plans to create the first national symphony orchestra in the Arab world, and the initial group of young Omani musicians was about to leave for Vienna for seven years' training.

"His Majesty marches to his own drummer," one of his ministers said, and I couldn't take issue. Kaboos has struck a close alliance with the United States, giving Washington access to Oman's mili-tary facilities in the event of an international crisis. He has kept Britons in posts as military and political advisers—an oddity in an age when Arab governments pretend they do not depend on non-Arab friends—and while most other Arab leaders were condemn-ing the Egyptian-Israeli treaty in 1979, he was calling the accord a significant, though less than perfect, first step toward peace. He was deeply suspicious of the Soviet Union's global intentions and pri-vately critical of other heads of state who waste too many idle words espousing the cause of Arab unity.

Kaboos runs an authoritarian monarchy—there is no constitu-tion, no suffrage, no political parties—that is something less than absolute. But he appears to have maintained the loyalty of his people. Like a desert chieftain, he achieves consensus through con-sultations with cabinet ministers and the leaders of Oman's two hundred tribes, and he keeps his hand on the national pulse by tak-ing three-week safaris each year, moving across the desert in a cara-van of Land Rovers. He spends the day talking to villagers and sleeps each night in his tent.

Under Kaboos, Oman has remained aloof from the Middle East's turmoil, yet trouble is never far from its shores: Kaboos wor-ries about the export of radical Islamic revolution and the security of his borders, where, until North and South Yemen merged in 1990, South Yemen was the only Marxist state in the Arab world. He casts a leery eye at the turbulent Horn of Africa. As a result, entry into Oman is carefully controlled. Western businessmen, for instance, can easily obtain visas, but Libyans and Iranians are persona non grata, and Palestinians and citizens of Eastern Bloc countries are granted visas only after intelligence checks that can take weeks. When I asked one government official why Oman had a policy that seemed to discriminate against Arabs, he replied, "Because Englishmen don't plant bombs." That, I thought, summed up an important characteristic of the Middle East: Arabs may embrace their brethren, but they don't necessarily trust them.

The sultan, blessed with a small population of manageable size, has succeeded where others have failed by putting an Islamic and Arabic overlay on the Western-inspired modernization of his country. Two cultures have met but have not collided. The Omanis believe they are moving at their pace, not his. They view Kaboos as Oman's religious leader as well as its head of state, thus bestowing a legitimacy on him that the shah of Iran did not enjoy. Having experienced the unpleasantness of being forced to step back into the past, they thirst for a taste of tomorrow as long as they do not have to sacrifice their Islamic and Arabic identity for it. Today, for example, if a father does not enroll his daughter in school, he is visited by an official from the Ministry of Education and encouraged to reconsider. If he refuses, believing that a Muslim woman has no need of an education or a profession, the matter is closed and his daughter is allowed to dwell forever in the realm of the ignorant.

The lesson of Oman, I think, is that change does not have to be threatening to the Arab world if people are made to feel that they have a choice, that they have control and are the masters, not the victims, of their destiny. New ideas eventually become a greater force than religion. Whether it is in the United States or the Arab world, the strength of the Moral Majority ebbs and flows, the attraction of religion swings like a pendulum. One may cling tenaciously to the past, but change becomes inevitable and the smell of it in the wind is irresistible, especially to the young, who find the call of fundamentalism compelling. The challenge is to graft what is good from other cultures to one's own society, not to reject out of hand all that is foreign. It is, as Sultan Kaboos has shown, not an impossible task, *inshallah*.

CAIRO GRIDLOCK

IN THE blissful still of early morning, when Cairo is bathed in the soft blue of desert dawn and the Nile's waters are smooth as silk, I could see from my balcony the vestiges of beauty in a city that was once among the grandest and most important on earth. Unlike the new, sterile Arab cities built by oil money, Cairo has soul and substance. Its streets throb with life, its open-air cafés are crowded until the wee hours with men who discuss the cost of bread and the price of peace over countless cups of sweet, thick coffee. In many ways, Cairo is to the Middle East what London is to the English-speaking world; it is an emotional magnet, a place where an Arab has only to step off the plane to know immediately that he is *home*. He may hate Cairo's filth and congestion and nerve-racking noise, but for him there is no more wondrous city anywhere.

The name for this thousand-year-old city in Arabic is Al Qahira, which means victorious. On the southwestern edge of the metropolis are the three Great Pyramids of Giza. On the northeast is an obelisk that marks where—according to legend, at least—Plato once studied. The French that Cairo's elite still speak is a legacy of Napoleon Bonaparte's scientific and military expedition here two centuries ago. And the architecture—the Romanesque stone doorways, the sand-colored mosques, the wrought-iron balconies reminiscent of Paris, the mullioned windows and the domes of the Mamluks, all darkened with age—is a reminder that Cairo remains a juxtaposition of new and old, of East and West.

"Cairo, like Rome and Florence, lives upon tourists who, if they are not beloved, are welcome," wrote Winwood Reade, a British author, in 1873. "The city is lighted by gas; it has bucolic gardens in which a native military band performs every afternoon; an excellent theater for which Verdi composed Aida; new houses in the Parisian style are springing up in the streets and are let out at high rents as soon as they are finished."

Our apartment was on the top floor, the fifth, of a dusty building overlooking the Nile. On our side of the river, where wealthy Egyptians gave catered cocktail parties, wore tailormade suits and spent their holidays in Europe, rents for expatriates averaged two thousand dollars a month. On the other bank, perhaps a hundred yards away, people wore the flowing robes of peasants and paid fifty cents for one-room flats without water or electricity. Their brick buildings were crumbling, as though hit by wartime bombardments, and they stretched in endless layers toward the horizon, finally disappearing from view in a haze of sand and polluted fumes. The river divided two worlds that were mutually exclusive and strangely independent of each other.

From our balcony I could count the minarets of twenty mosques—tall, graceful spindles that towered above palms and dwarfed everything in sight. Each morning before sunrise a sudden explosion of amplified cacophony would thunder from the mosques, shaking the neighborhood awake and summoning the faithful to prayer. "God is great. I testify that there is no god but God. . . ." Cairenes would pour out of their dark doorways and move through the empty streets to fill their chambers of worship. The muezzin's call would drift off and fall silent. Cairo was magic in those moments, hushed and peaceful, a grand old lady who still looked beautiful in the half-light of dawn. I used to sit on my balcony with my first cup of coffee of the day, waiting for the tempo of the streets to pick up. Soon the heat and the noise would become overwhelming and drive me inside. Loving Cairo was difficult; hating it was impossible.

IT WAS never easy to know whether Cairo—and Egypt as a whole—belonged to the First or Third World. After all, how can you speak of civilization's birthplace as being a "developing" nation? Yet never have I seen a place where the past seemed so distant and irrelevant, the present so unmanageable, the future so unimaginable. "A fascinating city but oh, my God . . ." Western visitors would say, shaking their heads in disbelief. Indeed, time has not been kind to Cairo, and yesterday's grandeur has become today's urban nightmare. The capital is sinking under the weight of people, people and more people, and Egypt itself seems in danger of becoming a Bangladesh on the shores of the Mediterranean, an impoverished land gripped by lethargy and decay, its illiterate population growing by more than a million a year, its daily bill for imported food already in the millions of dollars, its infrastructure held together by freelance fix-it men with glue and tape and bits of string and wire.

I had been given the name of a fix-it man my first day in Cairo, and when my toilet started gurgling, then overflowing, I called him immediately, reaching Mr. Darwish on the eighth or ninth try. "Hello! Hello!" he shouted into his phone. The connection was poor, and there was a lot of static. "Speak up!" he yelled. "I cannot hear you."

After a few minutes I managed to convey that I had a plumbing problem and needed help. Mr. Darwish said he did not like such work, preferring to repair air conditioners or typewriters or eggbeaters. But he had known my predecessor and after a moment's hesitation he replied, "All right, I will be there within ten days."

On the twelfth day, he mounted his bicycle in Heliopolis, a tattered suburb once favored by princes and magnates. He wore a faded blue necktie and a ragged jacket and carried a briefcase full of string, wire, bottles of glue, nuts, screws, a pair of pliers, two hammers, and some cooking oil. It took him an hour and thirty minutes to weave through the hazardous traffic and reach my apartment on the other side of town.

Mr. Darwish rolled up his sleeves and was at work at once, stopping only briefly to join my cook for noontime prayers on the kitchen floor. He fashioned a loop of string, attached a piece of wire, wrapped a loose joint with tape, tossed two ounces of cooking oil into the reservoir bowl and jiggled the handle. The toilet flushed perfectly and no water leaked from its base.

"There you are," he said, stepping back, an artist admiring his work. "Just like new."

I asked what I owed, and Mr. Darwish said, "As you like." A tough bargaining session followed, and we finally agreed on eight pounds, then about ten dollars. Mr. Darwish gathered up his paraphernalia and was off, biking down Abu El Feda Street to the next job, a broken radio.

The toilet worked fine for two weeks. Then the string broke, the wire became slack, the tape around the joint gave way and all hell broke loose in my bathroom. But no matter. Mr. Darwish was only an hour or so away by bicycle and for eight more pounds I knew he could give my toilet another two weeks of life.

There are thousands of fix-it men in Cairo like Mr. Darwish, and all are the benefactors of a system that has never rewarded competence and has seen its skilled craftsmen head off for better-paying jobs in the oil-rich countries. In their absence, janitors become clerks, farmers become builders, cooks become mechanics. When the results are predictably disastrous, the ever-tolerant and patient Egyptians merely shrug and say, "*Malesh*" — Never mind.

Cairo is a city of eleven million people, and had — when I lived there — five hundred thousand cars, eighty thousand animal carts and one motorized street sweeper. It is the largest city in Africa — four times more populous than its closest rival (Lagos, Nigeria) — and it dominates its region as no other capital does on any continent. It is the intellectual, religious and educational center of the Arab world, the seat of filmmaking, journalism and book publishing, virtually the only place where political debate is lively and foreign policy is bold and far-reaching. If you drew four circles, one each around the nonaligned, Arab, Islamic and African nations of the world, the lines would converge very close to Cairo.

Like many Arab cities, Cairo is bone-dry, receiving only an inch of rain in a wet year. The furnace-heat of summer bounces off the streets in shimmering waves that make everything look slightly out of focus, and the breathless days taste of sand. The sand is powder-fine and so pervasive that it sneaks through the tiniest cracks and clings to everything. Cairenes draw their louvered shutters tight, try-ing to seal themselves in a hermetic world, and live in darkness even in the dazzling sunlit days of July and August. They slip plas-tic covers around their radios and television sets, wrap their valu-ables in paper bags and flail away desperately with feathered dusters. But there is no escape. Open a book and there on page 105 is a fine coating of dust.

These hot, dusty summer months bring Arab visitors from the Persian Gulf states by the planeload to Cairo. Compared with, say, the Las Vegas Strip or London's Soho, Cairo is a fairly tame place, but by the puritanical standards of the Middle East it is Sin City, Arabia, offering belly dancers and nightclubs, young male and female prostitutes, whiskey and beer. This freedom from the restraints of home is a more powerful attraction than what Egypt has to offer historically or intellectually, and it was rare for an Arab visitor (or an Egyptian, for that matter) to explore the ancient mon-uments in the Valley of the Kings or gaze in wonder at the great Pyramids or be mesmerized by the King Tutankhamun exhibit at the National Museum. Instead the Arab tourists seemed more con-tent to sit, absorbing but not exerting. They shopped or watched movies on video recorders by day and spent the nights in outdoor tea gardens or in nightclubs dense with cigarette smoke, where the children and wives would nod off by midnight and their fathers and husbands would share two-hundred-dollar bottles of whiskey and cheer the plump, gyrating belly dancers until dawn.

Most Cairenes did not look favorably on these nouveaux riches from the Gulf, whom they called "gulfies." "They're crude. The Arabs don't know anything," a cabdriver with an engineering degree said to me. When I asked him if he didn't consider himself an Arab, too, he replied, "Not really. I'm *Egyptian*." His comment underscored an important change that has taken place in the Arab world since the 1960s: nationalism has replaced Pan-Arabism as the most powerful political force. The Egyptians and others have been told by their leaders for years that they had to sacrifice for Arab goals—the liberation of Palestine, the destruction of Zionism, rapid development that would lead to economic strength, Arab unity. But none of these objectives has been achieved, and the people, growing weary of political acrobatics, having had to surrender what little democracy they had to authoritarian governments, are now, more than ever before, looking inward, toward their own nations, for their identity.

WANDERING THE streets of Cairo, poking through the dark alleyways that smell of urine and are strewn with trash, you can stumble on dilapidated villas where orchestras were heard in their gardens on summer evenings long ago. Handsome Victorian-era apartment buildings stand mirage-like amid rows of tenements, their wrought-iron balconies draped with laundry, their shutters drawn tight against the assault of noise and dirt. Broad boulevards lead into expansive squares that hint of Paris; narrow alleyways that are scented with spices and crowded with goats and black-veiled women wind through mysterious, ocher-colored worlds, almost biblical in tone and texture.

Sometimes on the dusty shelves of unlit bookshops, you can find old guidebooks to a city that is no more. They speak of Cairo's fine opera house, of banyan trees and patches of green that stretched along the verdant promenade of the corniche clear out to the suburb of Maadi, of the splendidly pampered Japanese garden in Helwan and the excellent restaurant in Groppi's downtown pastry shop, of days when Cairenes could live and breathe and move easily in what was, until the 1950s, among the last of the twentieth-century Westernized enclaves in the Arab world. Cairo, in fact, was really two cities throughout most of the 1800s and 1900s: there was the Cairo for Europeans and the Egyptian aristocracy with manicured gardens, elegant hotels and palaces, fine carriages and well-dressed people, and farther back from the Nile, past the parks and villas, there was the crowded, dirty Cairo for everyone else.

One British writer, William Morton Fullerton, aptly described in 1891 how great the psychological gap was between the two Cairos: "With the polo, balls, the races and the riding, Cairo begins to impress itself upon you as an English town in which any quantity of novel oriental sights are kept for the aesthetic satisfaction of the inhabitants, much as the proprietor of a country place keeps a game preserve or deer park for amusement."

Napoleon had brought Western technology and culture to Egypt in 1798, and the Suez Canal—built by the Frenchman Ferdinand de Lesseps—established Cairo's reputation in the West as the sophisticated capital of a new and important power. The *New York Herald*, commenting on the canal's opening in 1869, noted that it brought Africa and the Nile "within a convenient distance for English colonization." Cotton was king then, and Egypt's viceroyalty embraced the Westernization of their country as surely as today's rulers reject it. Life was a lavish extravagance for the elite— much as it would be a century later for the Saudi Arabian oil sheiks—and from Europe came communities of British, French, Swiss, Italian and Greek settlers. Cairo had become truly cosmopolitan. It was a city of Christians, Jews and Muslims, of Europeans and Middle Easterners, of old monuments and new ideas. "Since God has given us the viceroyalty, let us enjoy it," said Ismail the Magnificent, the ruler from 1863 to 1879.

ON THE DAY that I was to discuss the decay of Cairo with Hassan Fathi, Egypt's internationally acclaimed architect, the local papers carried three items that caught my attention: two apartment buildings had collapsed, killing seventy people; a pedestrian had fallen into an uncovered manhole and drowned in raw sewage; and a student had jumped to his death from a bridge after being tormented for months by his neighbor's blaring radio—he had left a note that said, "Suicide is better than life without dignity."

Fathi's creative urban designs had been used in projects in Europe and the United States; his ideas for low-cost housing had been put into practice in India. But in Cairo, where he advocated the construction of satellite cities in the desert, no one had paid much attention. It was his great sadness that the people, *his* people who needed him most, had utilized his genius the least.

Thin and hard of hearing, Fathi was an old man when I visited him. He lived in one of the oldest parts of Cairo, in a rambling apartment full of maps and drawings and books written in English, French and Arabic. Every afternoon he observed the ritual of tea, making sure that each of his twenty cats shared his biscuits. He was, like almost every other educated Egyptian I met, gracious and kind and forthright with both his opinions and his hospitality. From the street below his open windows the din of blaring horns and raised voices swelled up, making it necessary for us to carry on our conversation in shouts.

"What is happening to Cairo is a tragedy, really," he said, cupping his hands to his mouth. "For forty years I have been fighting to save my city, and I have had no results. No one listens. Does anyone care? I'm not sure. Just look at those TV ads the government is running, then tell me I shouldn't grieve for Cairo."

The government's television campaign he mentioned was intended to bring a little order to Cairo, an undisciplined city whose population generally ignores all traffic regulations, most standards of sanitation and many rules of good neighborliness. The campaign consisted of several one-minute spots interspersed throughout soap-opera dramas. In one, a popular actor walks under a building and is suddenly splattered with garbage dropped from an upper apartment. Wiping the goo from his face, he asks: "Is that what our country has come to? Egyptians, say it isn't so!"

Alas, though, it is. An apathetic public, economic mismanagement and a wildly out-of-control birthrate have become the cancers of Cairo, sapping its strength and leaving its dazed inhabitants the victims of what is known in Egypt as the IBM syndrome: *inshallah* (if God is willing), *bokra* (tomorrow) and *malesh* (never mind). It doesn't matter what gets done or how it's done. If not today, then tomorrow. God decides anyway, so why worry? This sense of fatalism takes all responsibility out of human hands and puts everything—from the outcome of wars to the keeping of appointments—under the control of a Greater Power. That Cairo is being transformed into a vast slum of rural peasants, attracted to the city by the illusions of a better life, does not greatly concern the individual Cairene because, the reasoning goes, man does not really control his destiny or his surroundings.

But here's a curious thing: while Egyptians are content to live in filthy, battered buildings, the insides of their homes are always immaculate. Time and time again I trudged up darkened stairwells to apartments on the third or fourth floor, and when my host opened the door, I would step into an isolated world of elegance and cleanliness. The door would shut behind us and it was as though the blighted Cairo no longer existed. When I asked friends if anyone had ever considered a neighborhood block association or an owners' association to clean up common areas, they would chuckle and say, "Oh, *that* would never work here." No doubt it wouldn't. My friends did not feel that their responsibility extended beyond their own boundaries. That attitude, I thought, represented a troubling omen for the undisciplined Egyptian society as a whole and brought to mind the words that T. E. Lawrence spoke more than seventy years ago: "The Semitic mind does not lean toward system of organization. It is practically impossible to fuse the diverse elements among the Semites into a modern, closely knit state."

THE OPERA house mentioned in the old guidebooks no longer exists, having been set afire by a smoldering cigarette in 1971. Shepheard's Hotel, where John Speke and Captain James Grant were feted with public concerts and elegant dinners more than a century ago after their expedition to the source of the Nile, was burned down in the riots of 1952. The banyan trees lining the boulevards have been cut down to provide wider roads, and the patches of green along the riverfront have given way to high-rise apartment buildings that spill untreated sewage into the Nile. The streets of suburban Maadi are often knee-deep with trash and pocked by wide, deep potholes. The restaurant in Groppi's lost much of its business after a Kuwaiti bought it and banned the sale of beer. In Tahrir (Liberation) Square, out the back door of the Nile Hilton Hotel, the cluster of small gardens and the strips of grass have been paved over to make way for an outdoor terminal serviced by fifty-four bus companies.

Of the once splendid Japanese garden in nearby Helwan, a one-time health resort whose cement and steel factories now spew poisons over Cairo, the *Egyptian Gazette* commented: "Its ponds are broken and filled with dust, its flowers neglected and rusty tangles of barbed wire are strewn everywhere. Indeed, in Egypt today, we seem to have developed a talent for destroying beautiful things."

A generation ago, when Egypt produced a hundred or more feature films a year, Cairo's thirteen first-run movie theaters were as grand as any in London. There was not a filmmaker in the Arab world who had not studied in Cairo, not a successful actor or a songstress whose fame was not dependent on the acceptance of the Cairo audiences. Today no first-class theaters are left. And in the flea-ridden theaters still operating, the seats are broken, the air conditioners don't work, the aisles are littered with trash, and the audiences are made up almost exclusively of sexually repressed young men who hoot and holler in excitement when an actor and actress seem ready to touch.

"Our films used to change every week back when Cairo was the Hollywood of the Middle East," said Salah Abou Seif, a prominent director. "Opening night was really a gala occasion then. It was Monday at the Royale, Tuesday at the Metropole. Everyone wore tuxedos and gowns and the papers reported the next morning who had sat in what box and who had worn what. A fine era it was."

"The audience that used to support the first-class theaters just doesn't exist anymore," said one of Egypt's widely known character actors, Salah Zoufoukai. "Now it's a peasant society. My wife said the other night that she wanted to see a particular film that was playing in Cairo. I said, 'OK, I'll bring it home on video cassette, as long as you don't make me go into that theater.' Besides, who's going to go out into that traffic if you don't have to?"

At every major intersection fifteen or twenty illiterate policemen in soiled white, ill-fitting uniforms stand frantically blowing whistles and waving their arms, trying to unsnarl traffic jams they themselves have created. But the drivers pay them no heed, for Cairo's roads are an anarchist's delight. "We have complete democracy here—you can do whatever you want," a cabdriver chuckled as he bounced over a median divider and headed up a one-way street, the wrong way. Not to worry. Speed limits and safety restrictions are not enforced—a twenty-five-cent bribe will pacify most uncooperative policemen—and the only rule of the road is that he who honks loudest with the largest vehicle has the right of way.

Undeniably, though, lives were saved when Cairo's unruly drivers were immobilized by traffic jams of classic proportions, because the city's accident rate—eighty fatalities and six hundred injuries per ten thousand vehicles—is one of the highest in the world, according to a World Bank study. At that rate the United States' traffic toll would be 1.3 million dead and nearly 10 million injured every year. The American ambassador, Nicholas Veliotes, used to peer out at the long lines of motionless cars blocking every intersection in sight and spring from his bulletproof limousine with the words "The hell with it. Let's walk." And off he would head for his next appointment, jacket slung over his shoulder, followed by his Egyptian bodyguards.

Cairo's deterioration is of more than passing interest because the conditions that have allowed it to happen were largely avoidable. Yet throughout the Third World, dozens of cities are becoming the Cairos of tomorrow, buffeted by the same forces and awaiting the same fate. At some point even creative urban planning becomes irrelevant, and new overpasses to move the traffic and new apartments to house the poor represent not much more than a finger in the dike.

The first force of destruction was government centralization. Everything is centered in Cairo. If an Egyptian needs a new passport or has a question about his war pension, he must come to Cairo. Industry, government, education and commerce are all centered there. One in four Egyptians lives there. Cairo *is* Egypt and nothing of significance happens outside the capital. In Arabic the same word is used for both Egypt and Cairo: *Misr.*

Then there was the constant state of hot and cold war between Egypt and Israel from 1948 to the mid-1970s. Millions of peasants poured into the capital to seek safety during the '67 and '73 wars, and in the era of confrontation the nation's financial resources and its energies were channeled to the military, leaving nothing with which to build a nation. Every pothole in Cairo's streets is a legacy of the conflict with Israel, every eyesore represents a decision to buy a tank instead of repairing a building, a sewer or a telephone system. Besides which, Egypt's leaders never gave much thought to maintenance in the first place. They much preferred to spend money on grandiose projects that were flashy and new.

Compounding these problems were the policies of Gamal Abdel Nasser, Egypt's president from 1953 to 1970. In a burst of socialistic enthusiasm, he destroyed the power of the upper class, instituted mass education—in the process reducing school standards to the lowest common denominator—and pushed through a series of rent-control laws that destroyed landlord profits. Suddenly it was no longer economically reasonable for an owner to repair an elevator, hire a janitor or paint a building. Some large offices in Cairo still rent for less than the cost of a good meal at the Nile Hilton. Not a piaster has been spent on the buildings for a generation, and more often than not the elevators are dead, cobwebs cling to the ceilings, and the trash that has accumulated in the hallways needs to be shoveled out, not swept.

And finally there is the birthrate—the number of births per year per one thousand people. In Egypt the rate is twenty-five, compared with fourteen in the United States and eleven in Great Britain. Already the world's most populous Arab nation in 1985, Egypt saw its population grow by 22 million, to 68 million, over the next fifteen years. If the present trend continues, Egypt will need in the next decade four million new housing units and will have to import one seventh of all the surplus wheat in the world to feed its people. Cairo's population is growing at the rate of a thousand a day—seven hundred new babies and three hundred arrivals from the countryside.

"I am not a believer in calling on people to exercise birth control by decree or persuasion," Nasser once said. "Instead of teaching people how to exercise birth control, we would do better to teach them how to increase their land production and raise their standard. . . . If we direct our efforts to expanding the area in which we live instead of concentrating on how to reduce the population, we will soon find the solution."

He was wrong. In Cairo's most crowded districts the population density has reached two hundred forty thousand per square mile, which is tantamount to packing the entire city of Corpus Christi, Texas, into a single square mile. The United States has spent $67 million trying to help Egypt develop a family-planning program and has shipped in condoms by the carload, but to little avail; barely 25 percent of married Egyptians use any form of contraception (compared with more than 50 percent in Mexico, Taiwan and Colombia, three underdeveloped nations where family planning is working). Half the population is under age fifteen, and despite mass education, nearly half the population is illiterate and opportunities remain limited. Every year half a million Egyptians enter the job market to compete for jobs that do not exist, and every year forty thousand students are graduated from the nation's thirteen universities. Most find little meaningful employment and are forced to take jobs in government or to drive taxis or wait on tables. In the Ministry of Agriculture alone, there are two thousand Ph.D.'s, the majority of whom sit at empty desks without telephones or typewriters or notepads. (Until 1986 every university graduate was promised a government job—a policy started by Nasser; the bureaucracy as a result has grown from 370,000 to two million in three decades' time.)

Although educated, financially secure Egyptians often have only two or three children, the peasant majority still believes—with good reason—that large families are necessary to provide a financial safety net for old age. Some parents also believe it is their duty to promote the growth of Islam, a position that religious leaders do not discourage even though Islam's official policy on birth control is ambivalent. Even educated Egyptians see the empty desert all around them and, figuring that one day it will be conquered by Western technology and made habitable, ask, "What population problem?"

For Egypt, though, the population explosion means that serious economic planning is impossible. "By the prophet Mohammed," President Hosni Mubarak said after getting a report on the nation's economy, "if they brought in a government of angels, it wouldn't make any difference." For Cairo, the explosion means that life will continue to be a burden of endurance for all but the very rich, and that as the impoverished class becomes larger and more dissatisfied, the call of religious zealots for fundamental reforms in the system will have growing appeal.

Cairo's once-cosmopolitan population also is being transformed into a homogeneous one. The French and British communities either packed up or were expelled in the wake of Nasser's pro-Arab, antiforeign revolution. The Jews left in 1948, 1956 and 1967 because the Arab-Israeli wars had made their position insecure. The Greeks and Italians departed by the boatload as economic opportunities diminished under Nasser, with only a few remaining as restaurateurs and mechanics. The Egyptian royalty melted unobtrusively into society or moved abroad. The intellectual class became more isolated and less influential, its voice drowned in the sea of look-alike, think-alike peasants who have taken over Cairo and to whom politicians, educators, filmmakers and newspaper editors seem to believe they must cater.

ONE OF the few people I met in Cairo who had found a quiet, uncrowded place to live was a woman named Marhaba (meaning "hello" in Arabic) Hafez. Her home, in one room of an underground tomb, was cool and cheery. She and her three sons had painted the walls blue and hung an outdated calendar for decoration. They cooked their meals of beans on a cement slab beneath which were buried several members of a family, and they drew their water from another cemetery, a five-minute walk away. There was, Mrs. Hafez said, nothing spooky at all about living among the dead. Indeed, she was thankful for her accommodations and resented only the fact that she had had to make a one-time payment of $1,500 "key money" to the tomb owners for the privilege of renting her home.

Egyptians started living in cemeteries more than eight hundred years ago, and today the living population of the graveyards exceeds one million. Many of the residents think they are decidedly better off than those who live in Cairo itself. Their neighborhood is cleaner, quieter and less crowded than those in Cairo; the air is better; there's no traffic; their children have more space to play. The so-called City of the Dead even has its own post office, and here and there makeshift cafés and food stores have sprung up between the tombs. Many of the inhabitants tap into electrical outlets in nearby shops and equip their mausoleums with secondhand television sets and squeaky old General Electric fans. Few have any visible means of employment, but Egyptians are remarkably generous in taking care of both their own families and anyone less fortunate than themselves, and none of the graveyard dwellers lacks for food or even spare change to buy a cigarette or two or a leg of lamb for religious feasts.

"I'd rather be here than on a rooftop downtown, with a piece of bedding strung up for a ceiling," said Mrs. Hafez, who earned a dollar a day as caretaker for a score of tombs, sweeping and scrubbing and keeping them tidy for the owners. They came once or twice a year, on Islamic holidays and on the first day of spring, to visit the dead, an occasion that would be celebrated with a family picnic on the rocky ground just outside the tomb.

"We came to Cairo ten years ago, from Luxor," she said. "We gave up the farm because there was no money in it and Cairo had jobs. There was a lot of money here. But things didn't work out the way we thought, and my husband went off to Saudi Arabia to work in construction. It's a three-year contract. When he comes home we will have money to buy a house and raise a bigger family. *Inshallah.*"

The house she may need, but not the bigger family, for Egypt already has an uncommon problem: the country is larger than California, Nevada and Arizona combined, but 99 percent of the people are clustered in the narrow ribbon of green along the Nile that represents only 4 percent of the land. This cultivated strip, an area no larger than West Virginia, is the only habitable land in what is otherwise a desert wasteland. Each year urbanization is claiming forty thousand acres of the farmland, and while food production in

Egypt is increasing 2 percent a year, food consumption is increasing 5 percent.

Government officials know they are treading on a minefield of potential social unrest, and to keep the lid on the masses, they spend $3 billion a year subsidizing essential commodities, from food to fuel. The subsidies encourage consumerism and discourage conservation. Egyptians pay only 28 percent of the average world market price for gasoline and regularly feed their farm animals loaves of bread that cost only a penny and were made from wheat shipped by the U.S. government. The pricing structure got so out of whack when I was in Cairo that a gallon of gas in Cairo cost forty-eight cents, a gallon of milk sixty-eight cents and a gallon of purified drinking water $1.28. Teachers and middle-level bureaucrats earned forty dollars a month, about half what an illiterate maid could make working part time. A senior diplomat just below the rank of ambassador earned $138 a month and soldiers were so poorly paid (five dollars a month for a private) that most devoted more attention to their moonlight civilian jobs than they did to their military duties. At that rate of pay, it is not surprising that only 15 percent of the government's two million workers showed up on time for work and that the average workday for bureaucrats ranged from twenty minutes to two hours, according to one official report.

After my first six months in Cairo, I made an inventory of all my personal property because I fully expected the city to erupt one hot summer day in a frenzy of violent protest over horrible living conditions, intolerable housing, poverty-level salaries and the immense gap between rich and poor. But this never happened. In fact, Cairo didn't even have any crime to speak of. Muggings, house burglaries and car thefts were uncommon, even in the poorest sections of the city. Murder and rape and violence were rare. In a city of fourteen million, you could walk any street without fear. After a couple of years I tore up my inventory list.

What I had not understood at first was that the Egyptians, unlike many Arabs, had an escape valve for their frustrations and anger— a sense of humor. They joked constantly, about themselves, their leaders, their lives, about everything except religion, and it was only when you didn't hear jokes that you knew the nation's mood was glum. No matter how bad things got, they seemed able to make every day a tolerable, if not pleasant, experience. Their crowded existence reinforced their sense of community, and they laughed and argued and shouted with great gusto. Even in the worst of times, their optimism was unquenchable.

At the intersection below my balcony, I saw a collision at least once a day (there are no stop signs or right-of-way rules in Cairo), and the scenario was always the same: The two drivers would jump from their cars, cursing the other's stupidity, and square off as if to fight. A huge crowd of men would gather instantaneously to separate the drivers and to decide who was at fault. They would shout excitedly and try to direct the traffic that had come to a standstill with horns blasting. Soon reason would prevail. The shouting would subside, the traffic inch by, and the two drivers would embrace and head their separate ways, their fenders bruised but their dignity intact.

CAIRO IS a fan-shaped city wedged between the desert escarpments, narrow in the south, then widening in the north, where the Nile sweeps into a broad, fertile delta. Except for the river and a barren plateau known as the Mokattam hills that rises above the capital's eastern perimeter, the city is flat and featureless. Atop that plateau is a nameless village. The dirt track to it climbs steeply, and Fathi Zaki's donkeys must strain and heave to haul their precious cargo the final yards back into the nightmarish world of the *zabbaleen*.

Zaki was forty years old, going on sixty. His face was creased and leathery from the sun and his eyes were heavy from lack of sleep.

He reined in his donkey team outside a shanty at the end of the track and opened the tin door to his home. His two barefoot children scampered off the cart, and Zaki shoveled his cargo—ripe, wet garbage that he had carried the three miles from Cairo—onto the dirt floor of his living room, disappointed that the load contained no little treasures except food for his pigs.

"Look," he said to me, kicking at the pile. "Not even any good paper. People just don't throw away anything any good the way they used to."

Like the other villagers on the Mokattam range, Zaki was one of the rubbish barons of Cairo, the zabbaleen (a term that translates as rubbish collectors). They are Coptic Christians—Egypt's six million Copts represent the largest minority in the Arab world—who migrated from southern Egypt to the capital in the 1930s. They ended up in a medieval world of garbage, and there they have remained, finding no escape. The garbage sustains them and holds them in economic and social bondage.

Long ago Cairenes burned the garbage to heat water for Turkish baths or merely threw it into the street. Over the centuries so much garbage built up that entire communities grew atop layers of compacted trash, and today, as in Rome, one often has to walk down five or six steps to enter some old buildings that were once at street level. Early in this century a group of Muslims who had wandered to Cairo from the Western Desert developed a profitable business collecting garbage. When the zabbaleen arrived in the thirties, the wahiya (or bosses) put together a slick scheme: they contracted with tenants and landlords to dispose of the trash, then sold the zabbaleen the rights to pick it up and keep it.

The system still works that way, and routes are passed down among the zabbaleen from father to son. The wahiya charge both the zabbaleen and the tenants about fifty cents a month for an apartment. If one of the zabbaleen tries to collect the money himself from the tenants or if he does not make his monthly payments to the strong-armed wahiya, he is usually roughed up on one of his morning runs; his cart is smashed and his precious garbage is strewn over the street.

"It's very unfair, but it's an inherited kind of thing," said Father Saman Ibrahim Moussa, the young, bearded priest in the village. "The zabbaleen are forced into the system because without education there is no other way to break the cycle. They just accept that this is how it works, how it has always worked."

Each morning, well before sunrise, the zabbaleen take their children in tow, leaving the women behind to poke through yesterday's garbage, and head into Cairo in their rickety carts to collect the trash that no one else wants. Theirs is the only household collection service in the city, and for their labor—ten hours a day, seven days a week—the zabbaleen get no pay. They get only to keep the garbage, seven hundred tons of it a day.

Their little carts squirm through Cairo's bumper-to-bumper traffic, and their children crawl up the perilous spiral staircases that cling to the sides of ten-story apartment buildings where, at each narrow landing, tenants have placed the garbage. (If the tenants have servants, anything of value has already been removed.) The zabbaleen are scavengers as well as recyclers, and their municipal service is the most efficient one in Cairo, costing the city government not a piaster.

Back home, in their roofless brick houses that have neither water nor electricity and are shared with many barnyard animals, the rubbish is sorted by hand into various piles—garbage for the pigs, scrap paper that brings five dollars a ton, odds and ends like discarded toilet seats and broken pottery that may fetch a few piasters. What the zabbaleen can't use or repair they burn. Heavy clouds of smoke from the smoldering dump hang over their village night and day like storm clouds.

Except for the Coptic Church, there is almost nothing in the village but the cluster of living compounds that sprawls nearly to the doorstep of Cairo's magnificent, eight-hundred-year-old citadel.

There are no schools, health clinics or shops, and although a doctor visits the church two evenings a week, 40 percent of the children die in their first year, according to a World Bank study.

Virtually none of the twenty-five thousand zabbaleen have ever left their world of garbage, and few seem inclined to do so. I asked one teenage boy if he would leave if he suddenly found ten thousand dollars. He laughed at the foolishness of the question and said, "Of course not. Where else would I go? What would I do?" So he, like his ancestors, will presumably live forever atop a smoldering dump, and Egyptian Muslims, who place great emphasis on bodily cleanliness and wash themselves before each prayer session, will continue to scorn the zabbaleen as lazy, dirty people who supposedly grow rich on treasures mistakenly discarded by the rich.

"People who say the zabbaleen are wealthy have weak brains," Father Moussa said. "Just look around you. Does this look the way rich people live?"

Outside his pint-sized church, the stale air was abuzz with flies. Mounds of trash flowed up the hillside and spilled out of the doorways. Pigs and scrawny dogs wandered in and out of the cement-block homes and runny-nosed children played in heaps of garbage, as happy as any Western child turned loose on a sandbox. My shoes were caked with mud and slime, and as I turned to leave Mokattam, feeling disoriented and empty, I heard behind me the sound of laughing children.

THOUGH THE zabbaleen may be trapped, more than three million Egyptians—or one of every eight adults—have left their country to work abroad, many as common laborers in the oil-producing countries, others as professionals in cities ranging from Los Angeles to Jeddah. The remittances they send home each year now represent Egypt's largest source of foreign exchange. Egyptian teachers are the backbone of Saudi Arabia's educational system; Egyptian doctors keep the hospitals in Kuwait and Qatar functioning; Egyptian academics, economists and businessmen have become prominent in dozens of American and European cities. Most give two reasons for leaving: the limited opportunities at home, where the per capita income is only thirteen hundred dollars and promotions are based on loyalty, not ability, and the stultifying pressures of Cairo that assault the senses like jackhammers, leaving even the most energetic souls drained and numb.

"I step off the plane in London or New York and my whole mentality changes," an Egyptian executive with Citibank said. "In Cairo, I know my work gets sloppy and I try to cut corners because no one really cares how you perform. But get me out of Egypt and I am a different person. It's amazing. Suddenly, I get excited about doing a good job."

The banker and I were picking our way across Tahrir Square, crossing one lane at a time as buses bore down on us, each packed so tightly that the upright passengers seemed in danger of suffocating. "Now," he yelled, and finding a small break in the traffic, we dashed across another lane. There was no room on the sidewalks—that's where cars park—and the streets were a swirling mass of pedestrians, colliding and bouncing off one another like windup toys. "Aaaagh!" My friend cried as a soldier's heel accidentally came down hard on his foot in the crush of people jostling for the next safety zone.

He hobbled along behind me to the Diplomatic Club, one of the last physical remnants of Cairo's old aristocracy, where we were to meet an acquaintance for lunch. The club had high ceilings, long faded drapes that covered the sooty windows, and the feel of lost elegance. The bar had been closed for a year and turned into a prayer room. We sat down in the dining room and ordered grapefruit juice.

"I haven't slept in days, or, at least, it feels that way," my friend said. He explained that a "maverick sheik" had taken over his neighborhood, and for hours on end, crouching in reeds along the Nile night after night, would shout out his own thanks to God over a megaphone. With each sleepless moment the chant would seem to grow louder, until my friend imagined that the sheik had actually entered his bedroom.

"There's nothing I can do," he said matter-of-factly. I asked if he couldn't call the police and have the man arrested for disturbing the peace. My friend, a Muslim who took an occasional glass of whiskey and believed religion was being carried to the extreme by too many people, looked aghast.

"Are you kidding?" he said. "You couldn't do that these days. Why, I'm the one who would be arrested, for being unIslamic."

THREE

SPREADING THE WORD

FOR MOST Arabs, the days before Islam are a blank page of history. Egyptian children know surprisingly little about their pharaonic heritage; the Iraqis seem hardly aware that they are the descendants of the great Mesopotamian civilization. For the real believer all history of consequence began in the sixth century, in a pagan town full of vice and corruption.

Mecca in those days was an important station for camel caravans making the arduous trek from Syria and Yemen to the Nile Valley and the Fertile Crescent, an overland route traders preferred in order to avoid losing their frankincense and myrrh to pirates on the Red Sea.[1] The town was set among the Hejaz hills of the Arabian Peninsula. It was a dry, isolated place, insufferably hot. But its status as a mercantile center had made it powerful and wealthy, and Mecca was known to every tribesman for hundreds of miles around: a poet's fair was held at neighboring Ukaz every year; Mount Arafat, which nomads visited even in pre-Islamic times, was located nearby, and most important, Mecca had the Kaabah, a cube-shaped shrine that housed the three hundred sixty idols, images of various gods and goddesses, that the tribes of Arabia came to pay homage to. Their annual pilgrimage brought profitable business to

---

[1] Frankincense is an aromatic gum resin used by both Jews and Arabs in ceremonies of worship and as a medicine. The pagan Romans used it to mask offensive odors that accompanied the cremation of bodies. Myrrh is a bitter-tasting gum obtained from thorny, flowering trees. It was used in costly incenses, perfumes, cosmetics and medicines and for embalming.

Mecca, and so, for the pagan merchants, the idols were a source of both worship and revenue.

The Bedouin who roamed the Hejaz were combative and belligerently protective of their honor. They proved their manhood raiding and skirmishing, and they considered bravery in battle and generosity to the poor noble attributes. They, however, did not rule Mecca. The Quraysh tribe did. Its members were sedentary and practical. They admired those who could drive a hard bargain in their marketplace and realized, as do their present-day Arabian descendants, that the only thing money couldn't buy was poverty.

In the year 570, about the time Europe was slipping into the Dark Ages and Indian tribes roamed over the wilderness of the Americas, a child named Abu al-Qasim Mohammed ibn Abd Allah ibn Abd al-Muttalib ibn Hashim was born into the Quraysh tribe in Mecca. Everything about his family and his early upbringing was ordinary, and had anyone suggested then that his birth was to be the single most important development in the history of the Middle East, that one day eight hundred million people around the world would speak his name with reverence, the pagans of Mecca no doubt would have scoffed.

Mohammed's family was the clan of Hashim, or Hashimites — the same clan that rules Jordan to this day — and was known to be impoverished, honest and reputable. His father, Abd Allah ibn Abd al-Muttalib, died the year of his birth; his mother, Amenah, died six years later. Young Mohammed, as was customary, was sent off by his uncle for a year or two to live with the Bedouin and learn the ways of the desert and its people. (The custom was followed well into the twentieth century by the noble families of the Hejaz.) The desert shaped Mohammed's life, as it has that of all Arabians. He learned the forbearance of the herdsman, the patience of the nomad, the sweetness of the language so loved by Arabs everywhere. He shared solitude, and came to understand the power of endurance and the strength of human bonding. Although latter-day Muslim biographers contend that his chest was opened and his heart cleansed by angels, there was in reality little to distinguish Mohammed from hundreds of other Arab boys consigned to Bedouin guardians.

Returning to Mecca, the young orphan moved into the home of his uncle, a successful caravan merchant named Abu Talib. He taught the boy about trade and transportation, and Mohammed became skillful in the ways of business. When he was twenty-five, a wealthy widow fifteen years his senior, Khadijah, entrusted her caravan to the Honest One, as Mohammed was known in Mecca. He acquitted himself so well that she proposed marriage. Their twenty-one-year union was apparently a happy one, and Mohammed took no other wives during her lifetime. (After she died, he married at least nine times, and his wives included the daughter of his best friend and the divorced wife of his adopted son.)

Mohammed was not happy with what he saw in Mecca, where, among other peculiar practices, the pagans interred live baby girls, believing them to be a curse. He felt that the Meccans' existence was an empty one; the town's leaders had become greedy and self-centered; their gods did not constitute a living faith. "The holier the city," notes an Arab proverb, "the wickeder the people." Perhaps, Mohammed reasoned, the Christians and Jews in Mecca had some of the answers to the problems that seemed to be corrupting society. And on many nights, Mohammed, who could neither read nor write, would leave Khadijah's side and go to a nearby cave to meditate.

One night in 610, during the month of Ramadan, Mohammed was shaken from his semitrance in the cave by the clanging of bells and a voice that exhorted him to read aloud. "I cannot read," he replied in terror, but the voice ordered again:

> Read: In the name of thy Lord who
> created mankind from a blood-clot.
> Read: for thy Lord the most generous;
> He has taught by the pen
> taught man what he knew not.

Mohammed dashed home, fearing he had gone mad, and asked Khadijah to cover him with blankets. There were more bells and more commands, and he lay on his bed, shaking and sweating as though in a fit. (Some biographers say he was an epileptic.) "O thou who are shrouded in thy mantle, rise and warn [of an imminent Judgment Day]," the voice demanded. Much to his relief, Khadijah's cousin—Ibn Nofal, a Christian by some accounts—finally convinced Mohammed he was not insane. What he had received, the cousin said, was a divine revelation from the angel Gabriel telling him he was God's long-awaited messenger. Mohammed pondered that for some time, wondering why God would choose an illiterate forty-year-old camel merchant as His prophet. He spoke with friends and relatives before coming to the awesome conclusion that his mission was real.

The new movement he started was a democratic one with no clerical hierarchy. It was known as Islam, an Arabic word that means submission—submission to the will of God. Those who submitted, who believed that "there is no god but God, and Mohammed is the messenger of God," were Muslims, a word whose root form is the same as that for peace, *salaam*. The Muslims compiled Allah's revelations to Mohammed in the Koran, 114 *surahs* (chapters) of classical Arabic in verse that represent the only divine scripture in Islam.[2] "No other book," wrote historian Arthur Goldschmidt, Jr., in 1983, "has affected so many minds so powerfully and for so long."

Between the Koran and the *Sunna*—the Islamic practices based on the sayings and deeds of the Prophet—the Muslim is given instructions on every aspect of life, even down to the proper positions for sexual intercourse; there is no need to question anything. From the laws on inheritance to the punishment for crimes and to

---

[2] The Koran was not recorded in a single volume until after Mohammed's death. Its organization is chaotic. The chapters are not arranged chronologically or thematically and appear to have no other order than that the longest (with 286 verses) is placed first and the shortest (with three verses) last.

the role of women in society as well as to the prohibition on gambling, masturbation and alcohol, all is there as the perfect guide for the ages. As with Christianity and Judaism, great emphasis is placed on tolerance, love, compassion, integrity, justice and righteous living.

Rigorously monotheist, Islam is closer to Christianity than to any of the other major religions, a fact most Christians seem uncomfortable recognizing. Muslims accept Jesus Christ as a prophet (though not as the son of God) and Mary as Jesus's mother. They venerate Adam, Noah, Abraham, Moses, Jacob and Job. They believe in the resurrection of the body and in the concept of heaven and hell, heaven being everything the desert is not—a cool place of gardens and gushing fountains—and hell being a place of eternal physical and spiritual suffering where sinners must drink molten metal until their skin burns away. Both Islam and Christianity originated in the life of a single man, though a major difference in the faiths is that Mohammed—a historically verifiable figure—was entirely mortal. The Koran was not written *by* him but was merely transmitted *through* him.

Mohammed performed no miracles and was not an object of worship. He did not cure the blind or raise anyone from the dead or walk on water. Muslims in modern times, nevertheless, have treated the Prophet with a respect that borders on idolatry. T. E. Lawrence, for instance, found Mohammed to be such an omnipresent force that he referred to all Muslims as Mohammedans. One Egyptian religious leader of the 1800s refused to eat watermelons because he was not sure whether the Prophet had eaten them with or without the rind. University students I knew in Cairo debated for weeks whether it was proper to use a bristled toothbrush because such things did not exist in Mohammed's time. To this day no one is permitted to produce a likeness of the Prophet, not even a rough sketch, for fear that idolatry and demeaning misrepresentation could result. The 1976 film extravaganza *Mohammed, Messenger of God*, produced and directed by Moustapha Akkad and starring Anthony Quinn as one of Mohammed's uncles, Hamza, lasted three hours and never showed the man the movie was named for. Not even his voice was heard or his shadow cast. Though historically accurate, the $17 million production caused such an uproar among fuzzy-minded Muslims that King Faisal of Saudi Arabia pressured King Hassan II into expelling the film crew from Morocco (the movie was finished in Libya); Kuwait withdrew its financial support; black American Muslim radicals took over three buildings in Washington, D.C., holding 132 hostages and demanding that the movie be withdrawn from U.S. theaters (it was); and Akkad, a Syrian-born American, was threatened with knives on the streets of London.[3] Islam, the protesters said, belonged in the hands of religious scholars, not those of moviemakers. As for the thought of staging a musical called *Mohammed Superstar*, that would be nothing short of blasphemy. For the Arabs, religion is a serious business that has room for neither interpretation nor levity.

In the three years after his first revelation, Mohammed managed to win only thirty converts for Islam, including his wife and his cousin Ali. They kept a low profile but were subjected to great persecution—harassment, abuse, even torture—by the pagan Meccans who feared that Mohammed represented a challenge to their wealth and power. Some of his followers fled to safety in Abyssinia (Ethiopia), and Mohammed himself was kept under virtual house arrest, spared only because his uncle, Abu Talib, who had never converted and was highly respected as an honest merchant, refused to turn him over to the Meccans. In 619, nine years after the first revelation, his wife, Khadijah, and Abu Talib both died, and having lost his protectors, Mohammed knew he had to leave Mecca.

---

[3] The film played for three years in Europe, although its life span in U.S. theaters was brief because of the radicals' violent protest. It was never shown in Egypt and Syria; Saudi Arabia and most Arab countries, however, later decided that their judgment had been prematurely harsh, and *Mohammed, Messenger of God* is widely circulated in the Arab world today as an honest portrayal of Islam and is used in Arab schools as a teaching aid.

The trek to Medina began the next year with seventy of Mohammed's followers setting across the desert in small groups. The wings of Islam were spreading, and that year, 620, became the start of the Islamic calendar. Medina (then known as Yathrib) was two hundred seventy miles north of Mecca. It had a large Jewish population and an oasis over which two pagan tribes frequently fought. For Mohammed, this was an opportunity to become an accepted prophet in a new city and to deal with a people, the Jews, who already worshiped a single god. At the request of Muslim businessmen in Medina, he arbitrated the differences between the warring tribes, and tried hard to win the loyalty of the Jews by emphasizing the similarities between Islam and Judaism. He observed the fast of Yom Kippur and led his people in prayer facing Jerusalem. He even offered to join forces with the Jews in order to form a monotheistic bloc against the pagans. But the Jews rejected him as an Arabian prophet, believing him to be an untrained, unlettered man unfit for such a task.

Religiously the Jews could not reconcile the differences between the Koran and their own sacred scriptures; economically there was competition for control of the marketplace. Relations between the Jews and the Muslims grew progressively worse. The Jews' rejection of Mohammed the Prophet turned to scorn; the Muslims' tolerance of the Jews was replaced with contempt. "To those whom the burden of the Torah was entrusted and yet refused to bear it," says the Koran, "are like a donkey laden with books." In other verses, the Koran denounces the Jews as cheats and associates them, along with pagans, as among the most evil enemies of Islam.

Mohammed, saying he had had a Koranic revelation, changed the direction of prayer south toward Mecca, instead of north toward Jerusalem. The twenty-four-hour Yom Kippur fast was replaced with daytime fasting during the holy month of Ramadan. The Sabbath observance gave way to Friday prayers. Islam was becoming more Arab, more sectarian. The first bitter seeds of today's Arab-Israeli conflict had been planted.

Two of the three Jewish tribes in Medina were expelled for conspiring with the enemy during battles against Mohammed's Meccan foes. Jews of the third tribe, the Beni Quraiza, which had refused to help the Muslims during their battles in and around Medina, suffered the cruelest fate. They fought Mohammed's warriors in Medina for twenty-five days, finally surrendering on the condition that their punishment be determined by the Arab chieftain, Saad Ibn Moad, who was sympathetic toward them. But Moad had been wounded in the battle for Medina and had no tolerance left. On his orders, six hundred Jewish men were beheaded with swords, and their women and children were sold into slavery. Mohammed had now taken control of Medina, and the legend of his prowess quickly spread. Muslims spoke of his superhuman qualities, and many believed that by touching his robes they would be guaranteed a place in paradise. The massacre of the Beni Quraiza tribe was the only incident of organized violence against the Jews in early Islamic history. Generally the Muslims tolerated the Jews as People of the Book and protected them as second-class citizens. Today, ironically, that role is reversed, and it is the Arabs who live as inferior clients of the Jews in the Israeli-occupied territories.

Mohammed preached compassion and justice, not revenge and conquest, but the early days of Islam were nonetheless combative ones, and from this history some militant Arabs today find justification for the bloodshed in the Middle East. To develop an economic base and self-sufficiency, Mohammed and his people started raiding the caravans that were controlled by the pagans and escorted by Bedouin tribesmen who received protection money from Mecca. They even attacked during the holy months when warring was forbidden and during the pagans' annual pilgrimage to Mecca. This shocked many Muslims, but Mohammed had a revelation that allowed the raiding to continue: "They will question you about the holy month and fight in it, say . . . dissension is more wicked than killing."

The Muslims made the caravan business so risky that entire

tribes started breaking with Mecca and making treaties with Mohammed in order to share in the booty. Although outnumbered three to one, they mauled the pagans at Badr, a village southwest of Medina, in 624; the Koran mentions the battle as a mark of God's approval of the Islamic cause, and Arabs to this day look on victory as divine approbation and defeat as divine disapproval. There were some losses after Badr—Mohammed was wounded the next year at Uhud—but the tide had turned in the Prophet's favor. In 630 he gathered an army of ten thousand men and marched on Mecca. No homes, Mohammed told his warriors, were to be stormed, no women, children, old people or cripples hurt. Mecca fell with little bloodshed. The Muslims occupied the city and entered the Kaabah to destroy the idols. Bilal, a black slave whose freedom Mohammed had purchased, scampered up the Kaabah's wall and cupped his hands to his mouth,[4] and for the first time the muezzin's call to prayer swept over Mecca: "God is great. I testify that there is no god but God. I testify that Mohammed is the Prophet of God. . . ." Almost everyone in Mecca converted.

Mohammed was now in charge of a powerful army, and Islam was becoming a small religious state. He sent letters to the rulers of the world—among them the king of Persia, the emperor of Byzantium, the negus of Abyssinia and the governor of Egypt—inviting them to submit to Islam. Though they ignored him, his gesture showed the extraordinary confidence he now had in his mission.

Two years later Mohammed fell ill. He called his people to him and said:

> O, mankind, listen well. I may not be with you much longer. The weak among you, feed them with what you eat, dress them as you are dressed. You will meet your God and He will call you to account for your actions.

[4] Bilal was to become such a popular figure that in 1975 the militant, Chicago-based organization known as the Nation of Islam adopted the name Bilalians for its black members.

Let those who are present warn those who are absent you are all descended from Adam, and the best among you is he who most regards God. Think deeply about what He says. Let all your feuds be abolished. You must know that every Muslim is one of another. Between Muslims there are no races and no tribes. Nor must you take anything from your brother except what is given freely. Do not oppress and do not be oppressed. O, my people, I am but a man. It may be that the angel of death will visit me soon and death will overtake me, but I have left you a book revealed by God—the Koran, which is light and guidance.

Mohammed died on June 8, 632, and was buried next to the mosque in Medina. Although he never formally named a successor, he designated just before his death his best friend and father-in-law, Abu Bakr al-Siddiq, to lead the public prayers in his absence, and it was on him that the mantle of Islamic leadership would fall.

To the tribesmen, Mohammed's death meant that they no longer had to pay *zakat,* a form of tribute, and they broke with Islam. "Whoever worshiped Mohammed, let him know that Mohammed is dead," Abu Bakr said, "but whoever worshiped God, let him know that God lives and dies not." Abu Bakr took the title of *khalifat rasul Allah* (successor of the messenger of God, usually shortened to "caliph" in English) and sent his two top generals to force the Bedouin back into the *ummah,* the community of Muslims. Such a move would be equivalent today to Nicaragua declaring war on the United States of America, but the Bedouin capitulated, and under the second caliph, Umar (who ruled from 634 to 644), they were pardoned for having renounced Islam and enlisted to expand the territory of the ummah.

Umar called himself the Commander of the Believers, and from a purely military standpoint the success of his campaign was astonishing. Within little more than a decade of Mohammed's death the Islamic armies had captured Rome's Middle Eastern possessions (Palestine, Syria, Egypt and Cyrenaica, in northeast Libya) and, during a battle in a sandstorm at the river Yarmuk, had defeated the Byzantines—and the Roman emperor who shortly before had rejected the letter from the unknown Prophet of Arabia demanding submission. Next to fall would be the Sassanian shahs of Persia.

The Christians, persecuted by the Byzantines and believing that the coming of Islam meant the end of tyranny, welcomed the Muslims and in some cases, as in Egypt, even assisted them. The Muslims proved to be tolerant in administering the conquered lands. At Damascus, Syria, for instance, the Muslim general Khalid ibn al-Walid—a pagan, converted by Mohammed, who took the title the Sword of God—signed a treaty that read:

> This is what Khalid ibn al-Walid would grant to the inhabitants of Damascus if he enters therein: he promises to give them security for their lives, property and churches. The city wall shall not be demolished, neither shall any Muslim be quartered in their houses. Thereunto we give them the pact of God and the protection of His Prophet, the caliphs and the believers. So long as they pay the poll tax, nothing but good shall befall them.

The Muslims' early raids were not aimed exclusively at conquest or conversion. Rather, they were simply part of the Bedouin skirmishing traditions and were carried out primarily for economic motivations—the booty and tribute that amounted to 50 percent of one's wealth were healthy incentives for impoverished desert warriors—and thus the spread of Islam was more an economic phenomenon than a religious one. Nonetheless civilizations and empires fell under the banner of Islam, and barely a century after Mohammed lay quaking on his bed upon having received his revelation, Muslim soldiers and traders stood from Spain in the west, across North Africa and the Middle East, to the borders of China in the east. A new empire had been born.

That Islam survived the death of Mohammed was remarkable. That it spread like brushfire across a frontier forty-five hundred miles long and a thousand miles deep in the span of a century was startling. It was even more startling considering that the Arab armies (which included some Christians) seldom numbered more than a thousand men and were not as well equipped as the Persians or the Byzantines.

There are several reasons for the rapid spread of Islam: The Arabs fought few battles, but their victories were decisive ones that enabled them to gobble up huge chunks of territory at a time. They used the desert to their advantage, trapping their enemy in sand-storms and dry riverbeds, and they relied on two animals that made the conquests possible: for mobility, the swift, sure-footed Arabian horse whose flaring nostrils can take in large quantities of air; and for endurance, the one-humped camel that can drink twenty-five gallons of water in ten minutes and survive for days on a diet of thorny bushes and dried grass—its double row of eyelashes and its ability to close its nostrils for long periods of time protect it from sandstorms, while its soft two-toed feet serve the same purpose as balloon tires on a dune buggy. And finally, the Persians and Byzantines had exhausted their energies and resources fighting one another, enabling the Arabs to step into a void and bring the diverse cultures of Egypt, Iran, Iraq, Syria, North Africa and Western Europe under a single religious banner.

For those who accepted Islam there were five obligations: accepting one God and Mohammed as His Prophet; praying five times a day in a set sequence of motions; giving a specified amount of one's income—usually 2.5 percent—to the needy; fasting from dawn to dusk during the holy month of Ramadan; and making the *hadj* (pilgrimage) to Mecca during the twelfth month of the Muslim calendar at least once in a lifetime. The *hadj* represents the renewal of inner spirituality and the pilgrims' cry fills Mecca: "*Labayk, allahuma, labayk*" "Here I am, O Lord, here I am." (Making the pilgrimage remains such a proud moment that many Muslims add the word *hajji* (pilgrim) to their names and paint the outer walls of their homes with vivid murals depicting their journey to Mecca.)

Sometimes a sixth obligation is included in the pillars of Islam: the *jihad*. The word generally is translated in the West as "holy war," though its real definition is much wider. It means "utmost effort," or to protect and strive for Islam. This could include armed conflict, but the word does not connote irrational militancy as most Westerners believe. Nor, in its proper context, should it be perverted to mean waging war, as today's radical Muslims do when they call for a jihad against anyone who does not share their fanatical views.

What Islam brought to the world was more than a religion. It was a new way of life, a political and economic system, a set of laws, a code for social behavior. All believers are equal, and each communicates with his God directly rather than going through a priest. Every life is a statement of Islam. There can be no real separation of church and state because Islam is interwoven into every fabric and every moment of the Muslim's life.

Muslims share religious beliefs that are largely universal except in one area: the question of who was Mohammed's rightful successor. And that disagreement between the Sunnis and the Shiites has produced a thousand years of internal strife and become a schism over which more blood is likely to be shed in the Middle East.

The Sunnis are the conservatives of the Islamic world, and in countries with mixed populations they are the more economically successful of the two groups. They represent 90 percent of the Muslim population and the majority everywhere but Iran, Iraq, Lebanon and Bahrain. Their name comes from the word *Sunna*, and they accept the ascension and the legitimacy of the caliphs who followed the Prophet.

The Shiites (meaning "partisans" in Arabic) are the underprivileged minority who carry a sense of being oppressed and wrongly governed. Although the theological differences between the sects are small, the Shiites believe that only Mohammed's descendants can rightfully be caliphs and thus that the first caliph should have been the Prophet's cousin Ali, not his best friend, Abu Bakr. In their doctrine, the twelfth and last of the Shiite imams—or successors to the Prophet—will return to earth from a cave, where he was hidden away eleven centuries ago, to rule the perfect, godly society. Until then, all states are at least vaguely illegitimate.

In the seventh century the Shiites' first leader, Husayn, sacrificed his life and those of his followers during a battle in Iraq in an attempt to realize Shiite domination over all Muslims. His martyrdom is still celebrated each year by young men who strike themselves bloody with fists and chains and swords in sorrow and exultation. Forty days after a death, Shiites traditionally gather to remember the departed—and if his death was violent, to think of revenge. It is no coincidence that Muslim fanatics who welcome death today on the battlefields of Iran and in the car explosions of Lebanon are Shiites, following their leader's path toward a society that they believe will be just and pious.

The schism, however, did not interfere with Islam's westward advance, and by the tenth century the Arabs had forayed to within 170 miles of Paris and had begun on the Iberian Peninsula a civilization superior to anything Spain had ever known. Córdoba alone had seven hundred mosques, sixty thousand palaces and seventy libraries, including one with half a million manuscripts and a staff of researchers and bookbinders. With a population of five hundred thousand, more than ten times that of Paris, it was the most sophisticated city in Europe, and it had the first streetlights on the Continent. Later, Arab kingdoms flourished in the mountains of Andalusia, and the Alhambra citadel in Granada, begun in 1238, was one of the wonders of the civilized world.

But even as the magnificent citadel took form the Arabs' golden age was nearing its end, a victim of the Arabs' inability to unite and of the Christians' growing military strength.

The Crusades of the twelfth and thirteenth centuries were in effect a Christian jihad. Pope Urban II in 1095 urged Christians to unite against the Islamic threat and to seize the Holy Sepulcher in Jerusalem from "the wicked race" of Saracens (a medieval word for both Arabs and Muslims). An army of noblemen and peasants pushed eastward as a frenzied mob. The Arabs were shocked. They could not understand what they had done to offend the Christians, and they could not comprehend the behavior of the crude foreigners who did not bathe or wear silks or walk on fine carpets.

On July 15, 1099, the Crusaders entered Jerusalem. They reclaimed the Holy Sepulcher, marking the site where Christ was buried, and plundered hundreds of silver and gold candelabra from the nearby Dome of the Rock, from which Muslims believe Mohammed the Prophet ascended on his one-night flight to heaven. They also carried out such wholesale slaughter of "heathen" Muslims and Jews that a Latin chronicler of the time wrote: "The heaps of heads and hands could be seen through the streets and squares."

Across Spain, the Christians pushed the Arabs back, town by town. Two North African dynasties, the Almoravids and the Almohads, came to battle the Europeans but ended up seizing power themselves and fighting each other. Finally, in 1492—the year Columbus set sail for the Americas—the merged kingdoms of Ferdinand and Isabella hoisted the flag of Christian Spain over Alhambra. The last Muslim king, Mohammed XI, rode into exile carrying a note from his mother that read, "Weep like a woman for the city you would not defend like a man."

THE CRUSADES achieved no permanent results in terms of military conquest. Jerusalem and most of Palestine returned to Arab hands; an Arab hero, Saladin, who was a Kurd from Mesopotamia, founded a new dynasty; the Christian warriors were shoved back to small coastal enclaves in the Middle East, remaining there as petty rulers until their final defeat by Egyptian Mamluks (soldiers who were originally slaves) late in the thirteenth century.

But the two centuries of conflict between Europe and the Middle East had other important and lasting results. The eastern

Mediterranean was opened to European shipping, and control of those trade routes would affect East-West relations for centuries to come. The Arabs came to understand that unity and survival were synonymous, that Western intervention posed a continuing threat to Islam, that isolation was the surest means of enduring. The Arabs do not remember that era fondly, but in the United States it is curious that so many sports teams today are named the Crusaders. (I doubt that there has ever been a team called the Saracens.)

No sooner had the Crusades ended than another group swept through the Middle East under the banner of God. These were the Ottoman Turks, and after taking Constantinople in 1453, they carried Islam to Greece and to the gates of Vienna before being pushed back. The Turks ruled much of the Arab world for three hundred fifty years but had little appreciation of anything Arab. A period of isolation and intellectual decline set in; the post-Renaissance era when Europe forged ahead so dramatically, using many of the contributions the Arabs had made to build a new world, passed the Arabs by. Islam became a cocoon, and the Middle East slipped into a state of lethargy, to remain there until shaken by two monumental events in the twentieth century: the creation of Israel and the discovery of oil.

THE EMOTIONAL soul of Islam today remains in Mecca. But its intellectual heart is in Cairo, on the campus of the world's oldest continuously operating university. Al Azhar sprawls across four city blocks as a cluster of low, dingy buildings set behind stone walls and wrought-iron fences. Its 120,000 students, representing seventy-seven countries, are all Sunnis, although the rector of the university told me that Shiites are welcome to apply if they choose. None do. In keeping with Islamic tradition, women on campus cover their hair and shoulders with veils and are segregated from the men in separate classrooms.

Al Azhar's great influence stems from the fact that its *sheiks*, or religious leaders, have been entrusted by tradition to interpret the Koran for Muslims throughout the world. Precisely what, for instance, does the Koran mean when it says, "And when ye meet those who misbelieve, then strike off the heads until ye have massacred them, and bind fast the bonds"? Or when it says, "O Prophet, tell thy wives and thy daughters and the women of the believers to draw their cloaks close round them . . . so that they may be recognized [as pious women] and not be annoyed"? As the explicators of the Koran, the sheiks have become the Arab equivalent of Western court justices, and Al Azhar has become the supreme court. "This is the place where the Koran can be saved from personal interpretation, which is the one thing that could destroy Islam," a university official said.

The university opened in 972, and the first classes were held in the open courtyard of the mosque, where a handful of students sat at the feet of sheiks, repeating the words of the Koran until they had learned them by heart. The students later returned to their villages as literate but uneducated men. Today's students, packed a thousand strong into sweaty classrooms, are largely from low-income families and often of peasant origin. They spend at least four hours a week studying the Koran, and their choice of majors runs the gamut from medicine to agriculture. But the most popular major is no longer religion; it is commerce. "The venerated halls of Al Azhar," complained the *Egyptian Gazette*, "are turning out graduate classes of disco proprietors and video salesmen."

For most of its years Al Azhar was a seat of political opposition. It was there, after the students and sheiks rejected Napoleon Bonaparte's plea "to give [his] soldiers fifty years to understand Islam," that resistance to French rule was organized in the nineteenth century. It was there that the seeds of rebellion against the British were planted in the twentieth century. And it was there that Gamal Abdel Nasser came in 1956 to rally the masses against the attack on the Suez Canal by France, Britain and Israel.

Until 1961, students studied only theology, Islamic law and the

Arabic language at Al Azhar, but Nasser saw Al Azhar's power—and Islam's as well—as a threat to his own political authority, and he secularized the university and opened its doors to women. Nasser was among the first of the Arab leaders to successfully manipulate Islam in order to achieve personal objectives, and he had no trouble finding sheiks willing to give Nasserite interpretations to the Koran. When, for example, Nasser, a socialist, caused an outcry by nationalizing the economy, he called on the sheiks for support— Mohammed, after all, was a businessman and the Koran encourages capitalism; they complied, ruling that the move was justified on grounds that the Koran says the rich should give alms to the poor. Later, Anwar Sadat needed the same kind of backing after negotiating an unpopular peace treaty with the Israelis at Camp David; the sheiks responded by saying there was nothing unholy about the alliance because Mohammed himself had once struck an agreement with the Jews.

Libya's leader, Moammar Kadafi, was so angered by the ruling that he called for a "popular invasion" of Al Azhar. And the Saudis were reported to have offered a big chunk of money to move the university from Egypt to Saudi Arabia. They complained that the university had slipped outside the mainstream of Islam and was too pro-Egypt to have unquestionable credibility. Al Azhar's rector, for instance, has cabinet rank equivalent in protocol to that of the prime minister of the Egyptian government and is appointed by the Egyptian president. This ensures that religious rulings largely reflect government thinking on important issues. Without that kind of support from a country's religious elite, no Arab government could survive for long.

WE IN the West have always been uncomfortable with Islam. We have tolerance for, even interest in, Buddhism and Oriental religions, but Islam—a faith followed by one sixth of the world's population—seems rooted in fanaticism and vaguely threatening. Many of us think of Christianity as standing *for* things and of Islam as standing *against* things.

Even Mohammed has taken his share of knocks in the West. While Muslims embrace him as the embodiment of religious virtue, of kindness, compassion and generosity, some skeptics have dismissed him as a fraud, a charlatan and a renegade. John Gunther compared him with Mussolini and Hitler. In *Inside Asia*, published in 1939, Gunther wrote:

> The temptation to include Mohammed in a gallery of living portraits is almost irresistible. His career of conversion, incitation and terrific conquest is extraordinarily contemporary. Half a dozen times in discussing his life and career, one comes across modern analogies. For instance, the ... flight from Mecca to Medina is startlingly like the March on Rome. Like Mussolini, Mohammed prepared the way well in advance, and did not travel himself until his underlings had arranged and guaranteed a good reception. He was—as Hitler is—a mystic, an anti-Semite and an expansionist.

My own initial images of Islam go back only to the 1960s, when groups of sullen-faced, nattily dressed young men known as Black Muslims appeared on America's streets selling newspapers that espoused the prophetlike wisdom of Malcolm X. (Did I subtly fear them because they were black or because they were Muslims?) "These are *bad* people," a police chief told me in Nevada, where I was researching a story on the organization. I had no reason to doubt him, and the story I wrote caused such a stir that the heavyweight boxing champion Muhammad Ali—then known as Cassius Clay—came to Las Vegas for a press conference to defend Islam. He shook his huge fist at me and roared, "How can you write such lies without knowing anything about Islam?" Before stalking out of the room, a member of Ali's entourage gave me an English-language translation of the Koran, but I never bothered to read it until I got to the Middle East twenty years later.

A lot of us, I think, are still held hostage by the same kind of ignorance I displayed. Mention Islam, and our vision is of mobs swirling around a U.S. embassy, chanting "God is great!" and "Death to America!" Or it's of bearded fanatics in the streets of Beirut who hold a Koran in one hand and a rifle in the other. Yet this isn't what Mohammed the Prophet taught at all, and the vast majority of Arabs condemn such behavior as being anti-Islamic. Islam is not typified by the war junkies in Beirut any more than Judaism is by the zealots who stone cars driving through their Jerusalem neighborhoods on the Sabbath.

Sadly, though, organized religion all too often is misused in the Middle East to justify unreligious deeds. In the Muslim nations, as in Israel, the Moral Majority is winning, and actions both good and bad are cloaked in a gown of divine righteousness. When Libya's Kadafi, a soldier of limited mental capacity, evokes the name of God to boast about the killing of Libyan dissidents, one wonders if he ever read the Koranic verse (VII, 199) that says, "Keep to forgiveness (O Mohammed), and enjoin kindness, and turn away from the ignorant."

THE MAKING OF TERRORISM

Let terrorists be aware that when the rules of international
behavior are violated, our policy will be one of swift and
effective retribution.

— *President Ronald Reagan, 1981*

MOAMMAR KADAFI, looking pale and tired, was content to let the
crowd wait a bit longer. He had entered the military complex quietly, three hours behind schedule, and now he stood with his
bodyguards, just out of sight of the parade grounds, tugging at the
sleeves of his uniform, patting his Afro haircut with an open palm
and fidgeting like an actor preparing to walk onstage.

Inside, gathered on bleachers around the parade field, the crowd
was starting to grow restless. It had been rounded up off the streets
by government security men and told to sit there to greet Kadafi's
arrival, but that was six hours ago, and the wooden seats were hard
and the heat was oppressive. "Be patient," a government man said,
moving among the people. "Brother Leader will be here any minute." From the surrounding rooftops, marksmen carrying rifles with
telescopic sights peered down on the crowd.

Patience was never one of my virtues, and I killed time drifting
among the graduating class of female soldiers who stood in a slop-
pily arranged military formation, attempting to engage them in
conversation. They blushed and giggled at my questions and didn't
seem very fierce at all. A plainclothes security man pushed his way

over toward me. "No talking to the people!" he shouted. "Now wait a minute," one of the American journalists next to me said, "if Libya is a people's democracy, can't the people decide for themselves if they want to speak?" But the security man was adamant. "The people are *not allowed* to talk," he said, offering what turned out to be a fairly accurate assessment of exactly how much freedom The People have in a Kadafiesque society.

For three years my telexes to Tripoli requesting a visa had gone unanswered, so for this occasion, the fifteenth anniversary of the coup d'état that had brought Kadafi to power, I had flown from Cairo to Rome and virtually camped out on the doorstep of the Libyan embassy. Kadafi didn't let journalists in for just wandering around his country, but in a controlled situation celebrating some revolutionary milestone, visas usually were not difficult to obtain, and mine was granted after three days in Rome. I checked into the ramshackle Beach Hotel, overlooking the Mediterranean in Tripoli, and together with several colleagues was put aboard a yellow government bus for the first event of the anniversary—Kadafi awarding diplomas to female graduates at the military academy. For the eccentric, unpredictable colonel, this represented a step toward his goal of militarizing the entire country and giving arms and training to everyone old enough to shoulder a rifle.

Kadafi appeared angry at something or other as he continued to fidget with his uniform behind the bleachers. His brow was furrowed and his fresh-shaven jaw was set rigidly. Then, like an actor, he ran both his hands over his face and his expression changed, the look of brooding darkness replaced by a glistening smile. He nodded to an assistant, and shoulders thrust back, his right hand swinging a gold-topped marshal's baton, he marched through the chain-link gate and onto the parade grounds with giant strides, closely followed by two Range Rovers loaded with security agents clutching machine guns and by his own silver-colored, bulletproof BMW sedan. The crowd let out a delighted sigh, "Ahhhhhh," then broke into wild cheers. Kadafi, playing to the audience, changed his expression again, this time to one of pleased surprise, as if he were startled by the warmth of the reception.

He settled into a chair near the honor guard and removed his wraparound sunglasses, as it was now early evening and quite dark. The visor of his military hat was pulled so low that he had to tip his head back to see, and that cocksure poise made him appear both arrogant and commanding. Kadafi is a handsome, youthful-looking man, olive-skinned, five feet ten inches tall, trim. He radiates a presence that makes it difficult *not* to look at him, and although he seemed bored by the graduation ceremony, whispering with aides and tossing the crowd a perfunctory clench-fisted salute at each mention of his name, I found his manner mesmerizing. He captured everyone else's stare, too, and I wondered if they, like me, were asking themselves what inner voices called to Kadafi. Was he at this very moment hatching some outrageous plot? Did he really not recognize the threshold that separates demons and saints?

Jaafar Numeiri, the former Sudanese president, once explained Kadafi's Machiavellian schemes by saying the man had "a split personality—both evil." President Anwar Sadat of Egypt called him "a vicious criminal, one hundred percent sick." And President Reagan, early in his administration, made him something of a folk hero among radical Arabs by calling him the most dangerous man in the world, quite an achievement for a semieducated, one-time goatherd who led a backward desert country of 3.5 million people, most of them Bedouin nomads. I'm not sure Kadafi deserves all the notoriety Washington has given him, but I do think he would make a fascinating case study for a psychiatrist: "Now tell me, Colonel Kadafi, how long have you been having these dreams about restructuring the world order? . . . When you were growing up poor, did you feel, ah, let's say, inferior to those who had money and power? . . ." Whatever the diagnosis, Kadafi has been adroit at getting the world to pay attention to his preposterous proclamations and policies. He has even managed to maintain a vague respectability within the

Arab world because the vision he espouses is that of the old Arab party line: the destruction of Israel, the formation of an Arab nation and the righteousness of Islam.

"I am the leader of a revolution that expresses the feeling of the whole Arab nation and the whole Islamic world," Kadafi said in the 1980s. "We in Libya are responsible for the Arab nation and our behavior must be respectable."

His delusions, though, don't square with the realities, for Kadafi gets the same kind of reception in the Arab world that an ex-convict in Bermuda shorts would get interviewing for a job at IBM. When he flew into Tunisia without an invitation and asked for a meeting with President Habib Bourgiba, Bourgiba hurriedly retired to his bedroom and said he had the flu. (Bourgiba didn't want to hassle with Kadafi, but he had the good sense not to want to offend him either.) And when Kadafi flew into Morocco, King Hassan greeted him on the tarmac with a brotherly Arab embrace, then had his security people disarm Kadafi's bodyguards. Yet few Arabs dared denounce Kadafi's ultimate goals. And none dared to remind Kadafi that without oil money, he would be as inconsequential a world figure as the president of Burundi or the king of Swaziland. Libya is, after all, 93 percent desert and gets 99 percent of its income from oil and all its notoriety from gun bearers. Take away the oil and the guns and Kadafi would be the leader of a cultural backwater ranking alongside the Djiboutis and the Somalias and the other forgotten nations of the world.

Kadafi was tough to ignore because he was an architect of a new phenomenon in the Middle East—state-sponsored terrorism. His government was probably the only one in the world that admitted murder and terrorism were part of official foreign and domestic policy, and Kadafi himself has never been able to distinguish between a code of civilized behavior and the use of violent means to reach supposedly righteous ends.

"Yes, I am a terrorist when it comes to the dignity of this nation," he said in 1985 as the majority of Arab leaders showed signs of moderation of which he did not approve. "I will take up responsibility and begin terrorism against the Arab rulers, threaten and frighten them, and sever relations. And if I could, I would behead them one by one."

His use of the words "dignity" and "responsibility" in justifying terrorism is curious. This is a man who has been accused of mining the Red Sea, plotting the assassination of the heads of state of the United States, Britain, France, West Germany and Saudi Arabia, planning the capture of the Grand Mosque in Mecca, calling on American blacks in the U.S. Army to revolt, supporting liberation and terrorist organizations everywhere, from Asia to Ireland ("Minorities are nations in search of their nationhood"), killing a score of Libyan dissidents abroad, blowing up Pan Am Flight 103 over Lockerbie, Scotland, and trying to buy an atom bomb from China. He also ordered an Egyptian submarine captain to ram and sink the liner *Queen Elizabeth II* with its passengerload of American Jews traveling to Haifa for Israel's twenty-fifth anniversary. The submarine captain radioed his government for clarification and was told to make an immediate accident-free journey back to Egypt, which he did.

Eventually the world called in its chips on Kadafi. U.S. bombers sunk two Libyan vessels and attacked a missile site in March 1986. A month later U.S. warplanes struck terrorist-related targets in Banghazi and Tripoli, coming within a whisker of taking out Kadafi himself. The Pan Am flight went down in 1988, and finally, in 1992, the U.N. imposed sanctions against Libya.

Then a funny thing happened. Kadafi faded from center stage. His public appearances became few, his bizarre proclamations, rare. His linkage to terrorism disappeared, at least from public view. He desperately wanted to see the sanctions lifted and his tarnished image burnished. His behavior became so respectable that when terrorists struck the World Trade Center and the Pentagon on September 11, 2001, killing 3,200, Kadafi joined in the condemnations of an act of terror.

MOAMMAR ("HE who builds") Kadafi was born in 1942 in a goatskin tent, the only son of an itinerant and illiterate farmer who raised barley and livestock. His Bedouin relatives belonged to a small tribe, the Ghadaffa, and were deeply religious people of simple tastes and tough-minded independence shaped by their environment. "Life is so severe in the desert," Kadafi said, "and it was that severity that gave me the spirit of struggle, of the fight, the power to persevere. You have to depend on yourself in the desert."

Kadafi's father, Mohammed Abdel Salam Ben Hamed Ben Mohammed, once told an interviewer that the inspiration to send his son to a nearby Muslim school "came to me from God." The boy did well and memorized the Koran by the age of eight. But young Moammar was filled with the bitterness of social injustice. He resented the slights he often received as a simple nomad, and he detested the Italians, who had been ruthless occupiers of Libya from 1911 until World War II and had killed his grandfather—or "martyred" him, to use Kadafi's word—during the 1911 invasion and wounded his father in a later battle. Soon the youth had learned a new word—revolution—and by the time he was fourteen, the year the Suez Canal war broke out, he was urging his classmates: "We must go into the army. That is the only way to make a revolution."

The Arab world then was a different place from what it is today. Israel in 1956 was only eight years old and did not seem militarily invincible, and the humiliating defeat in the Six-Day War was not to be experienced by the Arabs until eleven years later. The monarchy had been overthrown in Egypt, and colonialism had ended or would end that year in Iraq, Jordan, Lebanon, Libya, Morocco, Oman, Sudan, Syria and Tunisia. The Algerians had taken up arms against the French; oil was starting to flow in generous quantities; and in Cairo, eight hundred miles from Tripoli, the first and last hero of the modern Arab world, Gamal Abdel Nasser, president of Egypt, the one Arab country with cultural and military strength, had captivated millions with his visions of a Pan-Arab nation that would "drive Israel into the sea." The Arabs, brimming with confidence and exuberance, were coming of age.

Nasser's Voice of the Arabs was broadcast throughout the Middle East from Cairo in the 1950s. Its rhetoric was exciting and inflammatory, stirring nationalistic pride in a people who had known two thousand years of foreign rule at the hands of the Greeks, Romans, Fatimids, Mamluks, Ottoman Turks and European colonialists. The Arabs found Nasser's bombastic messages psychologically heartening, even though most realized his words were intellectually empty. But Kadafi took them seriously, and given his limited exposure to any world beyond that of the desert and religion, he was to remain an intellectual captive of those broadcasts forever.

Kadafi entered the Royal Military Academy in Benghazi when he was nineteen and immediately began recruiting classmates for a revolutionary cabal similar to the one Nasser had led in overthrowing King Farouk a decade earlier. He and his friends were pious and serious. They did not smoke, drink, fraternize with women or attend parties. In 1966 Kadafi was sent to England for six months to study armored warfare. It was his first trip outside the Arab world (he still knows little of the non-Arab world) and he loved it. He mastered English (which he generally refuses to speak in public today), took long walks through the countryside of Beaconsfield and Salisbury Plain and visited many English churches—he decided, to his satisfaction, that Great Britain was a very religious country. By 1969 Kadafi was back in Libya and was a lieutenant in the army signal corps. He and his friends were ready to strike against King Idris.

The king's regime was elitist, corrupt and pro-Western. (The British had two bases in Libya, at Tobruk and El Adem, and ten thousand Americans were stationed at the Wheelus Air Force Base outside Tripoli.) Idris left for a holiday in Turkey in August, and on September 1, 1969, the Revolutionary Command Council took power in a coup d'état that was bloodless except for the accidental shooting death of one soldier. Kadafi was twenty-seven years old. Today in reading the speech Kadafi broadcast to the Libyan people that day, I am struck by two points: first, no one should be surprised by his policies—he has acted exactly as he said he would; and second, how pained and vengeful and full of humiliation Kadafi was. He was still fighting the Crusaders war.

"Give us your hands," he said that day. "Open up your hearts to us. Forget past misfortunes and, as one people prepare to face the enemies of Islam, the enemies of humanity, those who have burned our sanctuaries and mocked our honor. Thus shall we rebuild our glory. We shall resurrect our heritage, we shall avenge our wounded dignity, and restore the rights which have been wrested from us."

Except for expelling twenty thousand Italians who had lived in Libya as colonialists, Kadafi was not vindictive in those first months of power. Some members of the former regime remained in power to help build a new country; others were allowed to start new lives at home or abroad. Negotiations to terminate the American and British military presence were handled amiably and professionally, and the U.S. ambassador, Joseph Palmer II, managed to convince Washington that Kadafi represented no threat to American interests. Kadafi handled negotiations to take national control of the oil industry from international companies so deftly that even Western oil men marveled at his skill.

In Tripoli, he moved quickly to ban alcohol and gambling, both forbidden by the Koran. He determined that functionaries were spending too much time drinking coffee and reading newspapers at their desks, so he ordered that most furniture in government ministries be hauled away. That didn't greatly inconvenience the civil servants; they adjusted quickly, brewing their coffee on the cement floors and leaning against corridor walls to read their papers. Kadafi walked into a hospital late one night, dressed as a nomad, his face half hidden behind a swath of cloth, and told the doctor, who was Chinese, that he must follow him immediately to his home. "My father is dying," Kadafi lied. The doctor refused and prescribed two aspirin. The new Libyan leader swept aside his veil and said, "Doctor, you will always regret giving such a prescription to a dying man. You are leaving this country. Not next week. Not tomorrow. Tonight."

Kadafi is in essence a tribal prophet on a sacred mission. He sees himself carrying the banner of the two most important figures in the Arab world—God and Nasser—and even after the 1967 Arab-Israeli war, when Nasser was spiritually exhausted and more moderate in tone, Kadafi continued to echo his mentor's time-worn message that was pro-Arab and anti-Israeli. By then more and more Arabs, though not Kadafi, recognized the failure of Nasser, who had nationalized—and wrecked—the Egyptian economy and committed his troops to a futile war in Yemen. All the while, Israel was growing stronger and the Arabs, as a unit, were becoming weaker.

Nasser came to Libya in 1970, a few months before his death, and bestowed the mantle of Arab leadership on Kadafi. "I feel a new strength, a new blood in me," Nasser told a public rally. "I feel that the Arab people recognize themselves in you [the Libyan people], and that they have rediscovered their determination. In leaving you, I say to you, my brother Moammar Kadafi is the representative of the Arab revolution and of Arab unity. My dear brothers, may God watch over you for the well-being of the Arab people. May you go from victory to victory, for your victories will be the victory of the Arab people."

Nasser was, in effect, paraphrasing the Koran, which says, "Lo! The party of God, they are the victorious." The torch had been passed, and Kadafi's mission confirmed.

Against this background—Kadafi's upbringing, his fascination with Nasser, his ability to think but not to reason, his access to a windfall treasure chest that in thirty years had transformed his wasteland nation from one of the world's poorest countries into one of the richest—the Libyan leader is neither unusual nor, by regional standards, crazy. He is the Don Quixote of the desert tilting at windmills. He is one of many men who have assumed a messianic role and passed briefly through Arab history with a raised sword. He is at once cunning and naïve, primitive but not mad. What makes him dangerous is that he, like Ayatollah Ruhollah Khomeini of Iran, has perverted Islam and manipulated it to fit his own warped image of the world order. Both men, I suspect, may suffer under the delusion of being the twelfth imam.

KADAFI'S ECCENTRIC social, economic and political ideas are embodied in three thin green volumes collectively called *The Green Book* and subtitled *The Third Universal Theory*. They are, in effect, a Bedouin version of Mao Tse-tung's *Little Red Book*, but their contents are mostly a mumbo jumbo of non sequiturs and perplexing observations. Example: "Woman is a female and man is a male. Man, being a male, does not menstruate and he is not subject to the monthly period which is a bleeding. . . . As the man does not get pregnant, he is not liable to the feebleness which woman, being a female, suffers. . . . Women are exactly like blossoms which are created to attract pollen and to produce seeds. A woman is tender. A woman is pretty. A woman weeps easily. A woman is easily frightened. Thus driving woman to do man's work is unjust aggression against the femininity with which she is naturally provided for a natural purpose essential to life."

The key idea in *The Green Book*—a blueprint for the development of an Islamic socialistic republic—is to abolish government and turn the nation into one giant town hall in which every adult directly participates in running the country. ("Representation is a denial of participation.") Even decisions pertaining to Libya's most sophisticated weapons would be in the hands of the masses. ("The army will become the people and the people will become the army.") In the Kadafiesque Islamic Utopia of *The Green Book*, there would be no laws, no money, no private enterprise, no rental houses or apartments. ("Man's freedom is lacking if someone else controls what he needs.")

The week I was in Tripoli, he had closed the pastry and barber shops—cakes and haircuts are now available only at state stores—and shut down all primary schools in a step toward his goal of eliminating formal education entirely. ("Ignorance," *The Green Book* says, "will come to an end when everything is presented as it actually is and when knowledge about everything is available to each person in the manner that suits him.") High school teachers had previously been given military rank; embassies abroad had been turned into "people's bureaus" run by "students" who used their diplomatic privileges to smuggle guns and explosives around the world; all money in excess of $3,300 in bank accounts had been seized by the government; and the salaries of all workers had been abolished in favor of "fees" and a share of profits, making everyone a partner in every factory and business. To encourage the demise of private ownership, Kadafi ordered all the country's land-tenure records burned.

The results were startling and far from Utopian. From the shores of Tripoli to the halls of the People's Palace, the capital exudes the grimness of an Eastern European city. Trash covers the boulevards that skirt the Mediterranean coastline, and in the shade of dying palm trees the gardens of old Italian villas have become tangles of overgrown weeds. Nowhere could I find a playground or a movie theater or a café with people in it. The streets, mostly deserted and filled with shuttered shops, feel ghostlike, and the well-intended but inexperienced people's committees that are running everything from the hotels to the government offices have elevated inefficiency to a high art form. At the international airport, the makeshift group of air traffic controllers had created such a dangerous mess that Kadafi had had to relent and call in a colonel to take charge.

There is, I think, ample evidence to suggest that Kadafi's self-proclaimed revolution is a fake. He has, for instance, exempted the three most important institutions from the structure of people's committees: the army, the oil industry and the central bank. What Kadafi is saying is "Power to the people, but don't let them touch the money or the guns." Because of sanctions and his own misadventures, Kadafi ended up running a country so impoverished and dispirited that the oil seemed almost irrelevant.

The people's congresses, which meet to discuss everything from foreign affairs to factory production and give a voice to everyone from illiterate Bedouin to slick army colonels, are smoke screens, camouflaging what is not a revolution in the accepted sense but only the remaking of a country by a single man. "Brother Leader"— Kadafi has done away with all official titles of state—has the final word on everything. Others' authority is limited to giving rubber-stamp approval to his decisions. And in the police state Kadafi has created, those who do not acquiesce are good candidates for exile, prison or death.

It is worth noting that Kadafi's meddling—sending troops to Uganda and Chad, trying to overthrow governments in Ethiopia, Gambia, Ghana, Morocco, Somalia, Sudan and Tunisia, promoting terrorism in Europe and the Middle East, sponsoring failed merger attempts with Algeria, Chad, Egypt, Niger, Sudan and Syria—has earned him not a single foreign policy success. Nor have the billions of dollars spent in the name of Islam and Arab unity bought him a single friend. In 1976, for instance, Kadafi flew into Bangui, capital of the Central African Republic, to offer Life-President Jean-Bédel Bokassa $2 million to become a Muslim. Bokassa pocketed the check with thanks and adopted the name Salah Eddine Ammed. No sooner had Kadafi gotten back on the plane to Tripoli than Ammed the Muslim announced that he had again become Bokassa the Christian.

But what about the Libyans themselves? Are they better off under Colonel Kadafi than under King Idris? Assuming that most Libyans are fairly simple, religious peasants who do not run afoul of the authorities, the answer is probably yes. Although his national achievements are embarrassingly negligible compared with what Saudi Arabia and other oil producers have accomplished, Kadafi has managed to build two hundred thousand houses and hundreds of schools, plant four hundred million trees, raise civil servants' salaries from $1,700 to $10,000 and draw up the blueprint for a national development plan worth a mind-boggling $62 billion. Prostitutes and beggars were banished from the streets. The literacy rate increased, medical care improved. He condemned communism and capitalism—the first two "universal orders"—for being atheistic and exploitive, respectively. He bought $27 billion worth of weapons from the Soviet Union, much of which is rusting and uncrated in the desert, but he never sold out to any foreign power. He prays five times a day, rides horseback with the skill and daring of a conquering warrior, lives an austere life in the army barracks, speaks of the liberation of Palestine as a sacred cause and returns often to the desert to sit barefooted and berobed in his father's tent. Who can deny that the blood of Arabia runs through his veins?

So the peasant class, which had nothing to lose anyway, is not unhappy; the army, bought off with perks that give its men elite status, professes loyalty; and the middle and upper classes don't matter because most of their members are living in exile. Kadafi has crafted an obedient nation. One day the alienation that surely festers beneath the surface may explode, most likely in the form of a military rebellion, but for now "Brother Leader" is free to carry on in his fiefdom like a bull set loose in a china shop. His strange ways are a reminder that money doesn't necessarily breed conservatism, and that ignorance and wealth can be a dangerous combination.

After three days in Libya, my colleagues and I were told that our visas had expired. The anniversary celebration was over. I boarded Alitalia Flight 883 for Rome, squeezing into a middle seat next to an Italian contractor, who kept mumbling something about being able to have wine with dinner when he got home. The Boeing 737 carried a full load of passengers (foreigners, not Libyans), and as it taxied down the runway and lifted off, Tripoli disappearing from view over the left wing, everyone in the cabin broke into applause.

MANY WESTERNERS had the impression that Kadafi sat in a command post, poring over maps and intelligence reports as he manipulated a network of Libyan, Syrian, Iranian and Lebanese terrorists, much as a general directs his troops in battle. Washington itself reinforced this conception by fingering Kadafi as the prime source of evil in the Arab world. Two points need correction: First, the terrorist network in the Middle East was a loosely knit one with no formal command structure and little, if any, coordination between governmental agencies and free-lance groups. Distrustful of one another, each jealously guarded its information, plans and methods of operation—which, after all, they had to use against one another from time to time. And second, Kadafi was a junior partner in the world of terrorism. Before a U.S. serviceman was killed in a West German disco bombing in April 1986—a bombing that led two weeks later to the retaliatory U.S. air strike against Libya—no American had been killed as a result of Libyan terrorist actions. Kadafi, though, was singled out by Washington because, with a wimpy army and his own penchant for bravado, he was an obvious and easy target. There was little risk that the Soviets or the Arabs would come to his aid with anything more than rhetoric. But Kadafi posed far less threat to the global order than, say, Syria's silk-smooth president, Hafez al-Assad, who condemned political violence at the same time that he was promoting it, and ridding the world of Kadafi would have had little effect on the scope and dimensions of state-sponsored terrorism.

Perhaps the most frightening aspect of this new growth industry is that no one has been able to deal with it effectively, and that no one is immune. The muscle-bound major powers have learned that force has its limitations—a lesson the United States remembers from Vietnam and the Russians from Afghanistan. The Arabs have learned that to be moderate—to speak of peace with Israel, alliances with the West, secularism within the so-called Arab nation—is to be vulnerable, and scores of Arabs who could have made the Middle East a better place have been murdered by Arab terrorists. And Israel has learned that to ignore the causes of terrorism and to fight violence with violence only begets more violence. Each year the number of terrorist attacks throughout the world is growing at the rate of 12 to 15 percent. In 1968 there were fifty acts of international terrorism; by 1986 the total had increased tenfold. The number of nations victimized annually by terrorism grew from twenty-nine to sixty-five in that period. For countries such as Libya and Iran, terrorism has replaced diplomacy as the prime tool of foreign policy. It enables nations to use surrogates to kill and maim, and then to condemn the killing and maiming of innocents. Terrorism has become institutionalized, and affects relations between countries and national policies, the way diplomats conduct business and expatriates live their lives.

A FEW minutes past 6:00 A.M. on October 23, 1983, an old yellow Mercedes-Benz truck caught Eddie DiFranco's eye as it circled twice in a parking lot next to the U.S. Marines' base in Beirut. The sun is just coming up over the Mediterranean at that hour, and Beirut is always deceptively peaceful and beautiful in the first flush of day. DiFranco, a lance corporal, had no particular reason to worry. The base was located on the perimeter of the international airport and cargo trucks moved through the area regularly.

I had been at the nearby port fourteen months earlier to cover the arrival of the marines as part of a multinational peacekeeping unit. A mood of relief swept over Lebanon's war-ravaged capital. Everyone, Muslim and Christian alike, believed—or wanted to believe—that the presence of the marines as a neutral force would end the Israeli occupation and the fratricidal fighting. The marines patrolled the streets of the Muslim quarter in small unarmed groups. The children waved to them, and the older boys, scruffy young toughs who carried machine guns as casually as most teenagers carry schoolbooks, let them pass through their checkpoints with a nod, if not a smile. Having the marines around gave me a sense of psychological security that I hadn't known before during the several hellish months I had spent in Beirut. But everyone who comes to save Lebanon ends up being destroyed by Lebanon, and the Americans were to be no exception. Slowly they were sucked into the labyrinth of violence.

In the U.N. Security Council, the United States stood as a club of one, vetoing resolutions that condemned Israel's invasion of Lebanon in the summer of 1982 and its subsequent brutal bombardments of Beirut. In Lebanon itself Washington worked hard to prop up the weak Christian-dominated government, and when a unit of the Lebanese army, commanded by Christian officers, was besieged by Muslim militiamen in a tiny, now forgotten mountain village above Beirut, President Reagan declared that Souk el Gharb was of strategic importance to the interests of the United States, and U.S. warships off the Lebanese coast opened fire on Muslim positions there.

"If Lebanon ends up under the tyranny of forces hostile to the West," the president said, "not only will our strategic position in the Eastern Mediterranean be threatened, but also the stability of the entire Middle East." His words were an echo of the past, an echo of those spoken by other chief executives about Vietnam, and they were ill-advised. Lebanon was important to Israel's security but had nothing whatsoever to do with U.S. interests.

By the time Souk el Gharb came under U.S. shelling, the marines at the airport had been drawn into combat by Muslim provocateurs who sought confrontation, convinced that the American role had gradually changed and that the marines were now in Beirut as the guardians of Israeli interests and the protectors of the Lebanese Christians. Shiite snipers fired away on them at will, mountain gunners lobbed mortar and artillery rounds on them. At first the marines had shown incredible restraint in an effort to maintain their neutrality. The shooting got nasty and the marines merely dug themselves in deeper, weathering the attacks in their foxholes and firing hardly a shot in return. Not until the barrages became so fierce that marines started getting killed did the Americans respond in kind. The world's largest battleship, the U.S.S. *New Jersey*, was called into combat for the first time since the Vietnam war, and its one-ton rounds brought terror to the Muslims' village strongholds. In the Byzantine world of Lebanese affairs, the marines had become just another militia. I remember standing on the corniche along the Mediterranean with several colleagues, hearing the deep-throated rumble of the *New Jersey*'s cannon. Several seconds later the repercussion of exploding shells would come spilling out of the mountains. Strange, I thought. When I had covered the Vietnam war as a correspondent, the bark of American artillery was comforting; I was relieved to know that that much firepower was on *my* side. But in Lebanon it scared the hell out of me, for I knew that each round the *New Jersey* fired was creating a new anti-American terrorist.

The truck that Lance Corporal DiFranco had seen gained speed after its second circling of the parking lot. Suddenly it crashed through a reinforced steel gate and headed straight for the marines' four-story battalion headquarters. The truck was loaded with six tons of explosives, and when it slammed into the headquarters that housed more than three hundred Americans, the building's roof lifted off like a piece of windblown paper and the floors collapsed, one on top of another, with a deafening roar heard for miles around. The final toll was 242 dead—241 American marines and the Lebanese truck driver.

DiFranco will never forget the suicide driver's expression as the vehicle raced past the guard post: "He looked right at me . . . and smiled."

The driver's name, motive and affiliation were buried in the rubble of the building, but two things seemed certain: first, that he was a Shiite Muslim, for whom martyrdom is life's ultimate reward ("Who fighteth in the way of God be he slain or be he victorious, on him we shall bestow a vast reward," the Koran says); and second, that he was no free-lance terrorist. His mission was a complicated one requiring excellent intelligence and detailed logistical support, and it almost certainly could not have been carried out without the support of at least one government. The suspects, though guilt was never proved, were Syria and Iran. Beyond the tragedy of the event itself, the attack was significant in underscoring how horribly effective state-sponsored terrorism had become as a vehicle of foreign policy.[1] Countries could commit limited resources to affect major policy change without having to accept responsibility for murder. The risks and costs were fewer than those inherent in conventional warfare and diplomacy. A handful of kamikaze zealots could neutralize the strength of a superpower. They were to make terrorism the great equalizer, and terrorism in turn was to become the United States' great vulnerability.

---

[1] The State Department in 1986 listed five countries as direct sponsors of international terrorism—Libya, Iran, South Yemen, Syria and Cuba. Iraq had previously been dropped from the list.

TERRORISM—WHICH derives from a Greek word meaning "to tremble"—is virtually as old as civilization itself and is by no means unique to the Middle East. State-sponsored terrorism is also an old weapon (of European, not Arab, origin), dating in its present form back to 1793–94, when in the midst of the French Revolution, as the English statesman Edmund Burke wrote, "thousands of those hell hounds called terrorists" were turned loose by the state against the populace. Burke went on to remind people that such evil succeeds only when good men do nothing.

There is as well a precedent for the suicide attackers of Beirut. Nine hundred years ago in the mountain of Persia (Iran) a group of Shiite Muslims, giddy from hashish and eager to experience the euphoria of heaven, launched daring suicidal raids against Christian Crusaders and Sunni Muslim foes. Their leader, Hasan al-Sabbah, taught them the importance of having blind and total commitment to their faith, and this group of young killers had a collective Arabic name that today has become part of the English language. They were known as the Assassins.[2]

More recently, when British rule was coming to an end in Palestine, both the Arabs and the Jews practiced terrorism against one another, and against the British. Jewish terrorists killed 338 British citizens in Palestine during the 1940s. They blew up the King David Hotel, the British headquarters in Jerusalem, in 1946, killing ninety-one persons, and perfected the lethal letter bomb, which later became a favorite weapon of Arab terrorists. I have in my files a photostat of a WANTED poster issued by the British colonial authorities about 1943. It shows the mug shots of ten men hunted as terrorists, pictured in alphabetical order; the first is that of a Polish

---

[2] For more on the Assassins and terrorism in the Arab world, I recommend Robin Wright's *Sacred Rage: The Crusade of Militant Islam* (New York: Linden Press, 1985).

clerk whose "peculiarities" are listed as "wears spectacles, flat footed, bad teeth." His name was Menachem Begin, and he and his colleague, Yitzhak Shamir, also a suspected terrorist, were to become future prime ministers of Israel. Begin would also become a winner of the Nobel Peace Prize, sharing the award in 1978 with President Sadat. In the Middle East the boundaries of respectability are not clearly defined: today's terrorist is tomorrow's statesman; one man's freedom fighter is another man's common criminal. By the 1970s Begin and Shamir were (quite correctly) accusing Yasser Arafat of being a terrorist, although all three men had used the same murderous tactics in their nationalistic fight for the same piece of real estate.

The important point here, I think, is that the Arabs don't have a patent on terrorism, and the major reason why the world didn't take a united stand against this scourge until two hijacked jetliners were flown into the World Trade Center was that many people disagree on what constitutes an act of indiscriminate political violence. When the United States shells Muslim villages near Beirut or bombs Libyan terrorist targets, killing civilians in the process, Washington may view the act as one of retribution, but those on the receiving end surely consider it terrorism. Israeli air raids that kill innocents in Palestinian villages may be carried out in the name of self-defense, but to the recipients—indeed to the Arabs as a whole—that is just a euphemism for terrorism. Why, they ask, is violence condoned as justified when undertaken by one group and condemned as uncivilized barbarity when committed by another? Terrorism executed at thirty thousand feet may be impersonal, but surely it's just as deadly as an assassin's bullet fired from a speeding car.

Arafat and the Palestine Liberation Organization endorsed terrorism as their official policy for the same reason that other groups turn to terrorism—desperation. Everything had failed and no one was listening to them. Israel had crushed the Arab armies in the Six-Day war of 1967 that was designed to "liberate" Palestine. It was apparent, even to the hard-line Gamal Abdel Nassers of the world, that the military option against Israel was futile. Not only had the Arabs failed to reclaim a single inch of Palestine, but the Israelis had expanded the size of their own territory by three times and moved into parts of Egypt, Jordan and Syria. In response, the P.L.O. tried a guerrilla war in the Israeli-occupied West Bank and Gaza Strip, but Israeli security was too good and it, too, failed. Arafat knew that if the Palestinian cause was to remain viable, he needed worldwide publicity and he needed to attack the Israelis somewhere other than in Israel. Because the Palestinians lived nowhere and the Jews lived everywhere, the struggle took on an international dimension. Outrage followed outrage, and if innocents were the victims, if the chosen targets were "soft" ones, usually with their backs turned, no matter; only the cause counts in the twisted perception of the terrorist, whose misdeeds are conducted in the fuzzy netherworld between war and crime.

Eleven Israeli athletes were massacred at the 1972 Olympic Games in Munich, twenty-one Israeli schoolchildren were slaughtered at Ma'alot, planes were skyjacked and blown up. In a single day in 1970, three jets—a Swissair DC-8, a Trans World Airlines 707 and a Pan American 747—were pirated and, after the passengers had been set free, destroyed with explosives; the hijackers walked away free men. The larger the headlines became, the bolder the terrorists got. What counted most was not the magnitude of the event but the amount of publicity it generated. In fact, without media attention, terrorism is a fairly useless exercise because, by definition, it is a psychological weapon that uses indiscriminate violence to coerce governments or societies into recognizing and accepting various demands. If the terrorist can't communicate his demands and articulate his causes, he fails.

Most Arabs say the implantation of Zionism in the Middle East is at the root of regional terrorism; many Israelis counter that terrorism merely reflects the Arab world's propensity for violence and that if the issue wasn't Palestine, it would be something else. Both statements have some foundation in fact. What seems most unsettling, though, is that terrorism in the Middle East has gained a certain respectability, particularly when camouflaged in the cloak of nationalism and religion. Consider the names of three major Arab groups linked to terrorism: Islamic Jihad (Holy War), al-Dawa (The Calling) and Hezbollah (Party of God), whose symbol is a rifle held in a clenched fist. With names like that, one can only suspect that the groups' followers believe that their guidance comes from no mere mortal.

The grand mufti of Jerusalem, Sheik Saadeddin Alami, once issued a religious order for the killing of President Assad of Syria, saying his assassin would be assured a place in paradise. Such a call by a spiritual leader anywhere else in the world would be considered extraordinary; in the Middle East it caused not a ripple.

Nor did many people find it peculiar that the Middle East's most notorious terrorist of the 1980s, Sabri al-Banna—whose nom de guerre, Abu Nidal, means "father of the struggle"—once had his own press spokesman operating out of Damascus, Syria, in a little office just two blocks from the U.S. embassy, or that Hezbollah had held press conferences to publicize its activities, or that Mohammed Abbas, accused of masterminding the piracy of the Italian cruise liner *Achille Lauro* in 1985, once had an aide working full time combing the Arab and Western press for mentions of his name. When an Egyptian soldier named Suleiman Khater went berserk in the Sinai and killed five Israeli tourists, what did Iran do? It declared him a hero, named a street after him and set aside a day honoring him. There wasn't even much public indignation in 1985 when a uniformed immigration officer at Beirut's international airport drew his revolver and commandeered a jetliner because he wanted more pay. The engine blast killed an elderly man on the tarmac as the plane took off on the twenty-minute flight to Cyprus, trailing an orange escape chute from one of its three open doors. The next day, after the plane's return, the hijacker was back on his job at the airport. He took time off only to appear at a press conference with none other than the minister of transport and tourism, Walid Jumblatt. (Both were members of the Druze sect.)[3] "I supported this [piracy] because . . . all means are justified for a good cause," Jumblatt said. The hijacker beamed broadly.

Fanatics in the Middle East regard terrorists as Spain does its matadors. They are young and glamorous and nationalistic and daring. They face death stoically, even seek out death. The currency they covet is not money; it is recognition. And in death they earn that recognition and are exalted. The faces of the martyred ones used to stare down at you from a thousand postered walls in Beirut and Tehran, and those whose causes they espouse—but who are not anxious to die themselves—view them with fascination. The posters are enlarged from snapshots and the pictures of the young men always seem to be slightly out of focus. I don't remember ever seeing a smile on one of their faces. It is as though they knew all along that they would accomplish more in death than they could in life. (Would anyone today remember the American revolutionary hero Nathan Hale if he hadn't been hanged by the British and said just before his death, "I only regret that I have but one life to lose for my country"?)

If there is a common denominator in the character of the

[3] The Druze faith is a secretive Islamic sect that originated in Egypt in the eleventh century. The name commemorates a Persian mystic, Mohammed ben Ismail al-Darazi, who died, ironically, in disgrace, dismissed by the people as a heretic. Unlike other sects, the Druze do not make the pilgrimage to Mecca, accept converts or marry outside their faction. They have their own scripture, codified in six volumes by the fifteenth-century scholar Jamaluddin Abdullah Janukhi, and they regarded Jethro, Moses' father-in-law, as their chief prophet. There are about three hundred thousand Druze in Lebanon, two hundred thousand in Syria and fifty thousand in Israel. They are the only Arabs subject to conscription in the Israeli army.

pre–bin Laden Arab terrorist, it is a sense of hopelessness. He is young, usually poor and has had only a limited education. He has never mastered anything, and he is as likely as not to bungle his assignment as a terrorist. If he is a Palestinian, growing up as a second-generation refugee in the squalid slums of Lebanon, the homeland of his dreams is more distant today than it was in, say, 1974, when Arafat addressed the United Nations with an empty holster strapped to his waist. He feels betrayed—by the West, which created Israel; by the Americans, who support Israel; by the Arabs, who encourage him with words and money but little else. The world is his enemy. He is less tolerant than his father, just as his children one day will be less tolerant than he. With a gun, he is important. Without one, he is naked.

Newsweek's Ray Wilkinson and Rod Nordland tracked the Middle East terror network through the Arab world and Europe during a two-month investigation for the magazine. They spoke with Abu Nidal's recruits, who had trained for six months in southwestern Iraq, running six miles a day, spending hours mastering their weapons, learning how to stalk, kill and escape, and with middle-class Palestinian mothers, who feared that their own well-behaved children might one day become terrorists if the present cycle of reprisal and retaliation in the Middle East was not arrested. They had the impression, as I often did, that many of the people who are terrorists today would be normal, perhaps productive citizens had they not lived in an environment battered by the despair and desperation of fruitless conflict. But in each of them some mental fiber had snapped, and their empty lives were now dedicated to revenge. The reporters wrote:

> Terrorists are not born, they're made, and nobody makes them better than the star-crossed Palestinian refugee camps in Lebanon. Sabra and Chatilla, vast shantytowns near Beirut, produced Mohammed Sarhan, the surviving killer [of the terrorist attack on

the Rome and Vienna airports that killed seventeen persons and wounded 116 in December 1985] . . . . Mohammed Abbas—the man behind the *Achille Lauro* affair—recruited his killers there. Bombed by the Israelis during their invasion, the camps endured massacres in 1982 of hundreds of men, women and children by Christian militiamen while Israeli troops stood by.

Sarhan lost his father, a taxi driver, in the camp massacres. His brothers and sisters fled the country afterward, and his mother died of an illness. Sayid, his friend, also lost relatives and joined another radical group. As a group of children gathered to listen admiringly, he praised Rome and Vienna. "It is essential to make our presence known everywhere in the world," he said and stubbed out a cigarette butt on his hand.

Captain Abou Obeida, an Egyptian artillery officer who deserted to join a small Palestinian guerrilla faction, is a classic case. His hate was fashioned in the Sinai when the Israelis humiliated his army in the 1973 war, but the finishing touches were put on it in the Chatilla refugee camp, where his wife and small daughter were killed in an Israeli air raid. Now he commands a battery of Katyusha rockets aimed toward Galilee [in northern Israel] from a cypress grove in the Lebanese village of Bhamdun.

In his quarters, Obeida perched on a cot covered by an olive-drab blanket. Above him was a portrait of his seventeen-year-old bodyguard, Mohammed Ali Hassin, who died driving a suicide car bomb into an Israeli column last year. He leaped from his seat suddenly, turned around and thrust his buttocks out. "Do you see it?" he demanded. What? "No tail!" He went on, "No hair on my face. No horns on my head. I am a man, not an animal. We are not terrorists."

Guevara, the nom de guerre of a teen-age guerrilla, is another product of the cycle of terror and reprisal. He ripped his shirt off to show six shrapnel wounds he received when the battleship U.S.S. *New Jersey* shelled the Chouf Mountains. "I have metal in

my body from the Americans," he said. "If there were a very successful mission I would kill myself gladly," he said. "Even if I
killed only one person, it would be worth it."

Financed and encouraged by Libya, armed and supported by
Syria, recruited and trained in Lebanon, Middle East terrorists of
the seventies and eighties, who were the forerunners of Osama bin
Laden's al Qaeda fanatics, put together lethal organizations that ran
the gamut from small groups of free lances to sophisticated Mafia-
style outfits such as Abu Nidal's Fatah Revolutionary Council.
Nidal, the son of a wealthy Palestinian merchant and himself a former shoolteacher in Jerusalem, had no more than five hundred
men at his disposal. But he launched at least a hundred operations
in twenty countries on three continents and always found a safe
haven—in Libya, Syria or Iraq, depending on who needed his
services at the moment and who was willing to pay the most for
them. He received an annual stipend of $5 million a year from
Kadafi, plus commissions for individual attacks. That was more
than enough to feed his passion for gunning down unarmed civilians, most of whom were Palestinian, not Israeli.

Nidal was expelled from the P.L.O. in 1973 after taking hostage
the staff of the Saudi Arabian embassy in Paris. As a result he and
Arafat were on each other's death list. After his expulsion, Nidal
dedicated his life as an executioner and extortionist to undermining
any moves toward negotiations with Israel and any Palestinian drift
toward moderation. When his nephew, Said Hammami, began
hinting that the P.L.O. needed to seek accommodation with Israel,
Nidal showed his displeasure by booby-trapping the cooking-gas
canister in Hammami's home. The resultant explosion killed Hammami's wife and two children.

With an expanding midriff and a balding pate, Nidal looked
more like an out-of-shape former athlete than he did a terrorist. He
had large hands and a steady, focused glare. He wore neither the
wild-eyed nor the glazed-over expression of some of his younger fol-

lowers. Everything about this uncommon man looked ordinary. Yet Nidal was so paranoid that he wouldn't eat or drink anything not prepared in his presence, fearing it might be poisoned, and he communicated through mail drops rather than over the telephone. He slipped from the limelight he once coveted into the shadows of his private Libyan underworld, and there, unhampered by the restraints of civilization, he lived secretly and largely alone, one man against the world.

According to intelligence sources, Nidal's men were trained in small cells of three to seven people each. These cells were then attached to larger units, which would spend weeks preparing for a particular attack, training in isolation from other units, keeping the participants' identities secret from even fellow terrorists outside each cell. They were assisted by "sleepers"—agents placed in Europe who, supported by a retainer fee, led normal lives for months or even years while awaiting an order to take part in an operation. The simultaneous massacres in the Rome and Vienna airports were carried out by two Nidal cells. Although Nidal may be little more than a mentally crippled hit man, his young recruits were motivated by injustice and ideology. On the body of one of those recruits, killed by security agents after the Rome attack, was a note expressing anguish and hatred so deep that remorse was impossible. It said: "As you have violated our land, our honor, our people, we will hit you everywhere, even your children, so that you should feel the sorrow of our children. The tears that we have shed will be washed away by your blood."

The whereabouts of Nidal—whose henchmen killed and wounded nine hundred people in the 1970s and 1980s—was something of a mystery by the year 2001. He hadn't carried out a known attack against the West in a decade. He had lost his sanctuaries in Libya and Iraq, but reports had him variously in jail in Egypt, ensconced in the Sudan, dying of cancer in an undetermined Arab hospital. His legacy was a chilling one, made all the more so by the fact that the man who replaced him as the world's most wanted terrorist, Osama bin Laden, seemed to have stolen his modus operandi from Nidal's blue book on putting together a terrorist operation.

Despite the horror and the headlines generated by political violence, terrorism has accomplished little that is permanent and remains primarily a tool of losers, whose struggles are often doomed to achieve nothing but the finality of death. The results of terrorism, in all but its most spectacular forms, are tantamount to those of a fist hitting water: there are waves and ripples but the surface remains unchanged. Nothing underscores the futility of Kadafi's wild dreams more dramatically than the fact that he has had to resort to international terrorism to keep them alive. In the end terrorism doesn't bring down governments or offer any alternatives except chaos. None of this, though, has deterred the terrorist. As governments have become more effective combating terrorism, the terrorist has adjusted. His organizations have become smaller and more secretive, making them tougher to monitor and infiltrate. His aggression has gotten bolder and deadlier, making defense almost impossible. Generally, he no longer tries to seize and hold a target, preferring instead to use guerrilla-style attacks that are safer and hidden bombs that cause more casualties with less risk.

"Contemporary terrorists have not been able to achieve their long-range goals anywhere," said Brian Jenkins, an authority on political violence at the Rand Corporation in Santa Monica, California. "They are able to attract publicity. They can cause alarm. They can create crises. Occasionally they can win a tactical victory.

"But thus far they have been unable to translate the consequences of terrorism into concrete political gain. In that sense, terrorism has failed. Yet terrorists persist. And that is the paradox that leads to increased bloodshed. Governments have become more effective in combating terrorism, yet internationally the problems with terrorism increase. As in war, when neither side prevails, escalation becomes irresistible." Nearly a hundred other planned attacks on Americans were foiled in 1985 by U.S. and foreign intelligence agencies.

"Why *us?*" was the question I heard over and over again from Americans when I returned to the United States. Most didn't know—and probably didn't care—that their country is perceived as being ignorant of and hostile to the Arabs and Islam. Whereas Arabs a generation ago had faith in America's inherent evenhandedness, even the moderate Arab mainstream today believes the United States has lost its interest in playing a neutral peacemaker's role in the Middle East. They consider Israel and the United States as co-conspirators and are not sure which is the dog that wags the tail.

If history teaches any lessons, it might be worth remembering that President George Washington, in his 1796 farewell address, warned against doing precisely what the United States has done in the Middle East. He admonished the young republic to be neutral and to "observe good faith and justice toward all nations," cultivating peace and harmony with each. The United States, he said, should avoid "permanent, inveterate antipathies" toward some nations and "passionate attachments" to others. Such attachments, he went on, engender a "variety of evils," and lead to "the illusion of an imaginary common interest in cases where no real common interest exists, and by infusing into one the enmities of the other, betrays the former into a participation in the quarrels and wars of the latter, without adequate inducement or justification."

It seemed odd that U.S. administrations appeared genuinely unaware for so long of the relationship between peace and terrorism. I am not dismissing the element of common thuggery in the terrorist network, nor do I think that legitimate grievances in any civilized society justify ignoble deeds. I also realize that terrorism in many ways merely mirrors the bad health of the world, where in 1986 forty conflicts of varying intensity, involving the armed forces of forty-five nations, were being fought. But it does seem clear that there can be no purely military or technical solution to terrorism. If you plotted the increasing number of terrorist incidents and the increased degree of official U.S. support for Israel, as measured by U.N. votes, arms shipments, White House policy statements and unchallenged Israeli actions, the two lines would run in tandem right up the graph.

As long as the peace process lies dormant, as long as the United States and Israel remain insensitive to the Arabs as a people, as long as weapons continue to pour into the Middle East like Christmas-gift toys and Arab governments provide their people with no demo-cratic outlets to express their grievances, terrorism will have an atmosphere in which it can flourish.

"In many areas of the world, the demarcation line between the superpowers is clear," said Ariel Merari, a terrorism expert at the Center for Strategic Studies at Tel Aviv University. "Here in the Mid-dle East it overlaps and is fuzzy. The danger of conflict between superpowers is so great in the nuclear era that these countries resort to low-level, indirect warfare, which is much less risky."

At some point American leaders are going to have to ask them-selves *why* there is terrorism. What makes a normal teenager pick up a weapon and be willing to die? How can one people's national-ism be admirable and another's unfathomable? When does the exercise of self-defense become an infringement on the rights of others who also want to live within secure borders?

Granted, the answers to these questions can present at best only a long-range solution to terrorism, and in the meantime the West—and particularly the United States—faces a dilemma: It can strike back against the terrorists, but doesn't the use of force usually back-fire and lead to more terrorism? It can be passive and defensive, but if the guilty go unpunished, doesn't that encourage terrorists to commit further outrages? The Reagan administration showed admirable restraint until April 1986, when, feeling it had to do *something* to *somebody*, twenty-seven American planes launched a predawn bombing raid on terrorist facilities in the Libyan cities of

Tripoli and Benghazi.[4] Kadafi escaped unharmed, but as many as fifty Libyan civilians died in the attack, and the wounded included his two youngest sons, four-year-old Seph and three-year-old Kamis. "From now on until I die, I consider America my own enemy unless they give Reagan the death sentence," said Kadafi's wife, Safia, a former nurse.

The raid may have given terrorists reason to pause and rethink their tactics, but massive retaliation has never been effective, representing as it does more a political statement than an antiterrorist strategy. It kills more innocents than terrorists and serves primarily to raise the level of violence. Often the retaliator becomes the ultimate victim, because anyone who trades an eye for an eye with his enemy is eventually in danger of becoming blind. Israel for years has matched each blow with a tougher counterblow and in the process has seen Mideastern terrorism increase, not decrease.

The most effective way to contain terrorism in the short term is to conduct not massive air strikes but a covert, selective assassination campaign against terrorist leaders. It is a difficult, time-consuming task that requires excellent intelligence and the cooperation of other governments—but it pays dividends. This, though, is precisely the capability the United States lost as it depended more on technology in its antiterrorism campaign and less on old-fashioned

---

[4] As a historical aside, I should mention that this was not the first United States "war" with Libya. In 1800, with U.S. merchants under frequent attack by Barbary pirates of Algiers, Tunis and Tripoli, President Thomas Jefferson ordered his Mediterranean fleet to cruise the Tripoli coast and sink or burn enemy ships. One U.S. vessel, the *Enterprise*, took on the polacre *Tripoli*, destroying its guns and killing most of its eighty-man crew, but another U.S. warship, the *Philadelphia*, ran aground on a shoal off Tripoli. Libyan forces overpowered the ship and captured its crew. American vessels then bombarded the city. Scores of other American sailors also were held hostage by the pirates, and the Barbary war continued intermittently until 1815, when Congress declared war on Algiers. The dey (ruler) of Algiers surrendered and gave up his ten American prisoners when the U.S. squadron sailed into his harbor. The fleet then set off for Tripoli, where the pasha turned over his prisoners and paid a fine of twenty-five thousand dollars.

methods with agents on the ground who speak the local language and gather intelligence by infiltrating outlaw organizations. "Once . . . one of the leaders has been assassinated, we found a long period of peace in the area," Brigadier General Gideon Machanaimi, an antiterrorist official in the Israeli government, said in an interview broadcast by Israeli radio. The Israelis enjoyed some quiet moments after using a car bomb in Beirut in 1979 to kill the leader of the Black September terrorist group responsible for the Munich Olympic massacre. And however much Americans have come to view "covert" as a dirty word, it should not be forgotten that undercover operations played a decisive role in the Allies' two world-war victories.

In 1986, I wrote: "In trying to combat terrorism, the West, I think, should pursue three courses simultaneously. First, assuming legal niceties don't apply to the Abu Nidals of the world, the assassination effort—combined with tougher extradition laws and better international cooperation—would undermine the terrorists' ability to plan and execute operations. Second, the political, diplomatic and commercial isolation of states that sponsor terrorism would make the costs of the crime greater than its rewards. It seems absurd that terrorists doubling as diplomats should have the sanctity of embassies to plot their campaigns for destruction, the cover of diplomatic pouches to smuggle their weapons and explosives, and the privilege of diplomatic immunity to avoid prosecution in the very countries they are planning to attack. And third, an honest examination of the causes of terrorism and, when appropriate, a reappraisal of national policies would address the grievances that have created the problem in the first place.

"Those three policies, contradictory though they may seem on the surface, represent a parallel approach toward a desired solution. They would not eradicate terrorism, but they could reduce it to manageable levels. The alternative is to do nothing or to continue a blow-for-a-counterblow policy that will put all of us in the expanding rings of security that already encircle airports, embassies, government buildings, housing complexes and, increasingly, corporate offices. We will live with our alarms, sensors, cameras and reinforced walls, and our lives will be focused through the distorted lens of fear."

Today, those earlier observations still appear valid and aren't out of line with the approach President George W. Bush has taken in his war against terrorism. But I never imagined we would ever really view our lives through the lens of fear, as we started doing after the attacks on the World Trade Center and the Pentagon. As Brian Jenkins of the Rand Corporation points out, terrorism is a subjective threat, not an objective one measured in body counts, and the increased security—the United States already spends more for federal security services than for all its police forces combined—will not make us feel secure. It will only remind us of our vulnerabilities.

Jenkins finds little reason for optimism, other than believing that the world will not end in terrorist anarchy. Assessing the future, he writes:

> Terrorists will escalate their violence, their attacks will become more indiscriminate. . . . Terrorism will become institutionalized as a mode of armed conflict for some, no less legitimate than other modes of conflict. The media will increase its ability to cover terrorist incidents; we will *see* even more terrorism. The extraordinary security measures taken against terrorism will have become a permanent part of the landscape, of our life style. They will not attract comment.
>
> That may be the most insidious and perhaps the most worrisome development in the coming years. Terrorism will become an accepted fact of contemporary life—commonplace, ordinary, banal, and therefore somehow "tolerable."

Three times in the 1990s the United States went into combat to protect Muslim populations—in the Persian Gulf, Somalia and

Kosovo—so it seemed unlikely that America's war on terrorism was, as the fanatics claimed, a war on Islam. Religion had nothing to do with it. The war was against a sophisticated terror network, treated as an honored guest in Afghanistan, that in a few years' time had grown from an obscure extremist group into a dangerous organization with global reach. Al Qaeda had been blowing up American embassies and killing American servicemen since 1998. It wasn't until it brought its carnage to the shores of the United States that the American public was jarred awake.

Al Qaeda's leader, Osama bin Laden, a billionaire Saudi whom Saudi Arabia had stripped of citizenship, offered no vision except that the world should be as it was in Mohammed the Prophet's time and had no political ideology except hate. He hated the moderate Arab states and he hated Saudi rulers for allowing U.S. military personnel to be based in the holy land. He hated Israel, he hated the West, he hated Russia. Most of all he hated the United States, which he saw as a cradle of infidels out to export a decadent culture and to destroy Islam. Armed with a gun and the Koran, he was a man who belonged to the past. Although reviled by the vast majority of Arabs, he found a following among the fanatics and the disenfranchised who were products of failed societies, and more often than not were failures themselves. What bin Laden and militant Islam offered was a new form of colonialism, seeking to enslave the bodies and minds of unsuspecting young Muslims for the perceived beauty of a martyr's death.

I felt sorry for the ignorance of the Arab minority who yelled "Death to America" on the streets of Arab capitals because they understood neither what America is nor who the Americans are. Perhaps, though, their anger is not beyond grasp. We are seen as bullies who are arrogant and attentive only to our own interests. Our opinions are swayed by lobbyists in Washington whose job it is not to be culturally sensitive. We find that American ideals and American policy are frequently at odds, as history shows us supporting dictators to the detriment of the downtrodden, and tending to believe that democracy and capitalism are a fix for every distant problem.

The world will be a better place with bin Laden dispatched to whatever awaits him in the afterlife and the terrorist cells of hate crippled. Even then terrorism as a phenomenon is unlikely to disappear. Suicide bombers have shown the civilized world's vulnerability, as have hijackers with penknives and box cutters who can challenge the power of a nation armed with nuclear weapons and cruise missiles. But the eventual demise of bin Laden will give the United States an opportunity to rethink its policies, to reconsider its our-way-is-the-best-way attitude and to ask why America is a target of anger. It is an opportunity I hope the country does not let slip by.

FIVE

AMONG THE FAITHFUL

RAMADAN, THE Islamic holy month of abstinence, is never easy, and when it comes in the crippling heat of summer, as it did in 1984, man's discipline and piety are put to a severe challenge. By the fourth day of the fast, I noticed that Ali, our vegetable dealer who worked out of a tiny dark shop three blocks from the Nile, was showing ill effects. His eyes were red as tomatoes, sweat dripped from his brow, and his mouth was so dry that when he swallowed, it sounded as though his tongue was scraping over sandpaper.

"In four hours I can have a drink of water," he said, looking at his watch, which read 3:00 P.M. "And I can have a cigarette. I do miss my cigarettes." But Ali was not unhappy. He was a frail old man with only one working eye, yet he said that this annual twenty-eight-day fast from sunrise to sunset made him feel stronger, more at peace with everything and everyone. He looked on Ramadan as a spiritual cleansing that moved him closer to God.

Ali wrapped my two pounds of potatoes in a piece of newspaper, and I left him slumped on his wooden stool, limp as a doll, his fingers working over a string of prayer beads as he silently mouthed the ninety-nine names of Allah. Driving back to our apartment in my Russian-made Lada sedan, I passed a group of thirty soldiers who had been dispatched the day before to dig up a leaking sewer pipe. They had put down their shovels and were all sprawled on the sidewalk, fast asleep. I watched their lieutenant try to rouse them.

Then, realizing the futility of the task, he, too, sank to the pavement and assumed a fetal position.

The prophet Mohammed excused pregnant women, travelers, the sick and soldiers at war from observing the fast. Others are expected to eschew food, drink, tobacco, gum, sexual intercourse and all forms of indulgence until the firing of a cannon each sunset sets off a wild dash for bountiful family banquets that go on until dawn and are replete with delicious pastries and freshly slaughtered lambs. Having life turned topsy-turvy like this produces such a strain on the nerves and stomach that Egypt moves the clock back one hour during Ramadan so that everyone can start eating as early as possible.

Hardships aside, the Ramadan fast—one of the five pillars of the Islamic faith—is a joyous occasion in the Arab world. It is a time for prayer and self-examination, for sharing good fortune with the poor and disabled, for visiting family and friends. The cities are decorated with bright paper flags and lanterns, and strings of colored lights draped from the mosques give the night a carnival atmosphere. In the old days Egypt's Fatimid rulers opened their palaces to the public during Ramadan. They built pavilions to serve scrumptious "breakfasts" each evening, and their chefs slipped gold coins into selected desserts. Today, even without the pavilions and coins, Ramadan brings with it the same sense of expectation and excitement of the Fatimid era a millennium ago as it sweeps out of the east each year on the wings of the crescent moon.

There was, though, a hitch to this Ramadan in the *hyjri* (Islamic) year of 1405—or 1984 on our Gregorian calendar.[1] Ramadan, the ninth lunar month, begins officially when the crescent is sighted by the naked eye at sunset. The fast starts at dawn, and dawn is consid-

---

[1] Unlike the Gregorian, or Christian, calendar, which starts with the birth of Christ, the Muslim calendar begins with the date of Mohammed's emigration from Mecca to Medina on Friday, July 16, A.D. 622. It has twelve months and 354 days. One day is added to the last month eleven times in every thirty years.

ered to be the time when the first rays of day provide enough light to distinguish a black thread from a white one held at arm's length. The Saudis, because of their eastern location and their role as Islam's self-proclaimed guardians, are usually the ones to declare the start and end of Ramadan and the times for daily prayer.

So when Saudi Arabia announced on a Saturday, a day earlier than expected, that "two private citizens" had sighted the crescent, the fast began. Policemen drove through Cairo's streets spreading the word over megaphones; cigarette butts were snuffed out from Muscat to Marrakesh, and over a million radios came the chant "Ha'loow ya ha'loow, Ramadan gana" (Welcome, welcome, Ramadan has come to us). But Kuwait's official astrologer said it was impossible for the moon to have been sighted on Saturday, and Kuwaitis began the fast on Sunday. Morocco and Iran said no, the Ramadan moon wouldn't be seen until Monday. The king of Saudi Arabia called in his astrologers and issued a proclamation confirming the commencement. The rector of Cairo's Al Azhar University demanded a retraction. The one person who could have ended the confusion was the one person no one consulted—Mohammed Fahim, a geophysicist who was director of Egypt's Helwan Observatory, the only major observatory in the Arab world. He had all the precise times logged in his computer. Besides, he knew that the moon cannot be seen by the naked eye with any great clarity until about ten minutes after sunset because of the sun's illumination.

But there was room to negotiate and everyone agreed to agree on one point: Ramadan would have a universal ending. That moment comes with the sighting of the next new moon—beginning the tenth month, Shawwal—and heralds the start of a three-day feast, Eid-es-Seghir. Early one morning, a day before the expected sighting, Fahim was awakened by the telephone. That in itself was a surprise because his Cairo phone seldom worked. He groped his way through the darkened living room and, picking up the receiver, heard an assistant's breathless words: "The Saudis are celebrating!"

"Well, they're wrong," Fahim recalled saying. "We've computed it and recomputed it and, by the moon, the feast doesn't start until three P.M. today." Fahim hung up and went back to bed, aware that science and religion were once again at loggerheads. He well knew that the ancient Egyptians were such skillful astronomers that they had used the difference in the sun's altitude at Alexandria and Aswan at the time of the summer solstice to measure the earth's radius with remarkable accuracy. But *that* was five thousand years ago, and it seemed reasonable to him that Arabs today should be able to use modern technology to avoid religious confusion. Just because the crescent moon had been sighted by the naked eye in Mohammed's time when there were no watches or computers, wasn't there now perhaps a more reliable method?

A few weeks after the Eid-es-Seghir celebration, I went to visit Fahim in his office. The controversy had faded, and he had turned his attention to a computerized study of the continental drift.

"Certainly, the Koran recognizes scientific theories, so there is no conflict per se," Fahim said. "The Koran speaks of solar systems, of people living in other places. This is science. Where we differ with the muftis [men who interpret the Koran and thus make religious laws] is in saying the moon must be seen with the naked eye. If you were in a closed room and were told that Ramadan had started, you would begin the fast, wouldn't you? So what's the difference? We're trying to get the muftis to see our point of view on this."

But the muftis, who hold extraordinary sway over the public, are hard-line traditionalists, and I doubt that they are ready to exchange their keen eyesight for IBM personal computers. In fact, during each of the three Ramadans I spent in the Middle East, there seemed to be a marked, progressive increase in the number of Arabs who unflinchingly abided by all the restrictions the Koran set forth for observing the holy month. In the first year total abstinence was, to a large extent, associated with the peasant class in many countries; by the time I left the region, even diplomats, professors and businessmen had fallen in with the pack—for public consumption, at least. And that movement toward complete religious obedience is, I think, the most significant trend in the Arab world today. The Middle East is becoming more sectarian and, in the process, less tolerant.

Young women are putting back on the veils that their grandmothers fought to remove sixty years ago as a symbol of oppression. The unique systems of Islamic banking and Islamic law have increasing appeal for millions of Arabs from all classes. The mosques are fuller than they have been for decades. Moderate governments are finding that they must appease the muftis in every major policy decision, and militant Islamic students have taken command of many universities. In Cairo, while I was there, they used fists and sticks to break up dances and concerts—both of which they considered religiously proscribed—and to force the cancellation of an international conference on Islamic literature because the introductory brochure had used three modern, and thus objectionable, words—science, technology and dialectics. When a college dean asked a student involved in one of the disturbances why he was shouting at him and not showing respect, the bearded young man replied, "Because I am stronger than you. *I* have the Koran."

There is no word in Arabic for "fundamentalism," and linguists have had to invent one, *usouliyya* (which translates roughly as "basic principles"). Fundamentalism, in any religion, asks the believer to put his intelligence on the shelf but in itself is usually harmless enough. When it has militant overtones, however, it is self-righteous, irrational, anti-intellectual and dangerous. The movement back to the mosque that we are witnessing in the Arab world does not represent an Islamic renaissance, as some religious figures suggest, because there is nothing about it that represents an intellectual or artistic rebirth. It is a religious revival. And as that revival becomes louder and angrier, demanding that the world revert to what it was in Mohammed's time, it becomes a force that divides society and threatens governments. Today there is not a government in the Arab world, including Saudi Arabia's ultrareligious one, that does not fear militant Islam as the major challenge to its stability.

Ironically, it was the Arabs' great hero, Gamal Abdel Nasser, who first recognized the potentially disruptive power of organized religion and who moved most forcefully to usurp its authority. After members of the Muslim Brotherhood tried to assassinate him in 1954, Nasser imprisoned thousands of fundamentalists, scores of whom were executed and tortured.[2] He undermined the strength of the sheiks at Al Azhar by secularizing the university—admitting women and introducing nonreligious courses into the curriculum for the first time—and his security agents infiltrated the mosques and institutions and treated all devout worshipers as subversive suspects. But by desecrating the mosques, he did not kill fundamentalism or the call for the creation of a pure Islamic state; he only managed to force the movement underground.

Nasser's successor, Anwar Sadat, who held the unpopular belief that church and state should be separate, took the opposite track. He set free Nasser's prisoners and encouraged the growth of fundamentalist groups on university campuses, believing that they would be a counterbalance to the political left. It was a fatal error in judgment. While attending a military parade near the Tomb of the Unknown Soldier on October 6, 1981, Sadat was assassinated by a group of fundamentalist soldiers. The court-appointed defense attorneys for the killers argued that the murder was justified as a

---

[2] The Muslim Brotherhood was founded in Cairo in 1928. Calling for the implementation of Islamic political, legal and social systems and opposing the importation of Western culture, it remained an important force in Egyptian politics until banned by the Nasser regime in the 1950s. Societies of the brotherhood operate in several Arab countries, but there is little coordination across borders. Though still officially outlawed in Egypt, the brotherhood now operates more or less in the open. It has lost much of its radical flavor, and its membership comprises mostly older, middle-class men.

means of protecting Muslim morals because Sadat had moved Egypt too far from the teachings of the Koran.

A former Egyptian minister of the interior, Ahmed Mortada al-Maraghi, wrote a book in 1952 telling how Muslim fundamentalists were brought into the fraternity of extremists. "Young men between eighteen and twenty were recruited," he said. "A small room lit with candlelight and smoky with incense is chosen. . . . Once the likely young man is selected he is brought to this room where he will find a sheik repeating verses from the Koran. . . . The sheik with eyes like magnets stares at the young man, who is paralyzed with awe. . . . They will then pray, and the sheik will recite verses from the Koran about those fighting for the sake of Allah and are therefore promised to go to heaven. 'Are you ready for martyrdom?' the young man is asked. 'Yes, yes,' he repeats. He is then given the oath on the Koran. These young men leave the meeting with one determination: to kill. . . ."

I went to the trial of the nineteen men accused of killing Sadat.[3] Hundreds of policemen with fixed bayonets and a dozen armored personnel carriers were brought in to guard the makeshift courtroom that had been set up in a pavilion on Cairo's international fairgrounds. The defendants' mothers and wives, covered like mummies from head to toe in black cloth, hunkered outside the building, near a row of foxholes manned by soldiers in full combat gear. A voice, singsong and dreamy, drifted out to them. It was that of one of the accused, a thirty-three-year-old teacher, Ali Salamouni: "Dear friends, for all human beings, it is Islam, Islam, Islam."

Walking into the pavilion, I was engulfed by chaos and struck by how deep the divisions in modern Arab societies were. The judge was a distinguished-looking, gray-haired gentleman who tried hard to keep order by banging his gavel on the bench. The army of chain-smoking attorneys was dressed in Western suits and appeared

[3] Egypt operates under a Napoleonic, or French, code of justice, although the government is under pressure to adopt the Islamic legal system known as the Sharia.

very businesslike. Off to the right of the bench, in a specially built twelve-foot-high cage, were the defendants, a motley group of soldiers, teachers, preachers and students in their twenties and thirties. They chanted *"Allah Akbar"* (God is great), and pointed accusing fingers at the judge and shinnied up the bars of their cage. Each time a television camera was turned in their direction, they laughed and howled, holding out the Koran and waving crude hangman's nooses they had fashioned from torn robes. Watching these men with their beards and robes and dark, intense eyes, I felt as though I had encountered creatures I did not recognize as human beings, and I was fascinated, much like a child who visits a zoo and for the first time sees wild animals.

The trial lasted three and a half months, an unusually long time because the killers kept feigning fits and had to be lugged out of their cage by security guards. When the verdict was finally rendered—two were acquitted, seventeen were given prison terms and five were sentenced to death—the men seemed delighted. They cheered and chanted verses from the Koran and unfurled a banner that displayed a bleeding Star of David and the words "The Muslims are Coming."

THE LUNATIC fringe represents the same tiny minority in Islam that it does in Christianity or Judaism, and I do not mean to imply that Arabs who have renewed interest in their religion are necessarily extremist or antiquated. The Western world, too, has passed through eras when science and religion were in conflict, when terrorist organizations, such as the Ku Klux Klan or the Irish Republican Army, bore no shame for evil deeds carried out by the few in the name of sacred causes. The Arabs may be intensely religious, but most find religious extremism and violence as abhorrent as blasphemy itself. "This [fundamentalism] is not religion," Sadat said shortly before his assassination. "This is obscenity. These are lies, the criminal use of religious power to misguide people." Even the sheiks at Al Azhar University have tried to discourage students from radicalizing Islam, yet that process continues in underground cells throughout the Arab world. It is a movement led by intellectuals but appealing largely to the masses, a crusade whose supporters have a voice disproportionately greater than their numbers. And if its momentum keeps gathering strength, and governments from Saudi Arabia to Morocco are taken hostage by religious extremists, Islamic fundamentalism could rank with Marxism and Third World nationalism as one of the most significant social phenomena of the twenty-first century.

The roots of the modern Islamic revival go back to 1967, when Israel routed the armies of Egypt, Syria and Jordan in the Six-Day War. Nasser's visions had led the Arabs into that battle, and with the defeat his dream of a Pan-Arab union was to be buried forever. The war enabled Israel to evolve as the Middle East's first regional superpower; it also destroyed the myth of Arab unity and created a new myth, that of Israel invincibility. Many Arabs viewed the military debacle as an expression of God's displeasure, believing that they were being punished for having drifted away from Islam. They started returning to the mosques to expunge the guilt they carried and to fill the emptiness they felt, and six years later, during Ramadan of 1973, Egyptian warplanes and soldiers crossed the Suez Canal in a surprise attack on Israeli forces occupying the Sinai Peninsula.[4] By the second week of the war, with the United States airlifting massive quantities of arms to the Jewish state, Israel

---

[4] Before the attack was launched, President Anwar Sadat had sought the advice of experts on Islamic law and decreed that his soldiers did not have to observe the Ramadan fast. But when he drove to the operations room just prior to the first strike, he saw that his senior commanders apparently were fasting. He scolded them, asking why no one was smoking or drinking and saying that the operation needed their utmost concentration. "I noticed they were very embarrassed," Sadat wrote in his autobiography, "so I ordered some tea for myself and lit my pipe—whereupon they began to smoke and order tea."

had taken the offensive, and by the third, the Egyptian army was in trouble; only Henry Kissinger's shuttle diplomacy and a cease-fire imposed by the United States and the Soviet Union saved it from eventual defeat. But the outcome was almost irrelevant. The fact that the Egyptians had managed to cross the canal and temporarily put the Israelis on the defensive represented such an important psychological victory for the Arabs that they convinced themselves that they had won a military victory as well. And in that climate of illusionary power, the Arabs moved to punish the United States for its support of Israel by instituting an oil embargo.

I asked one of Al Azhar University's vice presidents, Hassan Abdel Al, about the Islamic revival, and he attributed it, without a moment's hesitation, to the '73 war. But "winning" the war, he noted, had little to do with military tactics or strategy. "The Islamic people were getting away from Islam for a long time," he said, "but now they have come to understand that everything is prepared by God. This is what enabled them to conquer the Israeli army. When our soldiers crossed the canal at two P.M. on October 6, 1973, the only words they said were, 'God is great.' By those words they could feel safe and could trust themselves and their leaders. By those words they knew they would win the war."

Young Arabs also have turned to religion because they have been failed by and grown weary of all the "isms"—Arabism, socialism, Palestinianism, capitalism, Baathism (a socialist Islamic philosophy practiced in Syria and Iraq), Americanism, presidential cultism, the notion of destroying Zionism. They sought an alternative, just as young Americans did who became hippies in the 1960s and Moonies in the 1970s. And the alternative they sought was the only constant in the Arab world—Islam. Whereas moral values change in the Western world from decade to decade, in an Islamic society the moral commitment and codes are immutable. "One would not even dare speak of changing them," Abdullah Masari, Saudi Arabia's director of antiquities, told me. "Everything we believe, everything we do, is anchored in the principles set forth in the Koran. We owe everything to the Islamic faith. It is our stability." Everything a pious Muslim needs to know, even how to invest one's money, is in the Koran and the Sunna. The Arab world, then, is a civilization whose foundation is based on religion and whose future will ultimately be dominated by religion.

THE FAISAL Islamic Bank headquarters is an imposing cement-block structure on Corniche el Nil in Cairo. With forty branches and seven hundred thousand customers, it has become one of Egypt's major financial institutions, and on the morning I stood in the mezzanine with the bank's chief accountant, Magdi Badran, the floor below was awash with hundreds of people elbowing and pushing their way toward the twenty-one tellers' windows. There were no lines, no order. There was just one swirling mob that moved like a tide of rush-hour commuters, voices raised in an undecipherable din of shouts and commotion.

Overhead three ceiling fans cut through the thick heat and the haze of cigarette smoke. Veiled women, waiting for the crush to subside, sat on wooden benches by the door, where an attendant dispensed cups of lukewarm water to depositors, whose nerves, like his uniform, were frayed.

"You know, it's amazing," Badran said, just before the lights flickered and the electricity died. "We don't advertise. We don't have soft music like Citibank or Bank of America. We don't have air conditioning. Our photocopying machine is broken. And look at the business we're doing. They come in this hot weather and they queue up—well, sort of queue up—and wait for a long time because deep inside they feel they are doing what is morally right. They are claiming their place in heaven."

The Faisal Bank—named after the late Saudi Arabian king—is part of a revolutionary banking system that is based on the Koran and Mohammed's words, "Allah hath blighted usury and made alms-giving fruitful." Instead of the traditional creditor-debtor relationship between a bank and its clients, the two parties become partners under the Islamic system, and the bank's function, in addition to making a profit, is to help build society and assist the needy. Usury (an archaic word for interest) is prohibited.

If you are poor and want to buy a house, the bank may give you—yes, *give* you—the necessary money. It provides numerous college scholarships and donates 2.5 percent of the shareholders' profits to charity each year (a tithe known as *zakat*). You want to build a factory or start a business? The bank may write you a check, interest-free, that will make you a partner. You and the bank then share the profits or losses of the venture.

At the heart of the system are the Muslim beliefs that wealth is transitory, that money is not a commodity and that those blessed with abundance have an obligation to share with the less fortunate. The Koran urges individuals to labor and increase production, thus endorsing capitalism and fair profits. It encourages the acceptance of risk but forbids speculation.

The first formal attempt to put Islamic banking theory into practice took place in the Egyptian delta town of Mit Ghamr in 1962. The bank prospered, but President Nasser shut it down two years later as part of his campaign to undermine Islamic institutions. Then, after Nasser's death in 1970, came the oil boom with the great surplus of petrodollars and the religious revival. Islamic banking found renewed popularity and profitability. Returns of 18 percent on savings and other investments were common (although depositors receive no guarantee, as they often do in the West, of what their investments will earn).

Today Islamic banks stretch from Manila to Geneva. Most are well capitalized and competently managed by a Western-educated board of directors, which answers to a group of men trained in religion but not in economics. The latter usually does not interfere with day-to-day bank business, though it must approve all transactions and loans. Its members look for socially redeeming projects that provide jobs, further national development and strengthen the economy. They would not, for instance, provide money to build a brewery or a nightclub; on the other hand, they would support (as the Faisal bank has) numerous projects ranging from the construction of hospitals to the production of potato chips.

To apply Koranic principles, Islamic banks have devised enough regulations and plans to fill a mosque: *Murabaha* enables banks to buy commodities for clients, then sell them back to the same client at a higher price. Under *muamalat,* the bank purchases goods for a customer and is paid back in installments. When loans are made, commissions and fixed fees are involved, all of which sounds like just another name for points and interest. Indeed, many of the differences between Western and Islamic banking are cosmetic, but having been told how unsavory interest is, Arabs feel psychologically comfortable doing business in a religious environment. And governments encourage the presence of Islamic banks as a harmless way of appeasing the fundamentalists' call for a society based on the Koran.

Privately some Islamic scholars question precisely what Mohammed the Prophet meant by the word "usury." Since he was a merchant himself who found reasonable profit perfectly acceptable, why would he ban interest? These skeptics say he probably objected only to exploitative, exorbitant charges, not to fair rates. They also note that there were no banks in the Arabian desert thirteen centuries ago, and they wonder whether what happened there so long ago can effectively be applied to solve the complex economic problems of the twenty-first century. Interest, after all, is one of the major tools governments use for national economic management.

The bottom line is that Islamic banks are not about to replace traditional Western-style financial institutions in the Arab world, and what is evolving is a dual system of banking. The World Bank still makes an important contribution to the development of poor Arab countries, and when the big oil producers, such as Saudi Arabia and Kuwait, want a safe haven for their resources, they usually choose interest-bearing accounts in Europe and North America.

Still, Islamic banks have a good record of turning a profit, though not a perfect one: in 1983 the Saudi-backed, Geneva-based House of Islamic Funds reported losses of $28 million and did not pay its shareholders any dividend. It had invested heavily in precious metals, an interest-free transaction that turned sour when gold and silver prices plunged. But because profits are believed to be bestowed by God in the Islamic world, no great panic or unhappiness was reported among the investors. As the Prophet once said, though probably not about precious metals: "Do not set interest. God alone does that."

THE OVERRIDING impression many Westerners have of the Arab world is that living there is like dwelling in a giant mosque. I do not mean this derogatorily, because it is an unusual and beautiful sight to see an entire sidewalk of men suddenly kneel and face Mecca to communicate with their God at Friday prayers, and I never doubted the sincerity of the words in the Arab greeting *Salaam aleikum,* "Peace be with you." (The response is *Wa aleikum as-salaam,* "And on you be peace.") Yet not for a minute does one forget that one is in a region where religion's control over every aspect of life is growing greater by the day. As one Iraqi university professor told me, "Even if I wanted to, it would be impossible to escape Islam."

Television reruns, such as *A Little House on the Prairie,* are interrupted during prayer times with a message on the screen that says, "Please stand by," and the visual shifts to stock footage of Mecca. In Saudi Arabia religious policemen patrol the streets, tapping with canes on store windows to tell merchants to close down for prayers. In Morocco white flags are run up the sides of mosques five times a day so that the deaf, unable to hear the muezzin's call, will know when it is time to pray. In the Persian Gulf states, arrows pointing toward Mecca are affixed to desks in every hotel room so that guests

will know the direction to face for prayer. In Kuwait Christmas celebrations, even for expatriate residents, have been banned since
1981. In Egypt the government, pressured by the religious establishment, confiscated and destroyed in 1985 all available copies of
the Arabic literary classic *Thousand and One Nights* on the grounds
that several sexual descriptions violated public morals. Probably
nowhere in the world is more energy and time devoted to a single subject, for eventually every newspaper article, every conversation and presidential speech, and every television show get
around to focusing on Islam. Even Tunisia's food riots, sparked by a
government-ordered increase in the price of bread, took on an inexplicable religious overlay as student protesters rampaged through
the streets taunting their octogenarian president, Habib Bourguiba,
with "There is but one God and Bourguiba is anti-God."

Contrary to generally held beliefs in the West, the fundamentalist bloc is not monolithic. Over two hundred groups in the Arab
world have been identified with it, and their platforms are diverse,
with their leaders usually independent of one another. What the
groups do share in common, though, is that each represents a
protest movement. Their grievances target the failure of Arab leadership, economic and social injustices in societies that are more
elitist than pluralistic, Israeli policies that they see as expansionistic
and repressive, and American policies that they believe are anti-
Arab.

As long as these grievances continue to fester, fundamentalism
will continue to swell. It will not simply fade away as policymakers
in Washington seem to hope. As long as the peace process remains
stagnant, the United States' support for Israel remains unquestioned and Arab leaders remain primarily concerned with the perpetuation of their own rule, religion will be a powerful tool in the
hands of the weak.

Whether the majority of Arabs support the Islamization of every
waking moment—and the educated elite generally don't—is immaterial. Lacking a democratic tradition, the Middle East is manipu-

lated by the militant minority and by those who seek confrontation. Arab governments have dealt ruthlessly with radical fundamentalists who threaten national stability—Egypt imprisoned hundreds of them; Saudi Arabia beheaded sixty-three who took over the Grand Mosque; Syria killed twenty thousand innocents to clear one city, Hama, of a handful of Muslim Brothers—but at the same time regimes have had to move cautiously against reasonable demands for Islamization to avoid being branded unreligious, a fatal curse in today's Arab world. Inch by inch, governments have yielded to the fundamentalists until now they have little left to give. One demand that governments continue to resist is that for the adoption of the Sharia, the Islamic code of justice that is used in its entirety only in Saudi Arabia.

AT HIGH noon on November 4, 1983, as thousands of worshipers, their prayers ended, poured out of Jamia Mosque in the Saudi Arabian city of Riyadh, a black police van carrying a man and a woman drove into the empty parking lot outside and stopped next to a piece of cardboard that had been placed on the pavement.

Ali Fakieh and Mouvira Sabie stepped from the van, blindfolded and with their arms bound behind them. They walked on wobbly legs toward the piece of cardboard and the man who waited there—a muscular former slave of Ethiopian descent who carried a three-foot-long double-edged sword. He would earn about $350 that day for severing their heads.

The crowd stood shoulder to shoulder, pressing in toward police lines. Men in long white robes, fathers holding the hands of children and a salesman with two hunting falcons perched on his leather wristband all clustered together, silent and expectant. From the tower of a nearby government building an amplified voice boomed, invoking the name of God and reciting the sins of the murderers Fakieh and Sabie.

Fifteen years earlier, when they were in their twenties, they had robbed and killed a man. But the victim's son had not reached the age of consent and thus was not legally able either to approve the death sentence or to offer forgiveness, which under Islamic law would have earned them their freedom. So they had waited in prison for the young man to grow up and make his choice. Now the eldest son had become an adult and he had decided. They would die.

Fakieh, the man, was the first to kneel and bend on the cardboard, as though in prayer, according to eyewitness accounts. The executioner's assistant jabbed his ribs with a sharp stick. Fakieh's body stiffened and jerked upward in response just as the glistening sword came down with a whooosh.

The crowd watched wide-eyed but made no sound. Moments later, the curved sword, held by the executioner like a woodsman's ax, struck again, and Sabie, too, was dead. A doctor stepped forward to confirm the obvious. Two medical attendants tossed the heads and the two bodies onto a stretcher, placed it in an ambulance and drove off. The crowd drifted away quietly. Islamic justice had been carried out.

Sharia translates in Arabic as "the road to a watering hole," hence the path of God. It differs fundamentally from Western law in that it is not, in theory, man-made. It is divine, based on God's revelations to Mohammed, and since it is not case law, judges are not bound by precedent or the decisions of higher courts. The Sharia combines compassion and harshness through a system of checks and balances. Because of its punishments—public beheadings, amputations, floggings and death by stoning for adulterers and adulteresses—most Westerners tend to dismiss it as little more than an expression of medieval barbarity.

I had a good American friend who lived in Riyadh and held counterviews. Frank Vogel, a lawyer and a Fulbright scholar studying Islamic law for a doctorate at Harvard, had mastered the Arabic language and developed an admirable understanding of the Saudi culture. Frank was wonderfully even-tempered, and the only time I ever saw him bristle was one evening when we sat at his kitchen table drinking coffee—unlike many expatriates in boozeless Saudi Arabia, Frank did not produce bathtub wine—and I mentioned that amputation seemed a fairly uncivilized method of dealing with thieves.

"The Sharia has gotten a bad press in the West simply because it runs counter to our trends of thought," he said. "We treat morality and behavior as an individual matter. The Saudis treat them as social matters that are the responsibility of the entire society. Why is the Sharia effective? Because there's basically no crime in Saudi Arabia. In the United States how many women are raped each year? How many people are killed? How many billions of dollars are spent on burglar alarms and anticrime devices? So here they cut off a few hands of guilty people and avoid these horrors. Can you really say that makes them barbaric and us civilized?"

Frank went over to his cluttered desk, shuffled through some papers and came back with a file of government statistics. During 1982 in Saudi Arabia, a country of seven million people, there were only 14,220 major and minor crimes reported, including consumption of alcohol and adultery. Thefts accounted for 30 percent of the total, alcohol use for 22 percent and burglary for 20 percent. There were 97 premeditated murders and 31 suicides. For comparison, I asked my editors in California to get me similar statistics for Los Angeles County, which also had a population of seven million. The telex came back the next day: in 1982 there had been 1,415 murders and 499,499 *arrests* for felonies and misdemeanors. Over the years the numbers have changed, but not the validity of what they tell us.

I could not refute the evidence: Saudi Arabia was perhaps the safest, most crime-free place in the world. I am quite convinced that if I had left a hundred-dollar bill and my business card on the sidewalk in any Saudi city, they would have been returned to my hotel within hours. There was no need to lock your car, guard your wallet or look over your shoulder while walking an unlit street. To Westerners who have never known this freedom, I can only say we live so constantly with the danger of crime that I think we have forgotten what a burden it is. How much more pleasant life is when personal security is taken for granted, as it is in most of the Arab world, and all threats, real or perceived, are removed.

The Saudis attribute their crime-free environment to the Sharia, but I found it curious that apparently no one has done studies to prove conclusively the validity of this relationship. There is, in fact, no firm proof that the Saudis' harsh punishment does deter crime, any more than there is proof that the death penalty in the West deters capital offenses.

There were, I thought, some other possible explanations that should be considered before giving Islamic justice wholehearted support. Saudi Arabia is a country where virtually everyone is rich and no one is poor and there is no need to commit crimes. The Saudis are tribal people with communal bonds, a society that believes in the sanctity of the family and the inviolability of the home. They are also a religious, moral people who accept Koranic warnings about the evils of crime. But the crime rate is minuscule in every Arab country, even though most use a Western-style legal system. So maybe it is the nature of the Arab culture and the strength of the Arabs' faith, rather than the punishment itself, that account for the absence of crime and violence.

Under the Saudi system, anyone suspected of a crime is usually arrested immediately and required to make a statement without a lawyer being present. Investigations are carried out by the Ministry of Justice, which recommends to the provincial governor whether to prosecute. During the inquiry, suspects remain in prison, jammed into cells that may hold as many as sixty people..Unlike the United States, however, little violence occurs in Saudi prisons.

Judges in Saudi Arabia are recruited by the Ministry of Justice from the top law school graduates and are widely respected for their incorruptibility. They alone decide guilt or innocence and punishment. Their courts are generally closed to all but the accused's family, and no counsel is present at the proceedings. There is no jury, no bail, no writ of habeas corpus. Suspects can be held for months, even years, while investigations are conducted at a leisurely pace.

These may not be the conditions most of us would want to be tried under, but fairness, restraint and discretion are also built into the system. The circumstances of the crime are always weighed; a poor man, for instance, who stole food to feed his family would not be considered a thief and would be set free. A guilty verdict can be rendered only if there is a confession or if there are at least two male witnesses to the crime. Adultery and rape are proved only if four witnesses have seen the actual penetration, an occurrence that presumably does not happen often. Death sentences must be personally approved by the king—he approves only about a dozen executions a year—and if there is the slightest doubt about guilt, judges reduce the charge to a lesser offense. In addition, there are penalties for false accusation. The penalty, for example, for wrongly accusing a chaste woman of adultery is one hundred lashes. And any criminal can be cleared if the family of his victim offers forgiveness—the Koran promises great rewards for this act of charity—or if the family agrees to accept compensation (the cost of buying one's way out of a murder conviction is about forty thousand dollars).

As in most societies, punishment is based on retaliation ("a soul for a soul, an eye for an eye, a nose for a nose, an ear for an ear, a tooth for a tooth," the Koran says) and on fear. The Koran notes that the amputation of a limb "will be a disgrace for them in this world, whilst in the next a terrible punishment awaits them."

I met one of those tormented souls in the Sudan, the only other Arab country that in 1985 was using Sharia punishment. He was a dull-eyed, slow-spoken young man named Nodredin Ahmed Aissa, who, as an accused habitual thief, had lost his right hand and his left leg in a public "cross-limb amputation" at Kober Prison six months earlier.[5] "It was a massacre," he said.

Aissa lived in a junkyard in Khartoum, the somnolent Sudanese capital. He slept in abandoned cars, begged for food and, so great was his disgrace, had not returned home since that October morning when his limbs were severed by a sword imported from Saudi Arabia. As we talked he balanced on a crutch stuck under his left armpit, brushing away with his remaining hand the flies that clung to his soiled robes, and he flashed a brief, gap-toothed smile only when he said, yes, he still believed in the justice of Allah and the Sharia.

Aissa said he remembered throwing back the blindfold over his eyes at the instant the two swords cut simultaneously through his body. And in that brief moment before fainting, he recalled seeing the prison guard pick up his right hand and his left leg and, holding them high like a matador with the ears of a bull, parade them around Kober's courtyard to the cheers of the crowd.

"If I had been judged by the old English law, I would have been released from Kober at once with no punishment because I did not steal what they said." He held up his scarred half-arm to make the point, and the small crowd that had gathered around us in the junk-yard fell back a step. "I was a victim of [President Jaafar] Numeiri, not God. God's punishments are fair. The Sharia is a good thing."

Numeiri, who had been overthrown and had taken refuge in Egypt a week before I talked to Aissa, had indeed victimized his people with a failed Islamic experiment. Once a heavy whiskey drinker, Numeiri had suddenly and inexplicably found God some-

[5] The loss of the right hand, and thus having to use the left, is a particular stigma. In Arab cultures, the left hand is best reserved for the bathroom and cleaning oneself; eating with that hand is considered unsanitary and disgraceful. If an Arab child shows left-handed tendencies, his parents will force him to use his right.

time in early 1983. He may have been reacting to political pressures from the fundamentalists or to his own ill health and the desire to make his final peace. Whatever the reason, overnight he became ultrareligious and started speaking of himself as an imam. He surrounded himself with religious mystics and discarded Sudan's Western-style legal system, replacing it with "decisive justice courts"—each composed of a policeman, a soldier and a civilian judge—to implement the Sharia.

The rigid interpretation of the Koran works in Saudi Arabia because the Saudis are a like-minded community of believers, whose lives are indelibly imprinted with Islamic adherence over many centuries. But the Sudanese are a laid-back people, more African than Arab in attitude, and they liked washing away their desert thirst with a few beers and idling away the evening hours in the company of pretty women. Nor, with Muslim Arabs in the north of the country and black Christians and animists in the south, are they a cohesive people like the Saudis. There was, then, considerable discontent when women were banned from using public swimming pools and the sale and consumption of alcohol was prohibited. In the lobby of the Khartoum Hilton Hotel one day a Sudanese official walked up to an Egyptian banker, sniffed the air and slapped him in the face. "You've been drinking!" the official stormed. But most shocking to everyone was the cruel and un-Islamic way in which Numeiri started dispensing Islamic justice.

In one fifteen-month period fifty-four suspected criminals lost hands, and sixteen others lost two limbs as repeat offenders. (The first amputee died of infection two weeks after his hand was cut off, although a Saudi medical team had been flown into Khartoum to train the prison amputation squad.) In two cases, appeals courts added amputation to a lesser sentence—something unheard of in Saudi Arabia—and on three occasions men were sentenced to posthumous crucifixion after hanging, though the crucifixions were never carried out. Every Arab country, including Saudi Arabia, was appalled; pressure mounted on Numeiri to back off as suspicions grew that he was using religion as a political tool to intimidate his people and appease the fundamentalists.

One Sudanese who spoke out, saying that Numeiri's use of the Sharia "humiliated the people and deformed the image of Islam," was a seventy-six-year-old Muslim named Mahmoud Mohammed Taha. He was a widely respected moderate who held that some portions of the Koran were not necessarily applicable for all time and that modern interpretation was quite valid. Taha's simple dream was for a society of good Muslims in a peaceful world.

Taha and his four closest colleagues were arrested, charged initially with heresy, then with "apostasy" for "nonviolently opposing Islamic law." All were sentenced to death. On the day before the scheduled execution, Taha's four friends were shown on national television sitting at a prison table, cluttered with half-empty tea glasses, talking with six sheiks. The condemned men were told they would be spared if they denounced Taha and admitted they had veered from the path of Islam. Three signed. The fourth hesitated, promising to correct the error of his ways but saying he could not denounce his friend of thirty years. The sheiks said his recantation was not sufficient to save him from the gallows. He hesitated again, then signed.

The four men were set free, but Taha refused to admit to being anything less than a good Muslim. He was hanged. It was then that the U.S. embassy in Khartoum put together a forty-page analysis of what Sudan would be like in the post-Numeiri period. The report was prophetic, and three months later, on April 6, 1985, Numeiri was overthrown by the Sudanese army, with the backing of the populace, while en route home from a trip to Washington. That night joyful crowds broke through the twelve-foot-high brick walls of Kober Prison and danced around the trapdoor of the steel gallows. They freed the prisoners and chanted, "No more amputations, no more amputations!"

Numeiri's Islamic experiment failed because he had abused his people and misused religion, twisting it for personal and political reasons. The sigh of relief throughout the Arab world was audible, but short-lived. The democratically elected government that replaced Numeiri's dictatorship lasted less than three years, and under a new gang of fundamentalists the civil war between the Sudan's Arab north and Christian south raged on, economic ruin loomed and religious intolerance had become part of the national agenda. In no time at all Khartoum, a city laid out in colonial times in the pattern of the British Union Jack, had put out the welcome mat to some of the world's most-wanted terrorists. Among those who accepted the invitation to set up operations in the Sudan was Osama bin Laden.

A GULF OF MISUNDERSTANDING

arab *n* 1 *syn vagabond, clochard, drifter, floater, hobo, road-ster, street arab, tramp, vag, vagrant. syn* **2** *peddler, duffer, hawker, higgler, huckster, monger, mongerer, outcrier, pack-man, vendor.*

—*Webster's Collegiate Thesaurus*

Let me tell you 'bout A-hab the A-rab, the sheik of the burning sand. He had emeralds and rubies just a-dripping off of him, and a ring on every finger of his hands.

—*popular 1960s song by Ray Stevens*

THE QUINTESSENTIAL Arab is Goha, a man who lives in the fables and imaginations of the Arab world, and nowhere in the Middle East is there a figure more revered. He is lovable, eccentric, simple. His optimism is boundless, his generosity has no limits. He is said to be a fool, but he is clever and conniving and usually outwits every sultan he encounters.

A movie has been made about him in Lebanon. He is the star of a puppet show in Syria, the subject of books in Iraq. Parents tell their children stories about him in Morocco. A political satire about him in 1985, *Goha Rules the City,* ranked as one of Egypt's most popular plays since World War II. For the Arabs, Goha is the Walter Mitty of Arabia, the little man living out his fantasies, always triumphing over great odds. And for the Westerner, to understand Goha is to comprehend—to a small degree, at least—the character of the Arab.

When the sultan wanted someone to teach his pet donkey to read and write, Goha volunteered. He said the task would take three years, and to accomplish it he would need a villa with servants. The sultan agreed, and the next day Goha and the donkey moved into a splendid mansion. Time passed. Goha's friends came to visit him and found him lounging about in great comfort while the donkey roamed happily over the gardens. They warned him time and again that if he failed to come up with a literate donkey at the end of three years, he would surely lose his head. But Goha was unperturbed.

"I shall not give up hope," he said. "After all, one of four things might happen: the sultan may die, I may die, the donkey may die or—who knows?—the donkey may learn to read and write."

Goha is usually pictured as an old man with a white beard, a floppy hat and black robes. He is said to have been born in Iraq, though whether such a character ever really existed no one knows. But Goha stories have been passed down through the generations, and in the hearts of adults and children Goha lives today as the fool who proves himself more learned than the scholars, the buffoon who knows that every problem has a simple solution, the desert philosopher who is disdainful of authority and never gets rattled by life's daily obstacles.

His robe falls off a hook on the wall and Goha, forever the optimist, observes, "Thanks be to God, I wasn't in it." He avoids school by sending his donkey in his stead, and the donkey holds his own against students from all walks of life. He loses his money in the desert one night and explains to a friend that he is searching for it in his house because "it is dark outside and here I have light."

Like the peasant Arab, Goha is a man of wit and homespun wisdom. He is portrayed as poor, weak, ignorant and lazy, but by rely-

ing on charm, guile and common sense and never resorting to violence or the humiliation of adversaries, he always manages to dis-
entangle himself from the most difficult and perplexing situations.
He is religious and gentle, and cheerfully gives street beggars the
money his wife has advanced him for bread because the beggar's
need is greater. He does not waste his energy needlessly.

One day Goha went to a mosque, traveling as always with his
faithful donkey. He rose to address the people there and asked, "Do
you know what I am going to talk about?" The people answered no,
so Goha left, saying, "Then there is no use telling you something
you don't know."

He came back the next day and asked the same question. The
people said yes and Goha replied, "Then there is no use repeating
something you already know," and he left again. On the third day
when he returned, some people said yes and some said no.

"OK," Goha said. "Those who know tell those who don't know."
And he took his leave.

I liked the Goha stories because they added a human dimension
to the Arab character that one seldom saw in the West. Goha was
decent and innocent. He was crafty but not devious. He tackled
problems in a good-natured, delightfully absurd way, always out-
smarting those who were richer and more powerful, and spun folksy
homilies as appealing to the Arabs as Will Rogers's tales were to the
Americans. If he had traded his robes for slacks and his mosque for
a church, kids in the corn belt of America or the villages of England
would have understood exactly what Goha was all about.

As I traveled through the Middle East, spending time and sharing thoughts with so many Arabs I thoroughly enjoyed, slowly
accepting the notion that it was I, as the guest, who had to adjust to
their culture, not the other way around, I became increasingly
aware that the Arab is judged by a double standard in the West.
When he buys property in America, as Saudi Arabia's minister of
industry, Ghazi Gosaibi, pointed out, it is a minor scandal; when a

non-Arab buys the same property, it is a sound investment.[1] When an American acquires an expensive painting, he is considered cultured and refined; when an Arab does the same thing, he is thought to be decadent.

"You know, stereotypes cut both ways," a Saudi prince, Sultan ibn Salman al-Saud, mentioned one day as we sat in his office in Riyadh talking about the negative image of Arabs in the West. "I remember once, when I was very young, my parents said that we were going to the United States for a visit. I said, 'Great, as long as it's Los Angeles or New York.' But I told them I wouldn't go to Chicago. Chicago really scared me. I thought it was full of gangsters and that people were getting killed on every street corner. That's what TV had taught me."

Salman, not yet thirty, was a bachelor, articulate and elegant in his flowing white *dishdasha*, and as a member of the royal family, was presumably very rich. He was licensed to pilot executive jets; his father was the provincial governor; his degree was in mass communications from the University of Denver, where, yes, his classmates had kidded him about living in a tent and riding a camel. Unlike the political cartoons we in the West see of Arabs, Salman was refined and unassuming, with the build of an athlete and the good looks of a movie star. During our chance meeting in a government ministry he never mentioned anything about himself to make me think he was more than just another civil servant.

I didn't hear of Salman again until three years later, when I noticed his picture in the *Los Angeles Times*. He was dressed in a Western business suit and would not have attracted a second glance on any street in America. He had just become the first Arab to travel in space, having helped launch a telecommunications satellite, owned by the Arab League, during the eighteenth mission of the

---

[1] The Arabs are far down the line in the rank of leading investors in the United States. The top foreign investors in the United States are the Dutch with $9 billion; the British, $7.4 billion; the Canadians, $6.5 billion; and the Germans, $3.2 billion.

shuttle *Discovery.* The prince, who was headed for Washington to meet President Reagan in the White House, told the *Times* reporter how the mission had given him a sense of a world community. How foolish it seemed, he said, that astronauts had to carry passports.

"The first day or two up there," Salman said, "you try to recognize the countries, especially Saudi Arabia. It stands out. It's very distinct. Then you keep missing the countries and you look only at the continents. By the sixth day the whole world becomes a beautiful blue and white and yellow painting. Those boundaries really disappear."

Most Westerners never see an Arab like Prince Salman portrayed on television or in editorial cartoons. Most would be startled to read Will Durant's *The Story of Civilization* and learn that during Europe's Dark Ages the Arabs "led the world in power, order and extent of government, in refinement of manners, in standards of living, in humane legislation and religious toleration, in literature, scholarship, science, medicine and philosophy." And most, if asked to describe an Arab, would probably use the same adjectives Americans did in a public opinion survey published in the spring 1981 edition of the *Middle East Journal:* "barbaric and cruel," "treacherous," "warlike" and "rich." In short, the West sees the Arab as being a millionaire, a terrorist, a camel herder or a refugee, but not as a real human being.

Probably no ethnic or religious group has been so constantly and massively disparaged in the media as the Arab over the past decades. Being Arab is a liability everywhere but in the Arab homelands, for virtually everywhere else the Arab is stereotyped in negative terms. When a school in suburban Washington, D.C., held a Halloween costume party, eight of the children showed up dressed as Arabs. Their accessories included toy guns, rubber knives, oil cans and moneybags. Even *Sesame Street,* the widely acclaimed American children's television show, once used an Arab figure to portray the concept of danger. And in 1978, when U.S. federal agents posing as wealthy Arabs from Oman and Lebanon offered bribes to congressmen in return for political favors, they called their undercover operation Abscam (for Arab scam). Few people were offended, but I wonder what the public reaction would have been had they named their operation Jewscam or blackscam. No matter. The Arab is fair game, particularly on television.

"Most minorities have come into their own on the television screen," Jack Shaheen, an American scholar of Lebanese parentage, wrote in the 1980s. "Blacks have graduated from their janitorial and servant jobs to become doctors, lawyers and scientists. Latins are no longer seen as Frito Bandito or Chiquita Banana types. The American Indian does not massacre helpless whites. The Oriental no longer acts like the shuffling coolie or barbaric villain. Television, for the most part, has discontinued pejorative characterizations of women and other minorities. Only the Arab has been excluded from television cultural reorientation."

Arab-bashing in the media has diminished since Shaheen wrote those words. Although Arab Americans are still sometimes singled out for harassment by ignorant rednecks in time of crisis, such as in the aftermath of the September 11, 2001, terrorist attacks, discrimination seems to be slowly fading. In the war against terrorism, for instance, President George W. Bush went to lengths to defuse anti-Islam and anti-Arab sentiments. He visited a mosque, conferred with the Arab-American community and delivered several forceful pronouncements in defense of respecting America's ethnic and religious diversity.

In early movies (*The Desert Bride, Son of the Sheik,* and Rudolph Valentino's 1921 silent classic *The Sheik*) Arabs were characterized with what Shaheen calls innocuous exoticism. They had harems, did battle on the desert and seemed humorous in their base, bumbling demeanor.[2] Later, because of Israel's popularity in the West and because Gamal Abdel Nasser's shrill rhetoric about Arab

[2] Not until Moustapha Akkad's film, *Lion of the Desert*, released in the United States in 1981, did an American audience ever find itself cheering Arab "good guys." It starred Anthony Quinn as Omar Mukhtar, the Bedouin guerrilla leader who fought Italian colonialists in Libya between 1911 and 1931.

nationalism was perceived as a threat to the West, they became the villains, slippery and warlike. And with the oil embargo of 1973 they became the enemy. One auto-bumper sticker summed up the sentiment in the United States then: DON'T BURN OIL. BURN A SHIEK.

To be sure, the Arabs themselves are partly responsible for the persistence of an unflattering image. The playboy princes frolicking in London, terrorist ruffians taking credit for repugnant terrorist deeds, leaders who seem intent on establishing Arab identity by simply being noisy—none of this has done much to convince the average television viewer in North America or Europe that the Arabs are different from their stereotype. Yet these portraits do not represent the whole, any more than the twenty thousand murders committed in the United States every year make America a nation of killers.

The great majority of Arabs, in fact, have never slept in a tent, ridden a camel or even seen an oil rig. Statistically, they are poor, not rich; farmers, not entrepreneurs; political moderates, not fanatics; pragmatists, not idealists; capitalists, not communists; law-abiding, not crime-crazed. (I once told a Jordanian friend that the United States had *half a million* people in its jails and prisons and that the country's prison population was increasing at the rate of a thousand a week; he shook his head in disbelief.) Arabs abhor violence and terrorism just as other civilized human beings do. They may take issue with Washington's pro-Israeli policies, but they like Americans and find much to admire in the American way of life. Marxism is anathema to them. They believe that anything atheistic must be inherently evil, and were not comfortable with the Soviet Union's heavy-handed policies or its diplomats, whom they considered arrogant and crass.

Like many Third World people, the Arabs cannot fathom why no one understands them but do almost nothing to convince anyone to try. They are inept at articulating their causes and unskilled at using public relations to manipulate opinion. They rely on rhetoric when conciseness is needed and blame everyone but themselves when things go wrong. They criticize (and are envious of) the Israelis for exerting great influence over American politicians and the American public, yet, except for Egypt and to a lesser extent Saudi Arabia, their governments have never made much of an effort either at home or abroad to cultivate the foreign media, to lobby the politicians or to court the public. I asked one senior Arab diplomat who had been based in the United States for four years if he had ever spoken to a Rotary Club or church group, taken a journalist to lunch or visited a university campus. "No," he said, "but I suppose that would have been a good idea." He then went on to say that he didn't understand why the Arabs were still stereotyped in the United States.

I could never figure out why the Arabs had not made a serious attempt to explain themselves to the world. They had some excellent diplomats and many polished, Western-educated intellects who would have made credible spokesmen. But the Arab is an intensely private person. He is a fatalist who sees conspiracies everywhere. More than a few told me with a straight face that Moammar Kadafi is most certainly a C.I.A. agent and the tensions between Libya and the United States are only a façade arranged by both countries to cover his double identity and promote instability in the region, thus making a united Arab stand against Israel impossible. Many believed the attacks on the World Trade Center and Pentagon in 2001 were carried out by Israelis, hoping to prod the United States into a war against Arab extremists. Somehow it was just easier to believe that the West's antipathy for the Arabs and its amity with Israel were part of a larger plot and nothing much could be done about it.[3] The Arabs' own timidity, their unwillingness to denounce their ethnic brethren's misdeeds that violated the

---

[3] Hardly a day went by in the Middle East when I didn't hear or read about some outrageous new conspiracy. Example: On April 14, 1985, the editor, Mohammed el Hayawan, of one of Egypt's major newspapers, *Al Gomhuria*, wrote that Israel was cultivating drugs in southern Lebanon for export to Egypt. The purpose, he said, was to "convert the Egyptians into drug addicts who were prone to having natural relations with Israel."

decency of the majority, only served to reinforce the West's perception of a monolithic Arab bloc whose parts were indistinguishable. They believed that if the West came around to understanding them, fine; if not, they at least had someone to blame other than themselves for being misunderstood.

For a journalist, the contrast between working in Israel and in one of the Arab countries is striking. In Israel, resident foreign correspondents have red phones on their desks that ring when the government wants to disseminate news. Government officials are always available for interviews, even on short notice, and interviews over the telephone are common. Senior newspaper and television editors visiting Israel are treated as V.I.P.'s and within minutes of stepping off the plane at Ben-Gurion Airport in Tel Aviv are on their way to a series of high-level background briefings arranged by the government. By the time the morning is over, they have, as likely as not, met the prime minister, the defense minister and the opposition leader, and are on their way to the Israeli-occupied West Bank.

In Arab countries, it sometimes takes weeks or months to get approval for an entry visa. Once in the country, journalists can spend four or five days waiting in their hotels for confirmation from the Ministry of Information that requested interviews have been arranged. More often as not they are told, "Nothing yet. Call back tomorrow." Iraq and Syria have a single middle-level official who is paraded out for interviews with Western journalists, and usually no one else is available. Government officials in most Arab countries will not talk on the phone, which probably is tapped, and few will talk in person about anything controversial or anything that conflicts with the party line. Besides, what Arab officials say is frequently not what they mean, because pride and dignity are more important to them than what we in the West recognize as "the truth." The result is that it is far more difficult for journalists to get to the essence of Arab policy and thinking than to that of Israel policy and thinking; consequently, the Israelis usually get their point across in the media and the Arabs do not.

"We have nobody to fault but ourselves for the way Arabs are perceived," said Moustapha Akkad, the Syrian-born Los Angeles filmmaker who produced *Mohammed, Messenger of God.* "We can't blame the West, the Americans or anyone else. The finger of blame should be pointed at ourselves, for not coming forward and articulating our positions, for not tidying up our own houses properly. The problem is not with the strength of the other side, it is with the weakness of the Arabs. Something has gone wrong from within."

Among the losers in this lopsided battle for Western understanding are the 2.5 million Arab Americans, such as Akkad—the last U.S. minority to stand up for its rights. Their community is about half the size of the American Jewish population, yet its voice is all but silent. Unlike other large minorities, Arab Americans have not united for political action.[4] Their community is fragmented geographically, beset by the same cultural differences that divided their ancestors in the Arab homelands, and leery of the resentment that might result from high visibility. Many of the older, conservative Arab Americans see no need for Arab unity. So as a group Arab Americans have maintained a low, apolitical profile and have integrated quietly into the American system, sometimes dropping the Arabic names that Americans couldn't spell or pronounce in favor of anglicized ones.

Arab immigrants came to the United States in two waves. The first, between 1880 and 1920, comprised mostly unskilled, illiterate Syrians and Lebanese Christians. They were seeking economic gain, not fleeing persecution or famine, and they tried to be more American than the Americans. Parents often forbade their children to speak Arabic at home, and eventually membership in the

---

[4] Arab Americans began taking the first steps in the mid-1980s to ensure that their collective voice was heard. The American Arab Anti-Discrimination Committee, based in Washington, D.C., has fifteen thousand members and is combating demeaning stereotypes. And the National Association of Arab Americans is engaged in Washington as a lobby group for more balanced U.S. policies in the Middle East.

Maronite and Melchite Eastern Rite Catholic churches dwindled as the immigrants drifted to Western Roman Catholic parishes, where they mixed with other ethnic groups. The new Arab Americans worked as salesmen and tradesmen throughout the country, and although some Americans referred to them as Turks or even Chinese and South Carolina backed legislation in the early 1900s that would have prevented Arabs from becoming citizens, they generally found tolerance and opportunity in their adopted home.

The second wave, coming with the birth of Israel in 1948 and political upheavals in the Middle East in the 1950s and 1960s, changed the complexion of the Arab American community. These new immigrants from Palestine, Egypt, Lebanon, Syria, Iraq and Yemen were better educated than their predecessors and brought with them a sense of Arab nationalism. Most were Muslims or Orthodox Christians. They kept their Arabic names and nurtured their appreciation for the Arabic language and the Islamic culture. Like every other minority in the United States, they had found pride in their roots.

But escaping from the shadow of the Arab stereotyping is difficult. Newspaper editors still feel more comfortable dealing with the Middle East from the Israeli perspective. The public still treats Arabs as objects of curiosity and ridicule. Politicians, fearful of offending American Jews, still consider an association with Arab Americans a potential onus. During the 1984 presidential campaign, Walter Mondale responded to Jewish pressure by returning five thousand dollars in contributions he had received from four Arab Americans. A fifth contribution was returned to a woman simply because her name *sounded* Arabic. In 1986, James Abourezk, a former U.S. senator of Lebanese descent who is chairman of the American Arab Anti-Discrimination Committee, sent a personal check for one hundred dollars to help Joseph Kennedy, the son of Robert F. Kennedy, in his Massachusetts campaign for Congress. One of Kennedy's aides, Steve Rothstein, returned the contribution, saying it was too "controversial." When Vice President George Bush toured the Middle East in 1986 as a prelude to seeking the Republican presidential nomination, he brought along a private film crew to film him in Israel. The crew did not accompany him on the remainder of the trip to Egypt and Jordan because, as one official put it, "There is nothing to be gained schmoozing with the Arabs."

The sadness is that ethnic stereotyping benefits no one. It only reinforces ignorance and prejudice. It obscures the fact that the Arab American community has produced a high number of doctors and academicians of international stature, of corporate executives, attorneys, writers, artists and show-business celebrities.[5] And it makes possible an unwarranted violent backlash against a community of Americans when passions are stirred by an Arab-Israeli conflict thousands of miles away.

"I would like my two daughters to be able to say with pride that their grandfather is from Lebanon, that they are American Arabs," said George Gorayeb, a New Jersey businessman I met one evening in Bahrain's Hilton Hotel. "I know, though, that that's not going to happen, for a while anyway. I know that at show-and-tell at their school, or when kids wear ethnic costumes on special occasions, that there will be embarrassment, that they'll have to apologize for their heritage, and frankly that makes me angry as hell."

BEFORE MOVING to Cairo, I had spent a good part of my adult life living abroad. Four years in Asia, four more in sub-Sahara Africa

[5] A handful of prominent Americans of Arab heritage includes heart surgeon Michael De Bakey, singer Paul Anka, opera prima donna Rosalind Elias, former Governor John Sununu of New Hampshire, consumer advocate Ralph Nader, football star Doug Flutie, author William P. Blatty, former White House Chief of Protocol Selwa Roosevelt, presidential envoy Philip C. Habib, White House correspondent Helen Thomas, television and radio host Casey Kasem, Miami Dolphins owner Joe Robbie, former U.S. Senator George Mitchell of Maine, the late poet and artist Kahlil Gibran, actress Marlo Thomas, Oscar-winner F. Murray Abraham and Colonel James Jabara, America's first jet ace.

and two in Australia had, I thought, taught me how to adjust to new cultures. Not so. The Middle East was the most inherently alien place I had ever encountered. Everywhere else I had been able, without even realizing it, to take what I wanted from a culture, then retreat into what was familiar and secure. I could enjoy the mystique of the Orient while still remaining separate from Buddhism and Asian patterns of thought. In Africa the educated government officials, journalists and businessmen I socialized with wore Western-style clothes, went to Christian churches and had been schooled in Paris or London. Among the Australians I felt every bit as much at home as I would be in any community of Americans.

But to survive the Arab world, you have to yield. Fight it and you lose. Move with its rhythms or be jarred into mental exhaustion. There are no closets in which to seek refuge. You cannot tune out religion because Islam is everywhere and in everything. You cannot avoid the cacophony and traffic of Cairo because, more than any other single force, they dictate the pace of daily life for anyone who lives in that teeming metropolis. You cannot recognize any familiar chords in the Arab's music or any syllables in his language. To what does the Westerner relate? One reason Americans like Israelis is that they *look* like *us*. But the Arab is different. He can be white, olive-skinned or black. He sometimes has four wives. He may dress in robes and pray five times a day. Whereas many educated West Africans became, in effect, black Frenchmen and many Caribbeans speak with a cultured British accent, the Arab has never pretended to be—or wanted to be—anything but an Arab.

"The Arabs are strange people," Ernie Pyle wrote in 1942 while covering the Allied invasion of North Africa.

They are poor, and they look as tight-lipped and unfriendly as the Indians in some of the Latin countries, yet they're friendly and happy when you get close to them. As you drive through the country, Arab farmers by the hundreds wave at you along the road, and small children invariably shout their few American words — "goodbye," or "okay" — as you pass, and either salute like soldiers or give the "V" sign with their fingers.

In half a day's driving here I get more "V" signs than I saw the whole time I was in England.

I still haven't got the religion question straight. Some Arab women wear white sheets and hoods that cover the face, except for one eye sticking out. The soldiers call them "One-Eyed Flossies." But they are in the minority. Most of the women show their faces.

As far as I can figure out, the ones who cover their faces are the severely religious, just as at home only a few of the Jewish people are what they call orthodox. The rest are good people, but they don't observe the ancient customs and restrictions.

One of the most significant differences between East and West is the role of women in the male-dominated Arab society. By any standards I understood, the Arab world was replete with sexual segregation and sexual repression, and most people seemed to take seriously Mohammed's warning: "If a man and a woman are alone in one place, the third person present is Satan."

Without realizing the religious sensitivities involved, I wrote a story not long after I arrived in Cairo saying that Arab women were so oppressed they didn't even realize they were still third-class citizens. To some, those words were tantamount to an attack on Islam. One Cairo newspaper printed a full-page condemnation of my story, and another accused me in a lengthy editorial of "laboring under the delusion that exhibitionism and possible nudity are irrefutable proof of feminine liberty and hence a sign of great civilization." Scores of letters poured into my office. I had, they said, missed the point: Islam had liberated women, not enslaved them. They pointed out that women control a considerable amount of the wealth in the Middle East (Mohammed's first wife was, after all, a successful businesswoman), that women had fought alongside men in the early Arab conquests, that women did not take their hus-

band's family name in marriage, that 10 percent of Egypt's 392 par-
liamentarians were women, that Libya's Moammar Kadafi had surrounded himself with female bodyguards. True enough. Yet, for
reasons that are cultural as well as religious, the Arab world, like
many developing societies, remains a man's domain. There the
birth of a son is greeted with great celebrations and the firing of
rifles by Bedouin tribesmen; the birth of a girl brings quiet congratulations that are almost consolatory in tone, as though to say, "Next
time maybe it will be a boy."

Although Islamic doctrine specifies that women should be protected and respected, and that rape is one of the most heinous of
crimes, women are thought to be weaker than men in mind, body
and spirit and to need safeguarding from their own impulses.
"Men," the Koran notes, "are superior to women because of the
qualities whereby God has made a distinction between them. . . ."
Man's highest achievement is perfection in his relationship with
God. Women represent a threat to that ideal because any sexual
impropriety brings dishonor. By isolating women, their chances of
damaging man's integrity are greatly diminished. So to many in the
Middle East, women remain biological objects whose place is in
the home rearing children. The (non-Arab) Taliban regime in
Afghanistan wouldn't let girls attend school and beat women in the
streets who were not properly veiled, head to toe, or who walked
with a lively step instead of the required shuffle. As T. E. Lawrence
wrote early in this century (when one of the few careers open to
women was that of being a professional mourner at funerals),
although man is not the absolute master, a woman is often the
"object of his sensual pleasures, a toy with which he plays whenever
and however he pleases."

Religious authorities in Kuwait took steps in 1985 to snuff out a
feminist movement by decreeing that women did not have the right
to vote or hold seats in the parliament. "Islam does not permit
women to forfeit their basic commitments," the sheiks noted,
adding an observation by Prophet Mohammed that "No people

will be successful if they are led by a woman." The authorities also had trouble that year with an increasing number of female students who were walking around unveiled on Kuwait University's campus. They wrote a leading Saudi theologian seeking a remedy. The theologian wrote back with a simple solution: Women shouldn't be on campus in the first place.

For someone raised in the era of Betty Friedan, I felt that the calendar had been turned back. Seeing Egyptian men sunning themselves in brief trunks on the beaches of Alexandria while their wives sat alone in the sand, fifteen or twenty yards behind them, sweltering in head-to-toe black *abeyas*, is a sight I will retain forever. Nor will I forget walking for the first time into a Saudi Arabian restaurant with an American friend and having to use a separate side door because we had our wives with us. On the door was tacked a sign: "Women must behave in a modest and bashful manner at all times." I had no doubt that Sandy and Melanie intended to comply, but as soon as we sat down, a waiter surrounded the four of us with portable partitions so that there would be no gawking and no immoral thoughts carried on between tables. Later, leaving the restaurant, a municipal bus caught my eye as it rolled by. In the back, next to the women-only door, were two females—it was impossible to tell if they were old or young, ugly or beautiful, because veils covered their faces—separated by a solid grate from the other passengers. It somehow all seemed reminiscent of the United States before the civil rights movement.

In a court of law the testimony of two women equals that of one man. In Saudi Arabia, women are not allowed to drive cars or work in any job that would put them in contact with men. They cannot enter the country without a male escort or leave without the permission of a male relative. Throughout the Arab world, a man can divorce his wife merely by reciting three times, "I divorce thee," and is under no obligation to tell his spouse if he has taken other wives. In the mosque, women must enter through separate doors and pray in the rear so that male worshipers are not distracted by sexual thoughts. "Virtuous women," says the Koran, "are devout and keep intact in their husband's absence what God has prescribed to keep intact. If you fear that they will reject you, admonish them, and remove them into another bed; finally beat them. If they obey you, then worry them no more. God is high and great."

What surprised me most was that most Arab women are not outwardly unhappy with their lot in life. Even those who have been educated in the West and have returned home to the veil insist that they are liberated and are man's equal. It is, though, mostly a question of semantics: if they concede that they are not liberated, they are challenging the Koran and thus being un-Islamic. Women have, in effect, become Uncle Toms. The veil protects them from sexual abuse—it is like a badge that says, *I* believe in God and *you* owe me your respect—and they have no interest in competing with men anyway. They have educational and economic opportunities, and that is a lot to be grateful for. Whatever Western women are agitating for makes no sense to them. Besides, they ask, what does the West offer as an alternative—promiscuity?

ALTHOUGH POPULAR Arab television shows promote the idea that love precedes marriage, as in the West, this is usually not the case. Love, if it is to come at all, takes root as the marriage grows, for marriage in the Arab world is a practical matter based more on the propagation of the family than on companionship and starry-eyed romance. Many marriages are arranged, and as often as not the bride is only a bystander in the negotiations for her future. The failure to bear her husband a son is grounds for divorce.

An Egyptian friend of mine named Hassan was stopped near his home one day by a young man with whom he had a nodding acquaintance. The youth came right to the point. "Excuse me," he said, "but I have seen your sister, and I would like to marry her." Hassan's eighteen-year-old sister, Sahar, did not even know that her suitor existed, but that was unimportant. The young man, Fuad

Hakki, was from a good family, he was pious, he did not drink and he earned a respectable salary of two hundred dollars a month as a bank clerk. Hassan quickly agreed to arrange a meeting.

Three days later Hakki knocked on the door of Hassan's parents. He wore a gray business suit and had brought a box of pastries as a gift. Everyone was a bit uncomfortable at first, Hassan recalled. Then coffee was served and the business at hand came easily.[6] Hassan's parents quizzed Hakki about his job, his personal habits, his salary, his chances for advancement. Hakki then turned to Sahar, who sat alone on a small sofa, and asked her about her friends, her interests, her attitude toward having children. The questions proceeded as in a job interview. Hakki looked pleased when Sahar said she would rather be a housewife with a large family than to have a career.

Finally Hakki said, "This is very good coffee." That was a code phrase meaning that the meeting had gone well and that, yes, he did want to marry Sahar. That was all there was to it. The couple recited a verse from the Koran, and Sahar promised to consider no other marriage proposal. Hakki in turn promised to pay Sahar's father a *mahr* (bride payment) of two thousand dollars in gold for his daughter's hand. The wedding date was set for seven months hence.

During the courtship, Hakki and Sahar would meet only in the presence of family members. They would not go to movies or par-

---

[6] Coffee (*qahwah* in Arabic) is the enduring symbol of Arab hospitality and is consumed in great quantities throughout the day. "May there always be coffee at your house," an Arab will say, expressing hope that a family will know prosperity and friendship. Wild coffee plants are believed to have first been taken from Ethiopia to southern Arabia in the fifteenth century. But legend has it that as early as A.D. 850 an Arab goatherd, puzzled by his flock's peculiar behavior, sampled the coffee bush the animals had been nibbling. He was overwhelmed by a sense of exhilaration and proclaimed his discovery to the world. Because of its stimulating qualities, coffee was later banned as being against the teachings of the Koran. The threat of floggings, however, did not diminish coffee's popularity. Coffee drinking spread rapidly throughout the Arab world and is no longer challenged on religious grounds.

ties together, would not hold hands or share any moments of inti-
macy. If the two had engaged in any premarital sexual activity—a
rare occurrence in the Arab world—chances are that Hakki would
have promptly severed the relationship, considering Sahar immoral
and unworthy of marriage.

The sexual segregation that all young Arabs experience builds
pressure and frustration for which they have no outlet. In movie
theaters the all-male audiences break into a perspiring frenzy over
the vaguest sexual innuendo. In the streets of Cairo and Tunis,
Western women with blond hair are brushed and patted by numerous idle young hands in the jostling crowds, and to get into a taxi
alone is often to be propositioned. Unveiled and thus unprotected,
the women are perceived to be available—a perception reinforced
by old American television features such as *Dallas* and *Love Boat*
that still show on prime time and are as popular in the Arab world
as they were in the United States. An Egyptian peasant convicted of
raping a blond tourist in Alexandria told the sentencing judge that
he was dumbfounded by his victim's response. "She *screamed*," he
complained. This was not at all the way amorous women reacted
on the American TV shows *he* saw.

For the young Arab, there is no place for love to bloom, and
denied love is the pain that many must silently suffer. An unmarried
couple can never be alone, never touch, never feel the pounding
heart of arousal. Emotions must be dismissed; it is safer not to fall in
love.

"If you do slip off alone with a boy you care for," said a university
professor, Zenib Hosni, who was both beautiful and unveiled, "you
feel tremendous guilt because you know it is wrong, even if you are
only talking. You live with the fear that you'll be caught. To fall in
love in Egypt is to feel guilt and pain."

PROPHET MOHAMMED'S wives were veiled, though he never said
that all women had to follow their example, stipulating only that

believing women should lower their gaze and be modest. But with the Islamic revival in the Middle East, more and more women have started to cover their hair, shoulders and arms as a sign that they are in tune with their generation. It is their statement, as surely as long hair was the statement of America's youth in the 1960s. The veil— some of which have become quite colorful and fashionable—is a woman's way of saying she is something special and is separate from man. Sexual equality isn't the issue at all.

I asked a graduate student in political science why she had started veiling. "It just seemed wrong to be uncovered," she said. "God ordered that we be veiled, and if he ordered it, we should obey. It doesn't matter whether veiling is pretty or not, good or not. We should obey and show respect."

Ironically, the veil that Amina now wears is a mark of identity that women once fought to take off as a sign of oppression. In 1922 three Egyptian women returned from a feminist conference in Rome. A large crowd had gathered in Alexandria to hear their address. Suddenly one of the three women pulled off her veil. There was a gasp of disbelief. Then by the hundreds others started removing theirs. The "de-veiling" of the Arab woman had begun, and the movement would soon spread throughout Egypt and on to Syria and Lebanon.

The veil by no means disappeared, but its use was generally restricted to peasants, and covered women immediately identified themselves as being neither educated nor prosperous. Today the veil cuts across all classes of society, but I wondered how deeply ingrained the tradition really was. More than once, on flights from the Middle East to London or Rome, I would watch a nondescript veiled woman disappear into the rest room and then emerge a few minutes later looking quite gorgeous in a French-designed dress *sans* veil.

More women are being educated today in the Arab world than ever before, and that in itself portends eventual change in the status of women. Saudi Arabia, for instance, didn't even open its first girls school until 1956; today the kingdom's schools have an enrollment of four hundred thousand girls. But in the short run the growing influence of fundamentalism will probably prevent much advancement toward equality of the sexes. To these religious purists, any talk of sexual liberation is heretical. They subscribe to Mohammed's advice to women: "Stay in your houses. Do not dress up after the fashion of the days of obscurantism. Celebrate the service of prayer and pay the tithe. Obey God and his Prophet. God simply wishes to save you from defilement. . . ."

During one trip to Saudi Arabia I asked the Ministry of Information to arrange some interviews with prominent Saudi women. After several days an appointment was made with Hend Khuthaiha, vice dean of the Women's Study Center (enrollment: four thousand) at King Saud University in Riyadh. She held a doctorate from Syracuse University and had spent eleven of her thirty years in the United States. The ministry official said he was sure I would find no segregation in Saudi society, and I asked what time I should be at the university for my appointment. "Oh, *you* can't go there," he said. "Your wife will have to do the interview."

So Sandy set out that evening with a tape recorder. Mrs. Khuthaiha's point was that the Arab world had its own moral and spiritual values and wasn't accountable to the West for the way it mixed the sexes. There was nothing peculiar to her in the fact that if a male professor was teaching female students, he did so on video while being in a separate room. "When there is a need for change, things will change, but at our pace," she said. "Look what's happened already. When I was in the first grade, who could have predicted that in ten or twelve years I would be in the United States, getting my education? And my four daughters will have even more opportunities than I had."

Outside her window, dozens of female students milled about the cement courtyard, which was surrounded by tall buildings and a high fence. No veils covered them. Dark-eyed and smooth-skinned, theirs was the beauty of youth, and the white skirts and blouses they wore contrasted with the shapeless black forms that Sandy and I had seen drifting through the streets. The girls laughed and giggled and joked.

Then, the school day ended, they moved toward the main gate, where they stood quietly in line. Their names were called out over a loudspeaker and, one by one, they threw on their abeyas and stepped into the street, gaze lowered, again wrapped in the black clothes that made them indistinguishable as individuals. Each walked directly to a chauffeur-driven car, which sped away from the curb, whisking the girls back into the privacy and security of a world I will never fully understand.

THE AMERICAN CONNECTION

THE FIRST glimpse many Americans ever had of an Arab was in the newsreels of February 1945, when President Franklin D. Roosevelt, heading home from the Yalta conference, met with the founder of Saudi Arabia, Abdul Aziz ibn Saud, aboard the U.S.S. *Quincy* in the Great Bitter Lake of Egypt's Suez Canal.[1] Ibn Saud, who never before had set foot outside his desert kingdom, traveled from Jeddah to the summit on the American destroyer *Murphy.* To the astonishment of the American sailors, he and his entourage of forty-nine slept and prayed under tents they had pitched on deck and feasted on eight sheep they had brought aboard and slaughtered during the course of the two-day journey.

Only five years earlier, when aides suggested that the United States develop some influence in the unknown backwaters of Arabia, Roosevelt had scribbled in a White House memo: ". . . tell the British I hope they can take care of the King of Saudi Arabia. This is a little far afield for us." But times were different now. European Jews, homeless and haunted by the horrors of Nazi atrocities, were emigrating to Palestine in large numbers. Standard Oil of California had outbid the British, and oil was flowing in the Arabian

---

[1] Correctly, the king's full name was 'Abd al-'Aziz ibn'Abd al-Rahman Al Faysal Al Sa'ud; *ibn* means "son of" and Al means "from the family of." He was from the family of Sa'ud and is commonly known in the West as Ibn' Saud. The apostrophe, denoting a "glottal stop," represents the tongue-twisting Arab consonant '*Ain* and is often dropped in Western writing.

Peninsula. The British and French empires that stretched through Africa and the Middle East were in the early stages of decline, and the voices of nationalism were gathering vigor in a score of colonies. Perhaps most significant, the United States was emerging from World War II as the new power. It had inherited the earth.

Flushed with victory, America represented strength and glamour and respect for the aspirations of all men (except its own blacks), who were free or wanted to be free. Europe was the past, America the future. And to the Arabs, America was a seductive goddess: it offered knowledge, technology, money, righteousness and fairness, consumer goods, weapons and the promise of modern ways to those willing to reach for the great dream.

No two men could have been more unlike than Roosevelt—urbane, worldly, the leader of the world's mightiest nation—and Ibn Saud, a barely literate warrior whose isolated, primitive land mattered little except to the oil barons and the Muslims who made the pilgrimage to Mecca. Only his steel-rimmed glasses gave any hint that Ibn Saud had ever been affected by the world beyond. But according to accounts by Colonel William A. Eddy, then an American envoy in Saudi Arabia, the king believed Roosevelt worthy of trust and the summit went smoothly even if there was no agreement on Palestine.

Roosevelt had hoped to gain the support of Ibn Saud—the guardian of Mecca—for increased Jewish immigration to Palestine. With it, he reasoned, other Arab Muslims would consent and the Arab-Jewish problem would fade away. But the Saudi king was unswayed. He suggested that the Germans who had persecuted the Jews be forced to surrender part of their country for a Jewish homeland. Neither leader yielded, though Roosevelt was not unsympathetic to the Palestinian Arabs, and the American president promised Ibn Saud that the United States would make no policy decisions on the Palestinian issue without first consulting Saudi Arabia. It was the first of many pledges the United States made to the Arabs in the postwar era. Few of them were ever kept.

THE IRONY of the uneasy course that Arab-American relations would take during the next four decades is that the Arabs were America's first real friends in the vast Islamic world. It was a friendship that would extend through World War II when the United States championed the cause of independence for two French colonies, Morocco and Tunisia. Even today it is impossible to have a conversation with any Algerian official about Arab-American relations without being reminded that in 1957 a young American senator, John F. Kennedy, startled everyone by siding with Algeria in its war for independence against France. "In those days," an Algerian editor told me, "you Americans stood by the underdog if you thought he was morally right. Now you like the status quo, the establishment, right or wrong, as long as it's anti-Communist."

Arab-American relations began in the last days of the American Revolution. Many U.S. ships used to call at the Moroccan port of Tangier, and the Americans, having declared their independence and needing a safe haven from Barbary pirates and British warships, sought de facto recognition from Morocco. Sultan Mohammed ben Abdallah III—a forebear of Morocco's ruler today, King Mohammed VI—granted it in 1777, making Morocco the first country to recognize the United States. The next year Thomas Jefferson and John Adams signed a treaty of friendship with Morocco on behalf of the new republic. It is still in effect and is the longest uninterrupted treaty in U.S. history.

Abdallah, intrigued with this upstart nation that had cast off British colonial rule, wrote President George Washington to convey his people's good wishes. Not until December 1, 1789, fifteen months later, did Washington reply to his "great and magnanimous friend," whom he mistakenly addressed as an emperor instead of a sultan. His handwritten letter, which is preserved in Morocco's royal archives, expressed the conviction that the United States had a promising future and could be an important ally.

"Our soil is bountiful and our people industrious," Washington wrote, "and we have reason to flatter ourselves that we shall gradually become useful friends."

The sultan cemented the friendship in 1833 by presenting the American consul in Tangier, James R. Leib, with two Arabian horses and a lion. Leib sent an urgent message to Washington, suggesting that he keep the horses and send the lion to a zoo in the United States. Washington replied that he should send the horses, if they were any good, and get rid of the lion.

Knowing he would offend Sultan Abdallah if he sold the lion, Leib kept the animal for more than a year in the legation's stables. History does not record how he solved the problem, but it is known that his out-of-pocket food bill came to $439, representing a big chunk of his salary.

The United States also signed a treaty of amity and commerce in 1833 with Oman that said there would be "perpetual peace" between the two countries. Seven years later Sultan Sayyid bin Said—the great-great-grandfather of today's Omani ruler, Sultan Kaboos—sent the first Arab envoy to the United States. His confidential secretary, Ahmed bin Na'aman, reached New York on a Thursday morning in April aboard the three-masted ship, *Al-Sultanah*, that flew the blood-red flag of the sultan.

So many Americans flooded the docks to get a look at the beaded, dashing Na'aman and his officers that the city marshal had to be called to keep order. Na'aman was feted with receptions and dinners, welcomed with a resolution from the Board of Aldermen, and trailed by reporters from New York's ten daily newspapers as he visited a hospital, a penitentiary and an institution for the blind and rode the new Long Island Railway.

Like any good Arab trader, Na'aman did not arrive in New York empty-handed. He had two fine Arabian horses for President Martin Van Buren (Van Buren sold them at auction), and the *Al-Sultanah* also carried dates, wool carpets, Mocha coffee, ivory tusks, cloves and salted dried hides. The cargo brought $26,157, which Na'aman spent to buy American goods for the return voyage: cloth, china plates, rifles, gold thread, mirrors and chandeliers.

American missionaries had ventured by then into the Arab world, much of which was ruled by the (Turkish) Ottoman Empire. They visited Egypt, crossed Palestine, traveled through Lebanon (Greater Syria). Missionaries with medical and teaching skills were welcomed, but they won few converts.[2] What the Arabs wanted was knowledge, not Christian ethics. A missionary from Vermont, Daniel Bliss, understood this, and with the help of contributions from the United States and Britain, he founded and opened in 1866 the Syrian Protestant College in Beirut. The college, later known as the American University of Beirut, educated generation after generation of future Arab leaders for more than a century, and it stood, until the assassination of its American president, Malcolm Kerr, in 1984, as the symbol of the Arabs' affair with America and all that America had to offer the Arabs.

The Ottoman Empire, which entered World War I in 1914 on the German side, was the first to feel the force of Arab nationalism. T. E. Lawrence wrote in *Seven Pillars of Wisdom* that it was institutions like the American University that fostered this new Arab spirit because to teach was to politicize. "The American schools, teaching by the method of inquiry, encouraged scientific detachment and free exchange of views," he wrote. "Quite without intention they taught revolution." Large numbers of Arabs in western Arabia, Syria and Palestine revolted and fought with the Allies against the Turks, believing, as Lawrence did, that an Allied victory would ensure their independence or, at the least, their rights to self-determination. The Ottoman Empire signed an armistice in late

---

[2] The missionaries did inadvertently almost make one large conversion in the 1830s. When the Druze in the mountains above Beirut learned that Christians had been exempted from military conscription, they tried to convert en masse. Egypt, which then occupied Greater Syria, said they had to remain Muslims.

1918 with the Allies and the Arabs rejoiced. But their independence was not to be. Britain, fighting to maintain its own empire, had promised parts of the Arab world to others.

In a secret treaty known as the Sykes-Picot Agreement, Britain, France and Russia had decided in May 1916 on how to divide up the heartland of the Arab world. Under the terms of that accord and the Paris Peace Conference of 1919, Britain got Palestine and Iraq, thus extending its indirect control from the Mediterranean to the Persian Gulf; France got Syria and Lebanon; Jerusalem and a small area around Jaffa were placed under an international government to appease Russia, which wanted influence in the Christian holy places. The Arabs were left with only the barren Arabian desert.

They found just one glimmer of hope in the debacle of World Way I—President Woodrow Wilson's set of principles called the Fourteen Points. Wilson denounced secret treaties, proposed a league of nations to prevent future wars and gave his support to the concept of self-determination for all peoples. Point twelve of his declaration specifically advocated that the former subjects of the Ottoman Empire be given an "unmolested opportunity of autonomous development." The Arabs viewed Wilson as a hero, a symbol of America's fairness and concern for the hopes of the common man, but that sentiment became immaterial, for Wilson's plan was dismissed in the West. The Arabs had been awakened from centuries of lethargy by American missionaries, and then by the revolt against the Turks, and finally by the promises of Britain. Yet they had nothing to show for their revitalization. They had traded one colonial ruler for another. Zionism was becoming a stronger nationalistic force than Arabism. The United States was a secondary power in the region and would remain so until World War II, when Roosevelt decided to challenge the British, a challenge that was underscored by Roosevelt's discussions about Palestine with Ibn Saud aboard the U.S.S. *Quincy*.

Roosevelt died a few months after meeting Ibn Saud, and when his successor, Harry S. Truman, was asked to renew the American commitment to consult with the Arabs before deciding the future of Palestine, he replied, "I am sorry, gentlemen, but I have to account to hundreds of thousands of people who are anxious for the success of Zionism. I do not have hundreds of thousands of Arabs among my constituents."

THE U.N. General Assembly voted, 33 to 13, with ten abstaining and one absent, on November 29, 1947, to partition Palestine into an Arab state and a Jewish state, giving the Jews 56 percent of the land even though they represented only one third of the population. The Jewish community, haunted by the recent holocaust that had claimed six million lives in Europe, accepted the U.N. offer, but the Arabs, led by Egypt, rejected it and threatened war. On May 14, 1948, the Jewish state of Israel was born and Palestine ceased to exist. The Arabs, sensing easy victory, attacked with five armies the next day. It was the beginning of a futile Arab military campaign against Israel that would span a generation and more. In early 1949 Egypt, its army crushed, was forced to sign an armistice with the state that the Arabs saw as a creation of the West. When the war ended, Israel was one-third larger in size than it had been at its birth.

Ever since then, the Arabs have been fighting, with words or guns, to regain what they rejected at the negotiating table. Opportunities for peace have been offered to both sides in the Arab-Israeli conflict, and each side has let them slip away. As often as not the stalemate pushed American administrations into a closer relationship with Israel, which represents about 2 percent of the land and the people in the Middle East. The relationship grew so close that in 1982, during the Israeli invasion of Lebanon, President Reagan's secretary of state, Alexander M. Haig, Jr., told reporters in London, "We . . . lost an aircraft and a helicopter yesterday." The word "we" referred to Israel.

"OH, AMERICA, may you choke to death on your fury!" shouted
Gamal Abdel Nasser. The crowd roared in approval. The Egyptian
president looked down on his people at the outdoor rally in Cairo
and let them think about his words for a moment. They roared
again. The year was 1956, and in those days Third World leaders
were respectful and docile, not truculent and sassy, in their dealings
with the West. But Nasser was an ornery Arab. He had adopted a
foreign policy of "positive neutrality" and had the audacity to con-
clude a cotton-for-weapons deal with the Soviet Union in 1955 and
to recognize China in 1956. The American secretary of state, John
Foster Dulles, responded by withdrawing the West's offer to help
build the Aswan Dam. The $1.5 billion project to harness the
waters of the Nile was, Nasser said, "a matter of life or death" for
impoverished Egypt. In the streets of Cairo pro-Russian leaflets
passed from hand to hand, and in Jordan screaming mobs burned
down an American technical-aid station and attacked the U.S. con-
sulate with stones. A new era had begun in the Arab world.

The building of the High Dam at Aswan—thirty-six stories high,
more than two miles long, seventeen times greater in volume than
the Cheops Pyramid of Giza—had been the dream of Egyptians
long before Nasser.[3] With a dam, Egypt could regulate the flow of
the Nile, 40 percent of whose waters spilled into the Mediterranean
without bringing any benefit to the country. It could end floods,
increase irrigation and the number of harvests, reclaim two million
acres of desert for agricultural uses, solve national water needs for
two hundred years and provide living space for ten million land-
hungry peasants. Inside the dam would be giant turbines that could
generate electricity and develop an industrial base in Egypt, which,
authorities noted with alarm in 1956, already had a burgeoning

[3] The Aswan project was known as the High Dam to distinguish it from a
nearby smaller dam built upriver in 1902 by the British. That dam, which still
functions, was increased in height in 1912 and 1934.

population of twenty-two million—more people than it could feed, house or care for.

World Bank officials looked at the project and declared in 1953 that it was feasible. But with the independence movement gathering momentum in Africa in the 1950s, the Soviet Union was looking for a toehold on the continent and Egypt was a natural. Moscow offered $600 million in technical assistance and equipment to build the Aswan Dam (at 2 percent interest, payable in cotton and rice), provided that Nasser would accept a substantial Soviet presence. The West was dawdling in making a firm commitment, and Nasser sent his financial minister, Adbul Moneium al-Kaissouni, to Washington in late 1955 with an ultimatum: either the West had to come through by January 1 or Egypt would accept the Soviet offer.

A few days later Kaissouni put through an urgent phone call from Washington to Nasser in Cairo. "I've got good news," he said. "The High Dam is in the bag!" Anxious to keep the Russians at bay, the World Bank, the United States and Britain had agreed to offer $270 million for the initial construction phase of the dam. *Newsweek* magazine observed that "the West had won a resounding diplomatic victory. . . . There was reason to believe Egypt would veer Westward again, perhaps feel more disposed to compromise its bitter seven-year-old frontier quarrel with Israel."

The victory was an empty one. Dulles withdrew the offer on July 19, 1956, and seven days later Nasser, telling America to choke on its fury, announced that he was nationalizing the Suez Canal, most of whose shares were held by British and French interests. The fees paid by shippers using the canal, he said, would finance the construction of the High Dam. The West was stunned. Seventy percent of the oil reaching Europe passed through the hundred-mile-long waterway that links the Red Sea and the Mediterranean, and Britain's prime minister, Sir Anthony Eden, declared that if nationalization succeeded, "each one of us would be at the mercy of one man for the supplies upon which we live." To thwart Nasser,

Britain and France, in collusion with Israel, went to war against Egypt in an attempt to take over the canal.

For Arabs, the attack was confirmation that imperialism and Zionism posed a greater threat to their security than the theoretical menace of Communism. The U.S. government—in what was to be one of its last genuinely pro-Arab positions—condemned the "tripartite aggression," and President Dwight D. Eisenhower was instrumental in arranging a cease-fire and a withdrawal that restored Egyptian sovereignty. But he received little thanks from Nasser or the Arabs. The damage had been done. Nasser turned to the Soviet Union to build the High Dam; Russia had finally achieved the breakthrough in the Middle East that it had been seeking—and been denied by the West—for a century and a half.

Perhaps most important, as Western influence was diminishing, the Soviet Union was now winning respectability in the Third World as a result of its commitment to construct the dam. It had sided with the underdog against the imperialists and shown that it, too, could offer technological and development skills, not just guns and ideology. The U.S. administration tried to recoup with the Eisenhower doctrine, which offered military and economic assistance to any Middle East country that wanted to deter Communist aggression. Except for pro-Western Iraq and the Christian leadership of Lebanon, there were no takers. Communism was not the enemy. Nasser, in fact, told Dulles it was the British, not the Russians, who posed a threat to Egypt. "How can I go to my people," Nasser asked Dulles, "and tell them I am disregarding a killer with a pistol sixty miles from me at the Suez Canal to worry about somebody who is holding a knife five thousand miles away?" So with the failure of the Eisenhower-Dulles doctrine, Moscow had its entrée to the Arab world, and laid the cornerstone of a policy it would carry through Africa's approaching decade of independence—a policy of gaining influence by supporting anticolonialist liberation movements that would eventually come to power.

Work on the High Dam began in January 1960, and at its peak it involved one thousand Russians (plus two thousand of their dependents) and thirty-four thousand Egyptian laborers. The sleepy riverside village of Aswan was transformed into a bustling construction town. Heavy Soviet equipment moved upstream on barges from the Mediterranean port of Alexandria, five hundred miles away. Concrete was poured, roads were built, airstrips paved and pillars for hydroelectric plants laid. The course of the timeless Nile itself was changed with blasts of dynamite. The United Nations undertook the biggest salvation effort in history to relocate the ancient monuments of Abu Simbel and Philae on higher ground as what was to be the world's largest man-made lake—310 miles long and 8 miles wide—began to fill behind the emerging dam. Many thousands of Nubians—whose ancestors had ruled a mighty empire located between Egypt and Ethiopia from the sixth to the fourteenth centuries—were forced by rising waters and government edict to leave their homeland and move into sterile resettlement communities that seemed to desecrate the dignity and power they had once known. Slowly the High Dam took shape like a temple to Nasser, and all across the republic Egyptian schoolchildren sang a triumphal refrain:

> We said we will build, and we've built the High Dam.
> Oh, imperialism, we have built the High Dam
> With our hearts, our souls, our bodies and our arms.
> We said we would, and we have built the High Dam.

Nasser died in 1970, the year construction was completed.[4] And on January 15, 1971—a day that would have been Nasser's fifty-

---

[4] Nasser's funeral in Cairo on October 1, 1970, attracted four million mourners. The *Guinness Book of World Records* calls the turnout the largest in history for any funeral.

third birthday—Egypt's new president, Anwar Sadat, and Soviet President Nikolai V. Podgorny left Aswan together in an American-made black Cadillac Fleetwood and drove the ten miles to the construction site to inaugurate the Aswan Dam. A green ribbon had been strung across the highway that spanned the top of the dam, and as they moved forward to cut it, car horns blared in unison, boat whistles tooted at the edge of the Nile and Egyptian youths chanted slogans praising Egyptian-Soviet amity and unity. Next to them six blond Russian girls released a dozen white doves, which flapped and soared and soon disappeared over Lake Nasser. The two presidents unveiled a granite slab dedicating the world's largest earth-fill structure to the "untiring struggle for freedom and socialism." Fifteen years after Dulles had said no, the Soviet Union had finally become the patron saint of the Arab world's largest and most important country.

I FIRST visited Aswan in 1983 and was surprised to see that the dam was neither a beautiful nor a graceful creation. It straddled the Nile like a giant concrete fortress, austere and businesslike. At one end was a towering lotus-shaped monument to Soviet-Egyptian friendship; at the other, an antiaircraft position bristling with guns and manned by a single sleepy-eyed Egyptian soldier.

The dam had wrought no miracles—Egypt's population had soared past forty-eight million and the country was growing poorer, not richer—but it had accomplished much of what was intended: electricity had reached all four thousand Egyptian villages; farmers were harvesting two and three crops a year on land that used to yield just one; the disastrous floods that had occurred when the Nile overflowed its banks were a nightmare of the past.

It was, though, not the dam itself that was the subject of concern when I went to Aswan; it was the giant runners, or blades, that rotated inside the twelve turbines. Attached to the generator, the twelve-foot-high, 140-ton runners were driven by the flow of the Nile's waters and they had started to crack. Russian consultants, who had been summoned, said cracking was normal and recommended periodic welding to keep the turbines running. That explanation didn't satisfy the Egyptians, and they called in metallurgists from Sweden and France. After extensive studies, the Europeans determined that the manufacturers, the Leningrad Machine Works, had used faulty casting techniques, that poor welding had caused shrinkage and that a bad original design had given rise to an unsteady flow of water through the turbines, thus leading to pulsating and vibrating that caused unacceptable levels of stress. "The Russians just didn't know what they were doing," an American engineer told me.

Leaving the High Dam on the road that Sadat and Podgorny had traveled together more than a decade earlier, I turned left into "Sahara City," the drab housing complex where the Russian technicians and their families had lived. The three-story stucco homes were occupied by Egyptian families now, and trash and old newspapers blew through the streets. The community club was boarded up, and few of the new residents of Sahara City remembered how the Russians had once idled away the evenings in it, hunched over chessboards below photos depicting the life of Lenin. Nothing remained of the Russians, and at the bus stop outside, a large red-and-white advertisement for Coca-Cola was a reminder that times had changed.

Indeed they had, as they often do in the murky waters of shifting Arab alliances. Sadat, unable to get the weapons he wanted from Moscow, had thrown seventeen thousand Soviet advisers out of the country in 1972 and had abrogated Egypt's twenty-year friendship with the Soviet Union in 1976. The last Russian technicians had left Aswan in 1981. That same year Sadat's cabinet expelled seven Soviet diplomats, including the ambassador, and two Soviet journalists. The cabinet that day also voted to accept an $85 million contract with Allis-Chalmers Corporation, a Milwaukee-based heavy-equipment manufacturer, to design and construct twelve new runners for the Aswan Dam's hydroelectric plant.

The baton had been passed. The Soviet Union's most prestigious Third World project—the project Washington had scrapped partly because Nasser had recognized China, something the United States would not do for another twenty-two years—was now in American hands.

IRONICALLY, THE Middle East is one region where the interests of the superpowers frequently overlap. Neither Washington nor Moscow would be served by renewed warfare between the Arabs and Israelis. Both want continued stability in the Arabian oil fields and both fear the spread of religious extremism. The Iran-Iraq war that began in 1980 gave the superpowers a fine opportunity to turn the conflict into a proxy confrontation but neither took the bait; they stood back and let the unsavory governments in Tehran and Baghdad carry on their killing unimpeded.

Although the United States and the Soviet Union both have legitimate interests in the Middle East, Washington has managed to shut Moscow out of the diplomatic peace process there since the collapse of the United Nations conference in Geneva in 1973. But its policy of unilateral crisis management failed, and by trying to be the sole arbitrator and benefactor of the Israelis and the "good" Arabs, Washington has, I think, actually retarded the peace process, because there can be no lasting solution to the Arab-Israeli conflict until the two superpowers decide it is in their mutual interests to reach one. Until that happens, there is no pressure for the Middle East participants to make concessions necessary for peace because, as armies get bigger and weapons mightier, everyone, except the Palestinians, can live (in the short term) with the status quo of no war, no peace. The immediate priority for Israel and the confrontational Arab governments is not peace; it is military superiority—

having the capability of using military force to achieve political goals. The superpowers have been accommodating to their regional clients, with the United States putting together a Herculean military machine in Israel and the Soviet Union one in Syria. The problem is that neither Washington nor Moscow has much control over its own creations.

I now read the previous two paragraphs with the benefit of fifteen years' passage. Had I known when I wrote them that the Soviet Union would disintegrate in 1991, which of course I didn't, I imagine I would have thought that without a superpower rivalry, the Middle East would be a vastly improved place. But that didn't happen. There were still plenty of guns and animosities and problems to go around. The United States seemed a more effective dealmaker and negotiator when it was viewing the world through the prism of countering Soviet influence than it was when left as the sole remaining superpower. Ironically its political power in the Arab world seemed diminished, because its continued bias toward Israel raised into question its legitimacy as an evenhanded peace broker.

At times, particularly under the Clinton administration, the United States tried mightily to resolve the "Palestinian problem," but neither the Jews nor the Arabs had quite the heart to take the risks necessary for peace. It preached democracy but no one listened. It continued to bomb Iraq's southern no-fly zone more than a decade after the end of the Persian Gulf War, but Saddam Hussein remained in power, as mulish and devilish as ever. Then, with bloodshed mounting in the occupied territories where Israelis and Palestinians were killing each other with fearful frequency, it went to war in October 2001, to rid Afghanistan of Osama bin Laden's al Qaeda terrorist network. To build an effective coalition, it needed Arab support, which was difficult to do as long as the West Bank was a battlefield and Arabs saw the United States as Israel's partner in the attacks on and humiliation of the Palestinians. A possible scenario emerged: the United States might be forced to take a more principled, evenhanded stand in its balancing act between Jews and Arabs if it wanted to achieve victory in Afghanistan and peace in the Middle East.

If peace can be defined as the absence of war, then the Arabs and Israelis are at peace, however fragile that peace may be. The Israelis don't have to make concessions because they are in a position of strength and already have the land they want and guarantees of the continued, unquestioned American support they need; the Arabs don't concede much because they are in a position of relative weakness—a qualitative, not quantitative, weakness caused by disunity, historical failures and ineffective military commands. "How can I negotiate when I am flat on my back with a sword at my throat?" Nasser once asked. And if he had had military superiority, might not he have said, "Why should I negotiate when I hold the sword?"

The superpowers could have quite easily imposed peace on the Middle East. If Washington and Moscow had told Israel and the Arabs that they would no longer supply them with weapons or spare parts—a most unlikely prospect—and put the belligerents in a locked room, I suspect they would have found a considerable amount of common ground and would have decided rather quickly that they were willing to make concessions. But no one has ever exerted that kind of force, and over three decades the Middle East has become a graveyard of failed peace missions that bear the names of men, cities, countries and continents. Among them: the Australian Plan (1957), the Bourguiba Plan (1965), the Yugoslav Plan (1967), the Rogers Plan (1969), the African "Wise Men" Mission (1971), the Johnson Plan (1972), the Fahd Plan (1981), the Fez Plan (1982), the Franco-Egyptian Plan (1982), the Reagan Initiative (1982) and the Brezhnev Plan (1982).

None got off the ground, because none reconciled the Israelis' and Palestinians' claim to the same chunk of land and none addressed the psychological barrier of fear and distrust between Arab and Jew. The only effort that achieved limited success was the

Camp David Accord, which led to the 1979 peace treaty between Israel and Egypt.[5] It could have been an important first step toward a broader settlement, yet the Arabs denounced it as a nonstarter, accusing Egypt—after Sadat said, "Egypt first, Egypt last"—of making a separate peace. (A separate peace, it seems, is preferable to a wider war.) Israel, just as obstinate as the Arabs, has vetoed other proposals that would have required concessions, and I left the Middle East with the feeling that the will and courage it takes to make peace were absent, or, at least, dormant. Ariel Sharon, a hardline Israeli cabinet minister, was asked in 1985, for example, if Israel would be willing to negotiate on the basis of exchanging captured Arab land for guarantees of security. No, he said, the only thing that the Arabs would get in exchange for peace was peace. And P.L.O. Chairman Yasser Arafat, chased from Jordan to Lebanon to Tunisia by his own Arab allies, declared, "War is the only way," while knowing full well it wasn't.

Such attitudes don't leave much to talk about. They also help make the Middle East fertile ground for international rivalry. Both the Soviet Union and the United States—which rank first and second, respectively, as the largest arms merchants to the Third World during the Cold War—had few reservations about fueling an arms race that made the Middle East the world's principal weapons-importing region in a $35 billion-a-year arms-trade industry.[6]

---

[5] The Camp David Accords, designed by President Jimmy Carter and signed in 1978 by the Israeli prime minister, Menachem Begin, and the Egyptian president, Anwar Sadat, contained two principal parts: the first, a peace treaty between Israel and Egypt, has worked; the second, negotiations leading to "self-determination" for the Palestinians, has not. To the Arabs, self-determination was synonymous with independence; to the Israelis it meant, in its most generous definition, some form of vaguely defined autonomy.

[6] According to a U.S. congressional report, the Soviet Union's share of arms sales to the Third World in 1985 was 30.4 percent; the United States' was 17.8 percent. Western Europe—Britain, France, Italy and West Germany—accounted for 31.3 percent.

The Middle East has less than 3 percent of the world's population, yet it accounts for more than 8 percent of the world's military spending. Its governments spend $350 annually per person for military purposes, three times the world average, the International Peace Research Institute in Stockholm reported. Another study, prepared by Anthony H. Cordesman, vice president of the Eastern Analytical Assessments Center, and published in the *Middle East Journal*, shows that Middle East countries accounted for 42.6 percent of the world's arms imports in 1983. Between 1973 and 1983, those countries spent $542 billion on their military forces and increased the total size of their armed forces from 1.3 million to 2.1 million men.

The results are predictable. Cordesman estimates that from 1979 to 1986 some 3.5 million persons were casualties of various regional conflicts in the Middle East. Of that number, three hundred thousand to five hundred thousand were killed. "God," the author observes, "is neither Israel's real estate agent nor the Arab world's general."

Even with declining oil revenues, military budgets are usually the last to be cut. "In this world of lawlessness, in this world of anarchy, despite a decline in oil income, there is no alternative to arms, regardless of the cost," said Abdullah Bisharah, former secretary-general of the Gulf Cooperation Council. Oman in 2001 devoted 13 percent of its budget to defense. Saudi Arabia's defense spending exceeded $18 billion. Defense expenditures in the tiny United Arab Emirates increased fifty-fold in two decades' time. Egypt has more men in uniform today (713,000) than it did in 1979 (350,000) when the Egyptian-Israeli peace treaty came into force and has started its own fledging arms-for-sale industry that is earning the country $1 billion a year. One Arab country that bucked the trend toward militarization was Tunisia, which devoted the majority of its budget to education and social services and spent only 2 percent on defense. The result was that other Arabs dismissed Tunisia as insignificant, and Israeli pilots met no challenge in 1985 when they flew fifteen hundred miles to bomb the headquarters of the Palestine Liberation Organization on the outskirts of the capital, Tunis. (The United States had helped convince a leery but pro-Western Tunisia in 1982 that it would help advance the peace process by giving the P.L.O. a political home in Tunis; Washington said that the guerrillas would be so far away from Israel that there couldn't possibly be any trouble on Tunisian soil.) As one Western diplomat put it: "In the Middle East, if you've got no guns, you've got no respect."

The arms buildup there has been made possible by the largess of the major powers and by the almost unlimited financial resources of the oil-producing Arab states. Perhaps Africa and Latin America and other Third World regions would have spent just as much on weapons had they also had access to such generosity and wealth. And perhaps what is happening to the Middle East is merely symptomatic of the world's condition in the 1990s. It is a world where one of every thousand persons is a doctor and one of every forty-three a soldier.

Whom do the Arabs see as the enemy in their rush to arm themselves? Fifteen years ago it was Israel, and rhetorically it still is. But most Arab governments today neither seek nor expect renewed warfare with Israel. Sadat changed the focus of the Arab-Israeli conflict from the battlefield to the negotiating table, and the Arabs know well the lives, the money and the energy they have wasted trying to fulfill Nasser's pledge to destroy Israel. "From 1948 to today," said the man who succeeded Nasser and Sadat, President Hosni Mubarak, "what have we achieved?" Mubarak didn't need to respond to his own question. The answer was, Nothing.

For the Arabs, the real enemy today is within. It is religious extremists, the fear of Iran's fundamentalist revolution sweeping across borders, the rivalry between neighboring Arab states, poverty and ignorance. As for Israel, the majority of Arab governments would, I believe, be willing to cut an honorable deal that took into account the future of the Palestinians and the return of occupied land. Critics of the Arabs tend to forget what a long step toward moderation the majority has taken. It was, for instance, only in 1967 that Arab leaders, meeting in Khartoum, Sudan, voted unanimously to adopt a platform of negativism toward Israel: no peace, no negotiation, no recognition. A suggestion then that Israel's presence was permanent, that any Arab state should negotiate directly with Israel, would have been heretical.

By that yardstick, the Arabs and Israelis have traveled light years since the 1960s. Even through two *intifadas* in Israel's occupied territories, the Arabs did not contemplate war against the Jewish state, as they surely would have a few decades ago. The destruction of Israel has become an antiquated notion to all but the hard-core radicals. In turn, statehood for Palestine has become an accepted eventuality to all but the most dedicated Zionists. But the actions of extremists on both sides have torpedoed the achievements of moderates who are both Arab and Israeli. One step forward and one step back. The United States got involved, disengaged and usually came back to the position that Israel was its most important Middle East ally, even though its strategic significance had been greatly diminished by the end of the Cold War.

The United States has chosen Israel as its prime Middle Eastern ally for many reasons: guilt over the Holocaust; Israel's democratic tradition and consistently pro-Western foreign policy; its European heritage, which makes Israelis less of a mystery than Arabs; its powerful, disciplined and effective military machine; the influence of the Israeli lobby and Jewish organizations on U.S. politicians. But Israel, like the West's friends among the Arab states, pays scant attention to American interests when they don't coincide with their own concerns. And if Israel is a strategic asset, so is Saudi Arabia; if Israel has been a longtime friend, so has Morocco; if Israel deserves the right to live within secure borders, so do the Arab countries. If the Israelis are perceived as better friends to the West, as more trustworthy and unfaltering, than the Arabs as a whole, it is primarily because the West has been neither tolerant in considering Arab interests nor generous in extending to the Arabs the opportunities for a mutually beneficial relationship.

Eventually, I think, the United States is going to have to make a choice. It can't have it both ways. It cannot maintain a continued presence in the Arab world and hope to promote a peace process at the same time its tax dollars subsidize the building of Israeli settlements on Arab lands and its politicians pretend Israeli and American interests are identical (as with the Arabs, sometimes they are, sometimes they aren't). The choice Washington will have to make is not between Arab and Israeli, because there is room for friendship with both. The choice is between a policy that gives unquestioned support to the minority, often to the detriment of the majority, and one that recognizes the need to play by the same rules when dealing with decent people, be they Arab or Israeli.

MALCOLM KERR, who devoted his scholarly career to understanding the Middle East, represented the best of everything America had to offer the Arabs. He was born at the American Hospital in Beirut, and his father was a professor of biochemistry at the American University of Beirut (A.U.B.), the institution opened in 1866 by a Vermont missionary. His mother was the dean of women at the university. Kerr grew up in Beirut, back in the 1950s, when the city was a fine, cultured place, and he met his wife-to-be, Ann, a Californian, at A.U.B. during her junior year of study. From Lebanon he returned home to earn an undergraduate degree at Princeton and a doctorate at Johns Hopkins and eventually to become director of the von Grunebaum Center for Near Eastern Studies at the University of California in Los Angeles.

But even when he was elsewhere, his heart remained in the Arab world. He traveled there often, gave lectures in flawless Arabic, taught Arab students in Cairo and Beirut during his sabbaticals from U.C.L.A. and was known among his many friends as a fair, compassionate man whose sympathies lay with the Arabs and whose beliefs were not at ease with U.S. policies in the Middle East. As a symbol of the American dream he and others like him were different from those who had preceded them to the Arab world—the missionaries turned educators, the investors, the military salesmen, the diplomats and journalists. The Malcolm Kerrs came to give, not take, to share knowledge and build bridges. They complemented, rather than impinged upon, the Arab culture, and they felt as comfortable in the Arab world as they did in the world of America.

By 1983 Beirut had turned ugly and dangerous. Nearly a decade of civil war, an Israeli siege and invasion of the Muslim quarter, and months of anarchy sown by competing militias had destroyed the fiber of Lebanese society. The acting president of A.U.B., David Dodge, had been abducted on campus and whisked by gunmen into Iran, where he remained hostage for 366 days, and the university itself was slipping into financial and academic ruin. Thus Kerr's challenge was not an enviable one when he was chosen that year to become the new president of A.U.B. Shortly before leaving California and his hilltop home with its sweeping view of the Pacific Ocean and the city of Los Angeles, he said, "I'd like to participate in saving the institution. If I'm lucky, this is what I'll do the rest of my active life. But I believe your life insurance premiums go up when you take a job like this." Malcolm Kerr was fifty-one years old when he left for Beirut.

Although I had long known of Kerr through his reputation and his books on the Middle East, I met him only once, shortly after he arrived in Beirut. We had lunch together at the university, on the patio of his home, and he was far less pessimistic about the future of Lebanon than most of the rest of us. "I think given time, given help, given some breathing space from the influence of outsiders, they can sort out their problems," he said. This was a time when it was risky to be an American, especially a prominent one, in Beirut, and after the U.S. ambassador, Kerr was the highest-ranking American official there. He still maintained a high profile, traveling without bodyguards around the city, meeting Arab businessmen and friends, addressing groups, drumming up support for the university he wanted to save. I asked him if he shouldn't be more conscious of his own security. He thought for a moment, distracted, looking away. He sat surrounded by the trees and flowers of his gardens. The seventy-three-acre campus felt so quiet and peaceful. Down the hill from his lawn, past the students' tennis courts, the Mediterranean, smooth and emerald-green on this day, reached out across the horizon. Like the Pacific back home in Los Angeles, the vista of the sea was a great pacifier.

"No," he said, "you can only use common sense."

It took five minutes to walk from Kerr's home to his second-floor office in the center of the campus. On January 18, 1984, he left his home a few minutes before 9:00 A.M. in particularly good spirits. He had earned a rare victory the evening before against his weekly tennis opponent, a friend ten years his junior, and more important, he was making headway in his attempts to restore A.U.B.'s academic excellence. After meeting with a banker that winter morning, he entered College Hall. Across the pathway was an inscription, chiseled into a stone archway, that read: MAY THEY HAVE LIFE AND HAVE IT ABUNDANTLY. He rode the elevator to the second floor and turned left. Two young men with silencers on their pistols walked up behind Malcolm Kerr as he reached the outer door of his office and shot him dead.

I was in Cairo when I heard the news on a Voice of America broadcast that Kerr had been murdered. The Beirut police developed a composite picture of the assassins, but they never released it, and there was no real investigation into his death. The next day both the Muslim and Christian sectors of Beirut united in a rare display of unity to grieve for Kerr. The mourners numbered in the tens of thousands, yet their voice and their strength were pitifully weak compared with those of just two angry young men with guns.

I wondered whom his killers saw in their mind's eye when they pulled the trigger. Surely it wasn't Malcolm Kerr, the man. Was it the temptress America that had promised so much and delivered so little? Was it the America that had made Israel's invasion of Lebanon possible? Was it the America that had promised no harm would come to Palestinian civilians left behind in two shantytowns, Sabra and Chatilla, after Washington negotiated the evacuation of P.L.O. guerrillas from Beirut?

We will never know because in Beirut common criminals are not brought to trial and Kerr's murderers were no exception. But I do remember thinking on that January day in Cairo that with the murder of Malcolm Kerr the American dream was finished in the Arab world.

EIGHT

A NATION LAY DYING

HISTORY HAS a way of repeating itself in the Arab world. Animosities and alliances between capitals, Machiavellian deals between leaders, flirtations with and estrangements from various foreign powers all have roots that reach back into the past, roots that unite the Middle East in a web of intrigue. Nothing ever happens quite in isolation. And so it was that the assassination of Malcolm Kerr in Lebanon represented more than just the work of two demented gunmen. His death, like that of the Arabs' affair with America, was vaguely entwined, strangely enough, with a promising moment of peace that came to a forlorn stretch of desert known as the Sinai Peninsula.

On a map of Egypt, the Sinai looks like a wedge driven between Africa and Asia. About two and a half times the size of Israel, it is a place of sizzling heat and vast emptiness that seems as inhospitable and uninhabitable as the moon. Yet this little corner of desert hell has played a role in shaping the world's history. The Sinai is where the Old Testament says God gave Moses the Ten Commandments and the tribes of Israel began forty years of wandering, where ancient trade routes crossed, linking two continents, and where no fewer than fifty invading armies have marched and fought.

The last of those armies belonged to Israel and Egypt. In four days of ferocious tank battles in 1967, the Israelis vanquished the Egyptians from their land and began an occupation that would last fifteen years. The Sinai's position between the gulfs of Suez and

Aqaba give the peninsula strategic prominence, and its modest reserves of oil give it economic importance, but in defeat the Egyptians lost a place to which they felt no cultural or emotional attachment; in victory, the Israelis gained one that they cherished for its rugged, isolated beauty, its tranquillity, its historical significance. It offered them a quiet refuge from their own crowded, tense country, and Israeli tourists by the thousands soon began pouring into the Sinai. The Israelis built comfortable blackfront hotels, conducted archaeological digs and backpacked through rocky mountains that soared above the low desert plains. They came to think of the Sinai as theirs.

But the United States worked out a land-for-peace exchange between Israel and Egypt's Anwar Sadat, and in 1979, as part of the Camp David Accords, Israel began a phased withdrawal from the Sinai, to be completed in 1982. The day of the final withdrawal, April 25, approached amid great uneasiness. Jewish settlers had to be dragged out of one settlement by the Israeli defense forces, and Israelis of all persuasions debated the wisdom of surrendering land that had been won with Jewish blood. There had been several precedents for what Israel was doing—Great Britain, after all, had handed back its entire empire; the United States had not seen fit to occupy Germany and Japan indefinitely. Yet Prime Minister Menachem Begin was a wounded and bitter man: What had the Arabs done to deserve the return of their territory? "The spectacle of total Israeli withdrawal will not be repeated elsewhere. . . ." promised Israel's ambassador to Britain, Shlomo Argov.

So many journalists from all over the world flew into Cairo for the hand-over of the Sinai that the Egyptian government needed three buses and two planes to transport us all to Sharm el Sheik and Rafah, the two Sinai towns where transfer ceremonies were scheduled. A cool wind blew off the desert, and the sky was dark and threatening when our prop-driven plane landed at Sharm el Sheik, on the southern tip of the Sinai, at noon on April 25. By that time the last group of Israelis had been gone for several hours. They had filled some water wells with cement and driven off at dawn toward their new border, two hundred miles north. Only the Hebrew road signs, the abandoned stucco settlement known as Ofira and the empty Marina Hotel remained as testimony of the Jewish state's occupation.[1]

We gathered on a dirt parade ground just past the hotel. A small contingent of Egyptians waited there, and it was disheartening that such a momentous occasion in Arab-Israeli relations—the exchange of land through negotiations instead of warfare—would not be marked by handshakes and words of goodwill between two neighbors who were ending thirty-four years of hostilities. The ceremony was brief. There was an Islamic prayer, a short speech by the governor and the shout "Long live Egypt!" as Egypt's black, red and white flag unfurled in the sultry breeze. In thirty minutes it was over. Peace had come at last to the Sinai.

I wrote my story in longhand on the return flight to Cairo. It seemed that the Middle East had taken an important step toward ending the Arab-Israeli conflict, and driving from the Cairo airport to my apartment on the Nile, the sight of electric lights that had been strung from the mosques and government buildings in celebration added to the mood of optimism I expressed in my story for the Los Angeles Times. Diplomacy had accomplished for Egypt what guns could not, I wrote. Sadly, though, optimism is too often tantamount to naïveté in the Middle East, and all the journalists, myself included, missed the real significance of the Sinai transfer. By making peace with Egypt, Israel had in effect neutralized the most powerful army in the Arab world. Confident that Egypt would

[1] The Israelis returned all of the Sinai except for a section on their border known as Taba. It contained a tourist hotel and measured less than one square mile. They presumably kept Taba as a future negotiating point in an attempt to wrest concessions from Egypt. Israel and Egypt agreed in 1986 to submit the border dispute to international arbitration.

not intervene militarily on behalf of the Arabs again, Israel was now free to turn its attention to other Arab matters, and the most pressing of these was neighboring Lebanon, where the Palestine Liberation Organization had entrenched itself as a virtual state within a state.

ISRAEL'S NORTHERN border with Lebanon had been quiet for ten months when the Sinai changed hands, thanks to a cease-fire the United States had brokered between Israel and the P.L.O. The P.L.O. was continuing to stockpile arms in southern Lebanon, but for the first time in memory Palestinian rockets were no longer screaming into Jewish settlements, and Yasser Arafat, the P.L.O. chairman, was managing to make his restless guerrillas abide by the cease-fire as he shifted his strategy from terrorism to diplomacy. In return, he had Washington's word that Israel would not undertake major military initiatives across the border.

But Israel's defense minister, Ariel Sharon, and other hardline Israelis had long been obsessed with destroying the P.L.O., whose guerrillas lived among Lebanon's half-million Palestinian civilians. Israel also wanted to establish in Lebanon a Christian government that was supportive of Israel—a goal that, ironically, would entail going to war with Lebanon in order to make peace with Lebanon. Sharon outlined his plan in early December 1981, four months before the Sinai transfer, to American officials in Washington.[2]

---

[2] Details of Sharon's plan were revealed by Zeev Schiff, military editor of the Israeli newspaper *Haaretz*, and Ehud Yaari, Arab affairs correspondent for Israel television, in their book, *Israel's Lebanon War* (New York: Simon & Schuster, 1984), and by the *Washington Post* in an interview with the U.S. ambassador to Israel, Samuel W. Lewis, published in the May 23–26, 1985, edition of the *International Herald-Tribune*. In the *Post* article, Sharon denied he had outlined such plans and accused Lewis of a "gross lie" in the ambassador's recollection of a meeting in Washington between Sharon and President Ronald Reagan's envoy, Philip C. Habib.

Israel would launch a forty-eight-hour strike into Lebanon that would carry its forces all the way to Beirut and would install a Christian militia leader, Bashir Gemayel, as president. In the process, Israel would engage Syria and end its influence over Lebanon.

Although the U.S. ambassador to Israel, Samuel W. Lewis, later recalled being "rather dumfounded by the audacity and the political concept that this seemed to involve," the idea was not without appeal to Washington. Beirut was an evil place, a den of international terrorism and a haven for unruly militiamen and free-lance thugs, who charged twenty-five dollars to shoot off a kneecap and one hundred dollars to kill. The country was run not by a government or by an army, but by ninety-nine identifiable Lebanese militias, some of which controlled only a few city blocks. The militias were, in effect, sophisticated street gangs, a big-league version of what one finds in the slums of New York. They controlled ports, illegal businesses and arms shipments, and were commanded by men who had been killing the families of competing militia chieftains for years. The total strength of their private armies numbered close to one hundred thousand men and boys—about five times the size of the regular Lebanese army—and their arsenals included tanks and heavy artillery. They appeared to take particular pleasure in turning their cannon on residential neighborhoods on the premise that it is safer to hit the unarmed friends of one's enemy than the enemy itself.

Lebanon was Armageddon, and the forces of good had lost. The place was—and indeed still is—a microcosm of the fragmented Arab world and the explosive pressures at work in it. Torn by religious, tribal and criminal strife, thrown off-balance by the truculence of the P.L.O., beset by individual greed and the struggle between traditionalists and modernists, Lebanon was where everyone came to settle old scores. The Arab-Jew conflict, the Arab-versus-Arab hostility, the Sunni-Shiite struggle, the superpower competition, the Palestinian "problem" and the uncontrolled arms race—all were brought to bear on this country that is hardly larger than the state of Delaware. Lebanon couldn't cope.

Testimony to the fact that Lebanon was dying in the spring of 1982 was the plethora of militias and their anarchic behavior; after a decade of civil war between Christian and Muslim, Lebanon had ceased to exist as a real country—it was a Balkanized cluster of enclaves whose leaders gave top priority to settling feuds and accumulating power in the tradition of the Mafia. Each claimed to do so in the name of nationalism. Beirut had been so decimated by the fratricidal fighting that much of the city looked like a twentieth-century Carthage in its last days. Remarkably enough, Israel thought it could put this Humpty-Dumpty back together again. The United States agreed.

Israel, though, needed a pretext, and on June 3, 1982, it got one. Ambassador Argov was shot and critically wounded as he left a hotel banquet in London. Within twenty-four hours, waves of Israel's American-made combat planes swept into Lebanon in retaliation, bombing Beirut's sports stadium that the P.L.O. used as a training camp and the nearby Palestinian neighborhood of Fakhani. The raid killed more than a hundred people, but no senior P.L.O. officials or commanders. (Arafat was in Saudi Arabia that day.) The fifth Arab-Israeli war—and the first fought without Egypt—had begun, and two days later, 85,000 Israeli troops and an armada of Israeli tanks crossed the border in a full-scale invasion of Lebanon. "When someone steps on our foot, we chop off his head," Lieutenant General Rafael Eitan, the Israeli army chief of staff, said.

By then it had become irrelevant that Ambassador Argov's intended assassins had nothing to do with Arafat; they were Palestinians in the employ of Abu Nidal, the hired-gun terrorist who had been expelled from the P.L.O. after denouncing Arafat's leadership as unjustifiably moderate. The Israelis fought their way north, driving swiftly through crumbling Palestinian resistance. They called their operation "Peace for Galilee," and its announced objective was a limited one: the creation of a safety zone, twenty-five miles deep, that would push P.L.O. artillerymen out of range of Israel's northern settlements in Galilee.[3] This, Prime Minister Begin promised, would keep Galilee safe from P.L.O.-launched Katyusha rockets for the next forty years.

In the first two days of the invasion the P.L.O. command structure disintegrated, and the Palestinian fighters fled north, seeking refuge among the civilians in Beirut. The Israelis, supported by heavy air cover, passed the imaginary border of their safety zone and kept rolling toward the capital, leaving in their wake immense destruction and hundreds of Palestinian civilian and guerrilla casualties. In Sidon, an hour's drive south of Beirut, two hundred women and children hiding in the basement of a school were killed by Israeli bombs. Later the two biggest Palestinian hospitals in Beirut, Acre and Gaza, overflowing with war victims, took direct artillery hits. For the first time in an Arab-Israeli war the Israelis were not the underdog fighting a defensive campaign. They were now the aggressor, and they had at their disposal an American-equipped war machine of awesome power. The U.N. Security Council met on June 8 to demand an immediate Israeli withdrawal from Lebanon. The only veto to the resolution was cast by the United States.

I GOT to Beirut the evening of the U.N. vote, after catching a midnight flight from Cairo to Jordan, taking a five-hour taxi ride to the Syrian-Lebanese border and finding an old man with a 1958 Pontiac who said he would make the eighty-mile dash to Beirut for five hundred dollars. It was dusk, and just minutes ahead of Israeli bombers, we hurtled at frightening speed over the mountains, dodging around Syrian tanks and antiaircraft guns that were being hauled into place. We careered through cedar forests, past stately

[3] In the first hours of the war an artillery duel between Israel and the P.L.O. resulted in the death of an Israeli civilian and the wounding of three Israelis in Galilee. That was more casualties than the Israelis had suffered in the region in the previous eleven months of the cease-fire.

hillside mansions with red-tiled roofs and into the valley where Beirut stood, its back to the Mediterranean. The city, without electricity, short on food and fuel, its airport closed by the approaching fighting, was blacker than the deep of night. The Lebanese army had already abandoned its posts and retired to the barracks, as it usually did in times of danger, and the streets were empty except for groups of young armed men who were erecting earthen barricades and fortifications of timber and discarded tires. One of them waved my driver to a stop with his rifle and demanded my passport. He held it upside down, checking each page with a pocket flashlight to see if it contained any Israel entry stamps. "American, huh?" he said, handing the passport back, his finger still on the trigger of his Russian-made Kalashnikov rifle. "Good luck. You may need it."

We swung down deserted Hamra Street, once the poshest shopping boulevard in the Arab world. Mannequins in Paris fashions peered through the steel grates of stores, and with their blank eyes and sallow complexion they looked like ghosts. We turned right by a Palestinian machine-gun position. The Commodore Hotel, just ahead, had been surrounded by sandfilled oil drums to prevent cars laden with explosives from crashing into it. Its owner, Youssef Nazzal, a Jordanian of Palestinian and Colombian origin, paid the P.L.O. and the various militias $1 million a year in protection money, and the glow of cigarette butts in the darkened windows of nearby apartments told me that his own private soldiers were on duty, looking down on everyone who entered the Commodore. I paid off my driver and walked into the hotel, feeling like a man who had come to Beirut to attend his own funeral.

The Commodore was full of journalists, some of whom I hadn't seen since the fall of Saigon in 1975. Television gear was strewn about the Formica furnishings and shabby padded chairs in the lobby. Scores of reporters milled around, waiting impatiently for their turn on the telex machines. They talked in small groups, quietly trading stories about having been caught between the artillery duels of advancing Israelis and withdrawing Palestinians, and they speculated about whether the Israelis intended to make the final twelve-mile push from the town of Damour into West Beirut, the predominantly Muslim sector of the divided capital. Nazzal assumed that they did. He had stuffed three footlockers in his office with $1 million worth of Lebanese pounds, stockpiled a six-week supply of food in the basement, stashed machine guns and rifles behind the reception desk and dug two escape routes out of the unused nightclub in the cellar.

"Beirut could get very, very crazy," he said. I took issue only with his use of the word "could." Beirut—once the intellectual center of the Roman empire—already *was* crazy.

In the first hours of the invasion the Lebanese government had closed down. Its policemen went home; its firemen stopped answering calls; garbage began to pile up chest-high on every street corner. Tens of thousands of refugees fleeing the Israelis descended on Beirut to squat in the foyers of office buildings. The odor of human waste was overwhelming. Competing militias fought gun battles in the street for the right to take over apartments left vacant by wealthy Lebanese hurrying out of the country on ferryboats to Cyprus. Gunmen protected their territory with roadblocks, their heads covered with black pillowcases that gave them the appearance of Halloween ghouls. Teenagers with bazookas and automatic rifles raced about, wild-eyed with the exhilaration of adventure and authority. "I *love* this!" one of them said, crouching behind the frame of a burned-out car. "I *love* war!" The hospitals filled up with casualties—about 75 percent of which were civilian, not military, during the course of the war—as the Israelis pummeled Palestinian areas with American-made cluster bombs.[4] Doctors performed sur-

---

[4] Cluster bombs, housed in six-foot-long shell casings, release upon impact hundreds of smaller bombs that spray shrapnel in all directions at groin level. They are designed for use against dense concentrations of enemy troops. The United States sold Israel the bombs with the stipulation that they be used only if Israel was engaged in a major war against two or more countries. Washington protested mildly that the Begin government was in violation of the agreement. It briefly suspended cluster-bomb shipments, then resumed them.

gery with young thugs holding pistols to their heads lest their friends
receive anything less than attentive medical care. The days were
full of screaming ambulance sirens; the nights shook with the thunder of heavy guns and exploding cars, detonated by gangs getting
even with merchants who had not paid their monthly protection
money. I found a pharmacy that was still open, and bought a bottle
of tranquilizers.

This was not a good time to have blue eyes and an American
passport, for virtually everyone in the Arab world, including U.S.
diplomats, believed that Washington was in collusion with Jerusalem. I learned a new kind of fear in Lebanon, the fear of constant
vulnerability. Covering the Vietnam war for two years, I understood
where the lines were drawn. I knew who was friend and who was
foe. A sixth sense told me what risks were worth taking. Even on
combat missions with the marines, I felt strangely secure; I was with
my people and my life meant something to them. But in Beirut
there were no lines across which it was safe to trespass, no discernible differences between allies and enemies, no rationale to the
random violence. On the streets the gunsels, as we called the gun-
toting toughs, stared us down, sending butterflies aflutter in my
stomach. Cars squealed through the town with loudspeakers blaring in Arabic, broadcasting what I assumed were anti-American
messages. Israeli planes dropped leaflets on Beirut, saying Israeli
forces would soon enter the capital, and at night Israeli flares
attached to parachutes drifted over the Palestinian neighborhoods,
bathing the city in an eerie glow of soft blue light. Everyone waited.
The mosques fell silent, and the call to prayer ceased. In the Palestinian shantytown of Chatilla an old man hobbled up to me. He
said six members of his family had been killed the night before in
an Israeli aerial raid. "Why are *you* doing this to us?" he asked, half
pleading and half in rage. He even knew about the United States'
veto at the U.N. I could offer him no explanation and mumbled
something like No, of course, Americans had no argument with the

Palestinian people. I looked around at the rubble of stone and brick, at the swath of destruction our bombs had cut through this slum neighborhood, and for the first time in my life I felt embarrassed to be an American.

Each day the Israeli tanks drew closer. On the night of June 13, seven days after the invasion began, Lebanese Christian scouts led the Israelis up through the hills overlooking the city, and the next morning the half-million Muslims in West Beirut awoke with the turrets of enemy tanks zeroed in on them. We waited for the deadly firing to begin, but there was none. People peered cautiously out of their homes and saw no advancing troops. Then the damnedest thing happened. On the Christian side of the capital, Beirutis by the thousands streamed into the hills on foot and in cars to welcome—or to gawk at—the Israelis. So many of them came that policemen volunteered to leave the safety of their homes to direct traffic around the invading army's positions.

"This is fantastic!" said sixteen-year-old Wadih Abirached. "Now we'll get rid of the P.L.O. Do you know what we think of the Palestinians?" He raised his middle finger to show me. The Christians brought coffee, soft drinks and candy for the weary, unshaven Israelis and greeted them with the word "Shalom." "Here's a cold 7-Up," a woman said, handing a can to one soldier. "Don't you have a Pepsi?" he joked. "No," she said, "you bombed the Pepsi plant last Thursday."

We piled out of the Commodore, crossed the imaginary green line that separates West and East Beirut and drove up into the hills. The Israelis had been welcomed in their drive through south Lebanon by the Muslim Shiites, who wanted the arrogant P.L.O. guerrillas removed from their land at any price. Now they were being welcomed on the outskirts of Beirut itself. But the reception was deceptive. The young Israeli soldiers I talked to, thinking they had come as liberators, did not realize that they were feared and hated by the Muslims in West Beirut. Nor did they know that by pausing here in the hills they were giving the P.L.O. the opportunity to regroup and dig in for a long, costly battle. They asked what the Western press was reporting on the war and seemed stunned to learn that most of the articles reflected little sympathy for the Israeli tactics. Told that European relief workers were estimating that the Israelis had already killed ten thousand Lebanese and Palestinians, the vast majority of whom were civilians, an Israeli soldier born in New Jersey said, "That's impossible. We killed no one but terrorists."

It was unsettling talking to the Israelis because the relationship between us was one of being both friend and enemy. They spoke my language, they asked about major-league baseball scores, they had relatives in the United States, some even carried American passports. They thought of me, an American, as a confederate — had I not cheered their lightning victory over Nasser's Arabs in 1967 and marveled at the daring of their raid on Entebbe in 1975? Yet as long as I remained with the other journalists in West Beirut, covering the war from the Palestinian perspective, I could be, in their eyes, nothing but their enemy's accomplice. And the Israelis in my view could be nothing but the instrument that threatened my life and that of everyone around me. The roles and the balances had shifted. Over the past decade either I had changed or Israel had changed. Perhaps we both had.

"Don't worry, we're not going into Beirut," an Israeli lieutenant colonel, Amos Neeman, told a group of us that day on a hilltop overlooking the capital. "We have established our lines right here, and although we may move along the road a little, we are not going any farther forward. We will not carry any part of the war into downtown Beirut.

"What happens tomorrow, I don't know. I am only a military man. But we have accomplished our objective. The P.L.O. is destroyed as a military movement. We wiped out Syria's air defense system, showing what a combination of American technology and Israeli execution can do.

"You know, the shah of Iran used to be the policeman in this part of the world. He's gone now. And if we have to be the policeman for the Middle East for the next couple of years to make sure that there is peace, to restore some sanity to Lebanon, then we are ready to do it."

HINDSIGHT, OF course, is easy. But when I reread the colonel's remarks in my notes years later, I realized how flawed the Israeli game plan inherently was and how little Israel really understood about its Arab neighbors. Arab pride and Arab militancy alone precluded the possibility of any outsider—least of all, Israel—being an effective regional policeman unless it is willing and able to conquer, occupy and oppress. And by the time the Israelis came in 1982, there was nothing to save or restore in Lebanon. The country lay dying, a victim of its people, its neighbors and its own history.

In early times, dating back to 3000 B.C., Lebanon was the site of three of the world's oldest settlements, in Tyre, Sidon and Byblos. Its people were a mixture of Mediterranean cultures and conquerors—Phoenicians, Babylonians, Greeks, Byzantines, Crusaders and Arabs—and from the seventh century forward, its rugged mountains and sweeping valleys became a refuge for Christian and Muslim sects escaping persecution. The most significant of them were the Maronites, a Christian community whose members had lived in northern Syria and had supported the Crusaders in the twelfth century. They were to become the largest of Lebanon's sixteen minority groups.[5]

Mount Lebanon, as the country was then known, sustained a

---

[5] The Maronite Church is one of the group of Christian churches known as the Uniates. They are in full communion with the Holy See in Rome, but maintain Eastern traditions, such as prayers in Syriac. They believe that Christ contained two natures within one will. The Maronites take their name from a fifth-century hermit and saint, Maron.

semblance of unity because the various factions respected one another's turf and autonomy. The Christians and the Druze, a secretive Islamic sect, banded together in 1840 to confront Egypt, whose army had taken over Damascus, Syria, with the help of a renegade Turk, Bashir II. Two years later, the Ottoman Turks, seeking to end Lebanon's semiindependent status, partitioned the country along the Damascus-Beirut road, with the Christians given the northern district and the Druze the southern one. The division accentuated animosities between the groups; tensions heightened when France threw its support behind the Maronites and Britain chose the Druze. The foreign interests transformed Lebanon's sociopolitical conflicts into bitter sectarian conflicts, culminating in 1860 with the massacre of Maronites by their former ally, the Druze. As an Arab proverb says, "My brother and I against our cousin; my cousin and I against the alien."

The five great powers—France, Britain, Russia, Prussia and Austria—met with Turkey that year and decided that the partition of Lebanon had been a mistake. They reunited the country under a Christian governor appointed by the Turkish sultan. The first man the sultan chose was Du'ad Pasha, an Armenian. However harsh and disdainful of the Arabs the Ottoman Turks were, Lebanon's blend of foreign and Arab influences, of Islam and Christianity and of Western missionaries and Eastern traditions made the country uniquely cosmopolitan and tolerant. Intellectual life flourished in this atmosphere. Beirut became the focus of the Arab renaissance and the American University there became the most important center of learning in the Middle East. Arabic literature thrived; an active, critical press took hold; a tourist industry, bringing increased exposure to the outside world, was born; Arab nationalism germinated.

Turkish rule ended after World War I, and the Allies placed Mount Lebanon and Syria under French mandate. (Much of what is now Lebanon was then part of Syria.) The French devoted great attention to improving Lebanon's educational system, agricultural practices and standard of living, but they favored the Maronites over the Muslims, and in an attempt to weaken the cause of Arab nationalism, they divided Syria into five smaller units, one of which would become the Lebanon of today. International pressure grew on France to end the mandate, and after a visit to Beirut by Charles de Gaulle, Lebanon was given independence in 1943.

France withdrew its troops three years later, upon ensuring that the Maronites would continue their dominance over a divided land, a dominance that would give Lebanon favored status among the Jews when British-run Palestine became Israel in 1948. Under the terms of an unwritten convention drafted by France and agreed to by Christian and Muslim leaders, the Christian communities were to cease identifying themselves with the West, and the Muslims were to protect Lebanon's independence by promising never to merge with any Arab country; the Christians were to accept that Lebanon was an Arab country with an Arab language while the Muslims were to accept Lebanon's continued intellectual ties to the West, a linkage that had brought Lebanon more economic and social progress than its Arab neighbors had enjoyed; finally, the president of Lebanon was to be a Maronite, the prime minister a Sunni Muslim, the speaker of the house a Shiite Muslim. Parliamentary seats were to be apportioned on a religious basis with six-elevenths reserved for Christians.

The fragile balance on which Lebanon was based was sustained through a floating consensus on the part of the factional leadership. Unlike some Arab countries, the people of Lebanon were not homogeneous, and their identity was not international or civic — it was based on the religious tribe. What the Lebanese cared most about was making money, and as long as Lebanon prospered, which it did, the groups generally acquiesced. But many tensions showed through the veneer of nationhood. The Muslims, believing they had achieved numerical superiority, were resentful that Christians filled a disproportionate number of senior positions in the civil service, the army and the private sector. The Christians were fearful of—and unresponsive to—the Pan-Arab mood sweeping the Middle East in the Nasser era of the 1950s. Egypt had merged with Syria. The editor of *Al-Talagraph*, a Lebanese daily known for its outspoken Arabist views, had been assassinated, sparking an insurrection in Beirut led by a fiery Muslim rebel named Saab Salaam. The pro-Western regime in Iraq had been overthrown, and the entire royal family of King Faisal II had been killed. Opposition radio stations in Beirut suggested that the Lebanese president, Camille Chamoun, would be the next to go. Chamoun asked the United States to intervene.

Washington in those days equated Arab nationalism with Communism, and President Eisenhower was anxious to test the Soviet Union's resolve and his own doctrine of offering assistance to any Arab government that wanted to confront the Red menace. On July 15, 1958, the day after Chamoun's request, U.S. marines landed on Beirut's Ouzai Beach. "I believe the presence of the U.S. forces now being sent to Lebanon will have a stabilizing effect which will preserve the independence and integrity of Lebanon," Eisenhower told the American public in a television address. President Ronald Reagan would echo almost the precise words twenty-four years later when he, too, sent marines to Lebanon.

The Muslim rebels were armed with only rifles and a few machine guns, and the marines had not the slightest trouble, primarily because Salaam had told his people to put down their arms "until we see how this all turns out." As the leathernecks splashed ashore, girls in bikinis and vendors selling ice cream on the beach cheered their uncontested advance. The marines moved into downtown Beirut the day after their landing in three columns, preceded by Lebanese policemen in jeeps and on motorcycles. People applauded along the route. Asked why they had come, one corporal from Massachusetts said, "I guess the rebels cause trouble here. I'd like to clean 'em out and get the hell home." But the leathernecks never even had a chance to fire a shot. The insurrection faded away and the marines left Lebanon after three and a half months without suffering a single casualty. They had, in effect, stepped into an internal revolution and thwarted the evolution of Muslim politics.

Salaam, a Sunni Muslim, went on to become prime minister in several governments. He was a respected moderate who believed in nonviolence, a man who cultivated friendships in the West and cared deeply about Arab dignity. When I met him in the summer of 1982, he was nearly eighty, balding and white-haired. He lived in the same three-story house on which ships of the Sixth Fleet had trained their guns in 1958. He puffed on a big cigar and laughed at the irony of it all. On this day the gunboats in the Mediterranean that he could see from his window belonged to Israel.

"The Eisenhower people made a big mistake," he said. "They thought if they finished me off, there would be no more problems in Lebanon. It's the same mistake Israel is making today. They think if they get rid of the P.L.O., there will be no more Palestinian problem. I'm afraid that's not a very sophisticated way to view the realities of the Middle East.

"You know, ten years after the marine invasion, in 1968, I was at the United Nations, and five of your marines who had been in Lebanon called me. They were colonels by then. I invited them over for breakfast and said, 'Now, aren't you glad you didn't finish me off?'"

DESPITE ITS fragility as a nation, Lebanon was an exceptional country when Salaam hosted his breakfast in New York with the five marines. It had the highest literacy rate in the Arab world; it was the banking center of the Middle East; it was the exile home of countless intellectuals, who with each Arab revolution fled the intolerance of their own governments in increasing numbers. With its Christian influence and Western ties, Lebanon never quite felt

Arab. A distinct code of life developed there, and Lebanon straddled many worlds. Women, who received the right to vote in 1953,
were treated as equals. Casinos with Paris revues were as elegant as
anything in Monte Carlo. Grand seaside hotels, such as the St.
Georges in Beirut, attracted the rich and the famous from around
the world. They skiied in the mountains overlooking the capital in
the morning and sunbathed on the Mediterranean in the afternoon. All those descriptions of Beirut in the tourist brochures—
Pearl of the Mediterranean, Switzerland of the Middle East, Paris
of the Arab World—may have been a bit overblown, but they were
close enough to the mark to confirm Beirut's preeminence as the
most vibrant, comfortable and cosmopolitan city for many miles
around.

For Western diplomats and journalists, Beirut was arguably the
most important capital in the Arab world. It was a listening post, a
place where information was exchanged and trends discerned. The
journalists could pay their dues in travels to other forlorn cities and
know that they had an alluring home to come back to. Granted,
Beirut was crazy and violent even then, but there was some vague
sense of order and decency that placed restraints on mayhem.
Occasional artillery exchanges in the hills or a few killings around
the corner didn't much disturb the civility of life. If an armed
teenager got out of hand, Kamal Salibi, Lebanon's leading modern
historian, had a simple solution: he would walk over and tell the
youth's mother or father. That ended any problem, for no matter
how threatening the youngsters might have seemed on the street,
the home was the focus of life in Lebanon, and around the family
dinner table the boys were as meek as house pets—they did what
their parents told them.

Lebanon worked, however artificially, then because one group,
the Christians, were clearly in control, lesser minorities were given
freedom to maneuver as long as they didn't get too uppity and
everyone who mattered was making money. Tensions and hostili-

ties festered only beneath the surface. But in 1970 Lebanon's deli-
cate balance was upset. The P.L.O..had been driven out of Jordan
in Black September by King Hussein's army, and it moved to
Lebanon, where the presence of a weak central government would
permit the organization almost unlimited freedom. Every Arab government that had offered hospitality to the Palestine Liberation
Organization had come to regret its decision, and Lebanon was to
be no exception.

Thousands of Palestinians, refugees who had fled Palestine in
1948, lived in Lebanon by the time the P.L.O. arrived to set up its
headquarters, and almost all were constantly reminded of their inferior status. They were poor, homeless and unemployed, except
when cheap labor was needed. By 1973 one in ten persons in
Lebanon was Palestinian. Stuck in squalid camps, exposed to the
grievances of Lebanon's Muslim minorities, abandoned by the
Arabs who paid them so much lip service, the Palestinians gradually
turned toward radicalized politics and armed themselves. Lebanon
was their last redoubt, and they intended to dig in for a long stay.

The splintered Lebanese government made a fateful error by giving the P.L.O. total control over their camps and the forward posts
along the Israeli border, thus putting the organization beyond the
control of Lebanese authority. In return the Palestinians promised
not to interfere in internal Lebanese affairs. P.L.O. gunners showered Galilee with rockets, and Israel responded with attacks on the
Palestinian bases in Lebanon—and later on Beirut itself. In one
attack just after Christmas, 1968, Israeli pilots destroyed thirteen
airliners of Lebanon's civilian Middle East Airlines at Beirut's international airport; the Lebanese armed forces fired not a shot in
return. President Suleiman Franjieh, a violent Christian of the
right whose living-room walls were decorated with daggers, swords
and nineteenth-century rifles, was helpless in attempts to control
the P.L.O. or to stop the Israeli infringement on Lebanese sovereignty, and his vacillation encouraged the Muslim groups to start

kidnapping Christians and skirmishing with the Christian-led army. Christian hatred of the Palestinians grew. The P.L.O. linked up with the Druze; Israel shipped weapons to the Christians. The lines for civil war were drawn.

If it is possible to choose a precise event that started the war, it was probably the Christians' ambush and massacre of thirty Palestinian civilians on a bus in April 1975. Beirut erupted. For the next nineteen months Christians massacred Lebanese Muslims and Palestinians; Muslims and Palestinians massacred Christians. The Christians wore wooden crosses around their necks, and the Muslims carried the Koran. Although the war may have been about economic oppression and political rights, religion was the dividing line, and Beirut became two cities—the eastern sector Christian, the western predominantly Muslim—as artillery flew between east and west. The great contributions Lebanon had made to Arab culture, Arab nationalism and Arab intellectualism were washed away overnight in an orgy of killing. Lebanon became synonymous with mindless death. The army never left its barracks during the war— Lebanon's leadership was too divided to know which side the soldiers should support—and national authority passed to the militias and to the young men who quickly learned that a gun brought quicker results than either the Bible or the Koran.

At first it appeared the Christians would lose the war. This made Syria nervous because it could have led to a partitioned Lebanon and Israeli intervention. So the Syrians, asked by President Franjieh to intervene militarily, sold out the Arab cause and entered the war with twenty thousand soldiers in support of the Christians, thus putting Syria and Israel, the bitterest of enemies, on the same team.[6]

---

[6] To those critical of Syrian involvement, the Syrians would reply that their intervention was no different from that of the U.S. marines who entered Lebanon in 1958 at the invitation of President Chamoun. Syria's entry into the civil war was also made in response to Anwar Sadat's peacemaking visit to Jerusalem in 1977. Believing that they were being relegated to a secondary role in

Later, when the Christians started winning, Syria switched sides and threw its weight behind the Lebanese Muslims and Palestinians. The war drew to a formal close in November 1976, when an Arab "peacekeeping" force of thirty thousand men, most of them Syrian, arrived to impose order. The tragedy for Lebanon was that no side won the war, and without a winner and the emergence of a strong government, the minorities would continue to battle—albeit at a sometimes diminished level of violence—for survival and superiority. Each in effect was waging its own civil rights war. As one weary American diplomat remarked, "There's nothing the matter with Lebanon that Mussolini couldn't fix in about a year."

The war took the lives of seventy thousand civilians, resulted in $1 billion damage and the destruction of much of Beirut, made half a million people homeless and sent a large segment of the country's educated elite scurrying abroad in search of new homes. The war also represented the final nail in the coffin of Pan-Arabism, for the Arabs had watched Lebanon burn with expressions of grief but not much else. The Palestinians learned, once again, that the Arabs would desert them in times of crisis, and the Christians learned that they had no one they could count on other than Israel. Lebanon was dead as a nation everywhere but in the history books, and it amazed me that Israel apparently didn't understand this when it came in the summer of 1982 to put Lebanon back together again.

ISRAELI MILITARY planners had figured it would take them about one week to clean up Lebanon, at a cost of no more than a hundred Israeli casualties. Had the Israelis moved into Beirut when they first

---

the Middle East, the Syrians started making friends with old enemies, mustering support among Arabs and taking stronger stands politically and militarily in the hopes of thwarting Sadat's peace moves. They consider Lebanon to be part of "Greater Syria," a political and geographical entity that the French and the British had carved up; it comprises Syria, Lebanon, Palestine and Jordan.

reached the hills overlooking Beirut, they might have succeeded. The P.L.O. was demoralized, the Muslim opposition was in disarray. But the Israeli army is best trained for large-scale conventional warfare, not street fighting, and instead of attacking, the Israelis ringed West Beirut with tanks and troops and tried to starve their enemies out in a siege that would last eighty days. That decision cost them the victory they had known in every other Arab-Israeli war. In the Muslim quarter, we bunkered down for a long summer. The skies were full of Israeli planes, and the streets teemed with gangs of crazed militiamen. No one seemed much concerned about whom they killed as long as they killed someone. Israeli bombs fell, often indiscriminately, on Palestinian refugee camps and Lebanese residential areas. The P.L.O. guerrillas turned civilians into sacrificial lambs by hiding among them, thus making civilians prime targets for Israeli attacks. The Muslim gangs fought one another when there was no one else around to battle, while the Christians in East Beirut gloated over the barbarity of their countrymen across the green line.

"You know, if you take us Lebanese as individuals, we are a very civilized people," said Nabih Berri, the leader of the Shiites. "But if you take us as a group, you'd think we were back in the Middle Ages."

That was the strange paradox of the Lebanese, for the country existed on two levels. The violence had become institutionalized, yet the façade of civilization never quite broke down entirely. The streets would be insane, but inside the homes there was a peculiar feeling of tranquillity. There I sat with professors, bankers, merchants and their families and talked about how, once all this was over, Lebanon would sort itself out. Somehow they still believed in their country, or, at least, pretended they did. I met kids who drove through the heaviest shelling attacks as volunteer ambulance drivers and a group of young businessmen who set up and personally staffed an orphanage. I met mothers who organized a peace march—they were turned back by fierce artillery duels—and doctors who ventured forth, going from door to door through murderous fighting in search of blood donors. Each night I went to sleep cursing Beirut, and each morning I woke up knowing that I cared about the place, hoping that its people would have just one more chance to make peace with themselves. The problem was that the people I cared about had no control over their national destiny. The voices of the decent majority had been silenced, and Lebanon had created a burned-out generation of degenerate gunmen.

At Berbir Hospital on the green line the wounded and the dead arrived in such numbers that they had to be stretched out on the sidewalk. The kitchen was turned into a morgue. A little boy of perhaps eight wandered among the bodies one day, idly playing with the fingers of corpses. "My God, get him out of here!" a Lebanese American doctor, Amal Shaama, shrieked at the mother. "He's too young to see this."

Later Dr. Shaama slumped into a chair, exhausted after a twenty-hour shift. "I shouldn't have lost my temper," she said softly. "I keep forgetting that these children have seen so many horrors that they're inured to death. Nothing fazes them. Psychologically they're old men."

As Israel tightened its blockade of West Beirut our world grew smaller by the day. The Western embassies moved into the relatively secure eastern sector. Washington evacuated all the Americans who wanted to leave Lebanon on a ship to Cyprus. The mail stopped, the airport remained closed, the telephone system ceased functioning, and medical supplies, food and water ran dangerously short. You could hardly find a Lebanese on the street who did not carry a gun. The Israelis kept bombing and the Palestinians kept digging in deeper. The U.N. Security Council passed a resolution calling on Israel to lift the siege. The vote was 14 to 0 with one abstainer, the United States.

I often wondered how New Yorkers would have reacted had they been subjected to a similar siege at a time when there were no policemen, no firemen, no government. I concluded that what I was seeing in Beirut was a fairly normal response to a highly unnormal situation. Beirutis had not a single national symbol to rally around. There was nothing to protect, nothing to believe in, except the clan and the neighborhood. The wars had gone on so long that everyone had debts to repay, and the violence had become so rampant that gunmen valued their weapon more than their penis as a symbol of manhood. (Doctors at the American University Hospital, in fact, treated several young men who had tried to castrate themselves in a fit of despair.) The Lebanese had lived for centuries with invaders—the Assyrians, Babylonians, Persians, Greeks, Romans, Arabs, Ottomans, French and now the Israelis, and they took pride in their resilience and rebelliousness. "We Lebanese," the people liked to say, "are easy to swallow and difficult to digest." Their children learned at an early age how to hide their guns from conquerors by burying the weapons inside rubber inner tubes smeared with cooking oil. That would preserve the guns for years and keep them safe for use against the next enemy.

The summer moved slowly toward its cataclysmic ending. President Reagan's personal envoy, Philip C. Habib, a career diplomat whose parents were born in Lebanon, negotiated for the evacuation from Beirut of Arafat and his twelve thousand guerrillas—a deal that would snatch the prey from Israel at the very moment it was so agonizingly vincible. Just as agreement was within reach, Israel unleashed its most savage air strike of the war on West Beirut, keeping the Muslim quarter under a relentless eleven-hour attack that forced Lebanese authorities to suspend the peace talks.

"What made Black Thursday so terrifying," wrote two Israeli journalists, "was the sense of brute violence run wild, given the sharp contrast between the progress in the negotiations and the savage attack on the city."

Reagan finally telephoned Prime Minister Begin to condemn the "needless destruction and bloodshed." But his words offered too little too late. To every Arab, America was the co-aggressor, as much responsible for the nightmare of '82 as Israel was. Apparently unaware of the depth of the Arab anger, the White House organized an interim international force to supervise the departure of the P.L.O. Key advisers counseled against including Americans in the unit. Secretary of Defense Caspar Weinberger said that the volatility of Lebanon would endanger U.S. troops. George W. Ball, former under secretary of state, warned that no nation with special regional interests or special relations with any of the contending parties should participate in the peacekeeping force. "We would imprudently hazard the lives of our marines to commit them to an area where anti-Americanism is a dominating sentiment," Ball told the Senate Foreign Relations Committee.

Israel, however, was mistrustful of any force that did not include Americans, and President Reagan succumbed to Israeli pressures. The multinational force that arrived in late August to oversee the P.L.O. evacuation included a unit of eight hundred American marines. In return for Arafat's agreement to leave, Washington guaranteed the safety of Palestinian civilians left behind in refugee settlements and offered assurances that Israel would not invade West Beirut. Before boarding ships that would scatter them throughout the Arab world, the P.L.O. fighters gathered at the port and unleashed such a wild volley of firing into the air that a score of people, including several guerrillas who had survived the war, were killed by falling bullets.

"I'll tell you what this war taught us," a bearded pharmacist turned guerrilla told me in perfect English. "It taught us that the real enemy is the United States. It is against you that we must fight. Not just because your bombs killed our people, but because you have closed your eyes to what is moral and just."

With the P.L.O. gone and the Israeli siege ended, a wonderful mood of euphoria swept over Beirut. The Reagan administration ordered the marines withdrawn after just ten days' duty, two weeks ahead of schedule, and the leathernecks boarded the assault ship *Manitowoc* under a banner that read, MISSION ACCOMPLISHED.

There was talk of peace, and for the first time in nearly three months
I did not feel weak-kneed when I walked out of the Commodore
Hotel each morning. Militiamen started burying their guns in inner
tubes; people emerged from their cellars and their dazed, glassy-
eyed expression soon faded; a few restaurants reopened. A group of
us went out to a little restaurant that an eighty-year-old Frenchman
by the name of Maurice Myse ran near the bombed-out part. We
asked about his son, Jean-Pierre, whom we had last seen during the
siege passed out at a table before noon, his hand clutching a half-
empty bottle of whiskey. His mother had pleaded then, "Please,
can't you do something? Can't you find someone at the French
embassy who will come and help him?" Myse said everything was
fine now. "Oh, he's well, thank you. His problems went with the
war. The worst is over for us all now, I think."

Optimism is the underpinning of the Lebanese resilience, the
safety net that has kept a fractured society from total disintegration.
"We always bounce back," the Lebanese say. They like to blame all
their problems on outsiders, and at the same time they desperately
want to place their trust in some foreign power that will come and
save them from committing national suicide. But Lebanon had
become a free-fire zone for the outsiders, and it was to the advantage of many of them that the country did not enjoy peace. Israel
armed two bitter enemies, the Christians and the Druze, because
the last thing the Jewish state wanted was a strong, united Lebanon
on its northern border. Iran wanted all Christians—and perhaps all
civilized people as well—out of West Beirut in order to cultivate
the seeds of Islamic revolution. Syria needed a weak Lebanon if it
was to fulfill its goal of bringing the country under the control of
Damascus. The United States did not want to see the evolution of
a Muslim-dominated republic that would be troublesome to Israel.
The Soviet Union was only too pleased to see Israel and the West
trapped in the quagmire of Lebanon. And so from every quarter—
from Russia, the United States, France, Britain, Israel, Iran, Syria,

Libya—arms flowed into Lebanon in immense quantities to subsidize the violence of one group or another. I should have realized
that the euphoria of those few days in August was an illusion.

On September 14 Israel's ally, President-elect Bashir Gemayel,
the thirty-four-year-old warlord who had led the Christian forces
during the civil war, was blown up with his top aides by a bomb at
his party headquarters in East Beirut.[7] He was buried in the family
vault, next to his eighteen-month-old daughter, who had been
killed by a hidden bomb three years earlier. Israel saw its costly
Lebanon investment going down the drain, and the next day, with
the announced intention of preventing a new outbreak of violence
in the Muslim quarter, its forces launched an unexpected and
unprovoked attack on an exhausted city, the first-ever Israeli invasion of an Arab capital. By now Israel was encountering something
never experienced before in an Arab-Israeli war: a hostile Western
press and debate in the West over the propriety of Israeli policies. Its
tanks ringed the adjoining Palestinian slum towns of Sabra and
Chatilla; its troops fought block by block through West Beirut's
Muslim residential and commercial areas. Within forty-eight hours
the Israelis were in control. One group of soldiers stopped an America TV crew from Cable News Network and confiscated its film of
an interview with Saab Salaam. When the sound man, Don Wells,
was asked for identification and produced an American passport, an
Israeli threw it on the ground and spat on it. Another group of
Israeli enlisted men entered the Berbir Hospital and took over Dr.
Amal Shaama's fifth-floor apartment as a sniper position. When she
was allowed to return to her flat a week later, she found defecation·
in her linens and cooking utensils.

[7] No one ever claimed credit for the assassinations, although many diplomats
suspected that Syrian agents had killed Bashir Gemayel because of his ties to
Israel. With Bashir dead, his older brother, Amin, became Lebanon's new
president. He spoke often of national reconciliation during his presidency but
answered primarily to Christian interests.

On the southern outskirts of the city, Israeli commanders moved into an eight-story building, which had previously been used as officers' quarters for the Lebanese army and was located two hundred yards from the perimeter of Chatilla. From its roof Brigadier General Amos Yaron, the Israeli commander in Beirut, and his officers had a clear view of the war-ravaged shantytown and of the Palestinians who moved among the rubble of mortar and brick. Chatilla and Sabra, just to the north, were a warren of twisting alleyways, two-story makeshift homes and tiny shops protected by sandbags. Pushcarts filled the bustling streets and vendors peddled vegetables and meat under striped umbrellas, shouting out the price of their goods to passersby. Each of the towns was a self-contained entity with hospitals, schools and social services administered by the now departed P.L.O. The inhabitants, many of whom had lived there since fleeing Palestine in 1948, were the poorest of the poor and had long since given up hope of ever escaping their hapless existence. The elders among them understood that they were the pawns in a larger international game—that when culprits had to be chosen and punished, they almost certainly would be the ones nominated.

Shortly after the Israelis took up positions around Chatilla and Sabra, about seven hundred Phalangists, a Christian militia force armed and supported by Israel, moved up from Damour and established a command center in the Lebanese University's abandoned business administration office, a hundred yards from the Israeli position.[8] Israeli and Christian officers mixed freely, and one presumes that the Israelis understood the depth of the Christians'

---

[8] The Phalange was a paramilitary political organization dedicated to preserving Maronite dominance in Lebanon. Its militia, known as the Lebanese Forces, was sectarian, not national as its name implied. The Phalange were founded by Pierre Gemayel, the father of Bashir, who visited Germany for the 1936 Berlin Olympics and was impressed by the spirit and discipline of Nazi youth.

hatred for the Palestinians, whom they held responsible for the bloodshed of the 1975–76 civil war. At nine o'clock that night, September 16, while Israeli flares lit the skies and the turrets of Israeli tanks pointed down on a largely civilian population, the militiamen entered Chatilla through the south gate.

From inside the camp, a Phalangist officer radioed his commander, who stood with other Christian militiamen and a few Israelis on the roof of the nearby headquarters building. He said he had found fifty women and children—what should he do?

The Phalangist commander radioed back: "This is the last time you're going to ask me a question like that. You know exactly what to do." The militiamen around the commander broke up with laughter.

The killing was slow and methodical. The Phalangists worked their way north through the main dirt street and down the side alleyways, going from house to house. Their assignment was carried out with rifles, knives, clubs and chains. Groups of ten to twenty Palestinians were lined up against walls and machine-gunned. Five youths were tied behind a pickup truck and dragged through the streets. Mothers died clutching their babies, fathers were castrated and shot. "Guns! Where can we get guns?" an old lady screamed. "They are killing everybody." Entire families spanning three generations perished. A dozen boys, some no older than twelve, fought to hold off the attackers with rifles and were quickly overcome. Panicked crowds tried to flee and found their escape routes blocked.

Milad Farouk, an eleven-year-old boy with black curly hair and eyes as round as saucers, made his way through the hysterical crowds to the door of Gaza Hospital at 8:00 A.M. on Friday. His mother, father and three brothers had been shot before his eyes minutes earlier, and Milad had one bullet hole in his right leg, one in his left arm, and one of his fingers had been shot off.

"We are all going to die," the boy told doctors, and for the most part he was right.

In scenes that were all too reminiscent of the horrors the Jews had suffered at the hands of the Nazis, Palestinians were segregated from Lebanese and pulled from their beds at Gaza Hospital; they were executed on the spot or pushed into cattle trucks to be driven to an unknown destination. Outside the south gate of Chatilla, a Phalangist officer sat on the ground, eating a can of American C rations given him by the Israelis. I asked what he was doing. "I'm just resting my men," he said. "We've got a group of a hundred cornered in there and we'll go back in after everyone rests up."

The shooting did not stop until 6:30 A.M. on Saturday. The militiamen withdrew in an orderly convoy, having suffered no casualties, and drove back to Damour. Nothing living remained in Chatilla and Sabra. Even the cats were dead.

THE EIGHT hundred victims of the massacre were buried in an unmarked mass grave that bore the message LONG LIVE OUR DEATHS, and the next day the Palestinians started rebuilding their two shantytowns. The little shops reopened, the mudbrick homes became livable again, with laundry hung to dry in windows that had no glass panes. Life soon seemed surprisingly normal.

An old man, Rafik Harrari, walked each day by the mass grave with its two withered wreaths. He always wore the same brown suit and the same wool ski cap. He paused only briefly by the grave, then shuffled on, his leather sandals stirring up little clouds of dust on the road.

"My wife and son are buried there," he said. "Almost everyone I know is buried there. We talked about getting a proper stone marker, but what does it matter? We have the memories. And there will be more deaths. One day someone will come to finish us all."

The Lebanese government never held a serious inquiry into the massacre, and no group was ever brought to justice. The commander of the Phalange killer squad, Elie Hobeika, a twenty-six-year-old banker turned militiaman, continued to maintain a high degree of respectability in the Christian community, even after his name was linked to the death mission.[9]

Only Israel conducted a thorough investigation, to determine its soldiers' involvement, although Prime Minister Begin had initially asked, "What's all the commotion about one set of *goyim* killing another and blaming it on the Jews?" The conclusion of the commission, headed by Chief Justice Yitzhak Kahan of the Supreme Court, was that Israeli commanders had not planned the massacre but shared culpability for allowing the Phalangists to enter the Palestinian settlements in the first place and for making no initial effort to stop the killing. Two Israeli generals were reprimanded and stripped of their commands for their roles in the massacre. One of them, Amos Yaron, was later made military attaché to the United States. Ariel Sharon, the defense minister, would become prime minister a generation later.

THE MULTINATIONAL force returned a week after the massacre. French and Italian soldiers moved into Sabra and Chatilla, and Palestinian women and children there clapped and saluted them. The U.S. marines—who thirteen months later would be the victims of the terrorist attack on their headquarters—took up positions on the airport perimeter, and the city's newspapers welcomed them back with banner headlines. I left Beirut a few days after the marines' arrival, never wanting to see Lebanon again. I felt sure that the killing wasn't over and that the eventual withdrawal of Israel wouldn't solve anything. My ship to Cyprus, the *Aphrodite*, a creaky ferryboat built in Belfast three decades earlier, pulled out of the port. Beirut was quiet and the hillside villas glistened in the sun. I felt overwhelmed by sadness, for the friends I was leaving behind,

---

[9] Hobeika was chased out of Lebanon in 1986 by other Christian forces after he signed on behalf of all the Christians a Syrian-sponsored agreement for peace in Lebanon that would have diluted the Christians' power. With Hobeika gone, the agreement with Syria collapsed.

for the people who had suffered through that long, ugly summer, for the Israel and the Lebanon that could never be the same again, and in a strange way for myself. I felt incapable of laughing or crying. I felt neither love nor hate. I just wanted to get away, to sit somewhere quietly and safely alone, and not be bothered by anyone or anything. Beirut had done to me what it had done to so many others. It had stolen my emotions.

The ship was crowded with Lebanese, most of them Christians, who had already figured out the destiny of their country. The passengers pushed against the rail as the *Aphrodite* slipped away into the Mediterranean, leaving Beirut stretched across the skyline. One of them, Vera Issa, started to cry. "I'm scared I'll never come back, that there won't be any Lebanon to come back to," she said in a whisper. "This Lebanese passport in my purse, what will it be worth next year? What'll I need—a Syrian passport, an Israeli passport— to come back to Beirut?"

Her friend, Dr. Michel Salhab, put his arm around her shoulder to comfort her. "No, there will always be a Lebanon," he said. "Maybe not as we knew it, but there will be a Lebanon. In fifteen, twenty years there could be peace. Now, wouldn't that be something?"

THE WAR was a tragic misadventure whose results were precisely the opposite of what Israel had intended.[10] Its great lesson was the same one the United States learned so painfully in Vietnam: political goals cannot be achieved through military force, and people

---

[10] The Israelis withdrew most of their troops from Lebanon in June 1985, having suffered more than six hundred dead during a three-year occupation. They created a six-mile-deep, fifty-mile-wide "security zone" along the border and set up, equipped and paid for an eighteen-hundred-man Lebanese Christian militia to patrol it. Israel also keeps about one thousand of its own troops in southern Lebanon. With the main-force Israeli units gone, the various militias turned their guns on one another and violence continued throughout the country.

with a cause that they see as just cannot be bombed into submission, unless one is willing to commit genocide.

The Shiites in southern Lebanon who had initially showered the Israelis with flowers, welcoming them as liberators for expelling the P.L.O., came to view the Israelis as occupiers whose "iron fist" policy was racist and repressive. Israel had made another enemy in the Middle East and had given a boost to Shiite nationalism—and Shiite terrorism. The multinational force that had come to save Lebanon ended up being its victim when terrorists killed 241 U.S. marines and 58 French paratroopers in the simultaneous suicide attacks on October 23, 1983. Syria, whose air force and missile sites had been destroyed by Israel in the early stages of the war, rebuilt its armed forces with Soviet help, replaced its lost missiles with more sophisticated SS-21s that had a seventy-five-mile range, expanded its army from 300,000 to 450,000 men and became the dominant power in Lebanon. The Lebanese Christians, who had sought Israel's protection, were weakened and by 1986 were losing their power bit by bit to the Muslims. The Palestinian guerrillas who had been forced from Beirut started drifting back to Lebanon in large numbers, and occasional Katyusha rockets started falling on Galilee again. The United States, which had staked its Middle East policy on Lebanon, lost its credibility with the Arabs and found itself acting not as a negotiator but as a messenger between Israel and the Arabs. And Israel itself was left as a divided nation, torn by the deeply troubling notion that it was creating the very conditions that had forced its own people to flee Europe forty years earlier.

The war, though, gave the Arabs in general and the Palestinians in particular an important opportunity. For the first time they had been perceived in the West as the underdog, and Israeli conduct and policies had come under reexamination and severe criticism. An atmosphere of sympathy for the Palestinians took hold. This was the time for the Arabs to go on the peace offensive, to take bold steps that would have capitalized on the prevailing mood in the battle for Western public sympathy. This was the time for Jordan and the P.L.O. to align and agree to direct negotiations with Israel, the time for the Arab majority to set aside the rhetoric and present its case to the world. But Arafat, insisting that Beirut had been a military victory, got on a plane and shuttled around the Middle East and never offered one idea that was fresh or original. Arab groups met, flew in and out of Washington, met some more, and finally everyone scratched his head and admitted he really didn't know what to do next. Clovis Maksoud, the Arab League's ambassador in Washington, resigned in disgust over Arab inaction. (The league's secretary-general in Tunis, Chedli Klibi, tore the letter of resignation in half and mailed it back to him without comment; Maksoud stayed on.)

Despite its inability to permanently alter Western attitudes, the fractured and dispersed Palestine Liberation Organization emerged from the war as a double threat to Israel—diplomatically through its moderate elements, militarily through its radical ones. The war and the Sabra-Chatilla massacre unleashed a frenzy of frustration, hatred and hopelessness among young Palestinians who had lived their entire lives in refugee camps. They felt they had nothing to lose by dying, and with the P.L.O. having lost any capability of fighting a conventional war, they sought alternative tools of confrontation. International terrorism took on a new, frightening dimension. Innocents from many nations died. But if Israel and Lebanon bequeathed one legacy to the United States from the war of 1982, it was that more often than not the targets of the terrorists were Americans.

THE LEGACY lingers but the Beirut I returned to years later was no longer a dying city. It had been rebuilt with Arab money, and new hotels and luxury condos stretched along the Mediterranean coast. Yasser Arafat and his lieutenants were long gone by then, resettled in the Gaza Strip, which was destined to become part of the future Palestine. But the Palestinian refugee camps remained, as did the

Syrian soldiers in Lebanon. Beirut was a vastly better place than the wartime city I had known, but somewhere, perhaps in the ashes of Sabra and Chatilla, I felt its soul had been buried. Beirut was no longer a beacon for Arab writers and intellectuals or for Western tourists or for foreign journalists covering the Middle East. It felt tired and old and worn, which is how most places feel when they are filled with too many memories.

NINE

THE TWICE-PROMISED LAND

IN THE midst of the Beirut siege, when Israel was pounding the hell out of the Palestinians, Bill Barrett, the Middle East correspondent for the *Dallas Times Herald*, received a telex at the Commodore Hotel from his editor in Texas. The message, which was in effect a request for a story, read: "Who are these Palestinian people and why don't they just go home?"

Whether intended or not, there was brilliance in that telex. In twelve words the editor had cut to the marrow. He had boiled the most complex of Middle East issues into the simplest of terms— land. The Palestinians couldn't go home because they had no home. Their land had been promised by the British after World War I to two peoples, the Jews of Europe and the Arabs of the Middle East. When it came time to fulfill that promise, the former got a state, the latter got dispossessed. And neither has known a day of true peace since.

The Arab-Palestinian conflict has probably caused more bloodshed on a sustained basis than any single global dispute since World War II. The battle is not about religion or historical animosities or economic superiority. Like the wars between Indians and settlers in the old American West, it is simply about land, a narrow strip of the Fertile Crescent that runs for a hundred and forty miles along the eastern shore of the Mediterranean Sea. Until 1948 that land was Palestine, named for the Philistines who once occupied it. Then it became Israel, named for the ancient Jewish kingdom that had existed there two millennia ago. No sooner had David Ben-Gurion declared the establishment of the Jewish state on Friday, May 14, than the Arab armies attacked. When he broadcast a message to the United States early the next morning, the sound of Egyptian aircraft bombing Tel Aviv could be clearly heard in the background.

It is sad testimony to man's insensitivity that the Israelis and Palestinians have spent so little time trying to understand each other, for if any two peoples in the Middle East share a heritage of common suffering that should engender empathy and friendship, it is they. The Palestinians—whom Egyptians call "our Jews"—and the Israelis are Semites. They often look alike and their respective languages, Hebrew and Arabic, share historical roots. Both peoples are stereotyped as being economically aggressive, pushy, clannish and obsessed with educating their children. Both believe that without a homeland they will cease to exist as "a people," and their leaders have been willing to use any means, including terrorism, to secure that homeland, or to reclaim it, as the case may be. Most important, they both have known the humiliation of oppression and the anguish of diaspora. All they want, they both say, is the dignity and the security due them as a people in a land granted them by God.

But as the losers, the Palestinians became a nonpeople, an irrelevant population beholden to whoever offered shelter, jobs and passports. Asked about the Palestinians in 1969, Israel's prime minister, Golda Meir, said, "It is not as though there was a people in Palestine considering itself as a Palestinian people, and we came and threw them out and took their country away from them. They do not exist."

That came as something of a surprise to the world's 4.5 million Palestinians. And it also comes as a surprise to many Westerners to learn that the great majority of Palestinians are neither refugees nor gunmen. They are, in fact, as a people the most literate, industrious and best-educated Arabs in the Middle East. Ninety-five percent of their children attend elementary school, and twenty of every thousand Palestinians have received a higher education, compared with four of every thousand for the Arab population as a whole. They are middle-class and politically conservative, They are secular and less fervent about religion than other Arabs. (About 12 percent of the Palestinians are Christian.) They wear Western-style clothes, have only one wife and speak English. They run newspapers in Jordan, banks in Lebanon, the civil service in Kuwait, construction companies in the United Arab Emirates. Within their ranks are poets in Syria, millionaire traders in Saudi Arabia, insurance brokers in London, importers in Los Angeles and professors at leading universities in the United States and Europe. Remarkably enough, each left Palestine in 1948 for various exile homes with nothing more than a suitcase.

"We worked two jobs—God, how we worked!—and we had a fixation with education because we knew we had lost everything but our brains," said Subhi Lughod, whose Lebanese television production company is one of the largest in the Middle East. "I was in Cyprus with a very modest salary and I was dividing it so many ways—supporting parents in Jordan, a brother in Cairo, my wife and children in Cyprus—that there often wasn't enough to feed us. My youngest son grew sick and died simply because I could not afford the food and medicine he needed to live."

Today Lughod is a wealthy man. One of his sons is an engineer in Chicago, another a surgeon in the Persian Gulf states. He is soft-spoken and unassuming, but in that summer of the siege his voice rose with bitterness: "We are terrorists? Ha! The people who stole my home and who are now trying to chase me away again dare call us terrorists? Such a contradiction. Do they really think I am on the wrong side morally?"

To be sure, the Palestinian society is as varied as any. It includes thugs, crooks and terrorists. But I was always surprised to talk to young men who had hijacked jets or blown up buildings and discover how rational and low-keyed they could sound on everything but Palestine. Many, I suspected, were living what would be the high point of their lives, and I could envision them in a generation's time sitting around V.F.W. lodges, retelling war stories and reminiscing about the good old days. The Palestinian society also includes more than a million refugees, uneducated peasants who are welfare wards of the United Nations. Many probably would not be particularly productive citizens no matter where they lived.

But precisely because so many Palestinians like Lughod have clawed their way out of poverty and succeeded, other Arabs, viewing the Palestinians as an economic and political threat, resent them. The Palestinians work harder than the citizens in most host countries. They stay in school longer and get better jobs. They are more adaptable and less concerned with changes wrought by Western-inspired modernity.

Although many Arab governments have claimed to represent the Palestinians' interests, what they really want is the increased political leverage that that representation provides. The idea of a peaceful Palestinian homeland in what is now Israel is an unsettling one to them, contrary to the tone of their voluminous rhetoric. It would deprive the Arabs of a bargaining chip with Israel and the West, negate the announced reason for their military buildups, create a new political entity that would dilute the power of individual governments and dash the myth that Arab unity will be achieved with the rebirth of Palestine. Let the Palestinians dream of the orange groves they left behind; dreams are harmless. In the end the unity about which so much is spoken is an intimidating notion to the Arabs.

"Leaving Palestine still haunts me after all these years," said Ludwic Tamari, whose seventh-floor condominium in Beirut is appointed with Persian carpets and mahogany furniture. "I shouldn't have left. If we'd stayed, if all the Palestinians had stayed, we'd be the majority in Palestine—Israel—today. Then what would the situation have been? I know that no one is ever going to chase me away again. And I know I don't ever want to have to start over again with ten dollars in my pocket."

Tamari was a wealthy citrus exporter when he and his family left

Palestine in 1948. He settled in Jordan, moved to Lebanon, got an education that included a master's degree from Cornell University in New York and built up another citrus business that made him prosperous again.

We were sitting by an open glass door that led to a balcony full of potted flowers. He put down his cup of coffee and lit his pipe, pondering for a moment the Palestinians' fate—and his own. "You know, I don't want to sound boastful, but I really think the Palestinians are decent, hard-working people. We're not afraid to work to succeed. And we do succeed. I think that's the one quality the Zionists fear most in us.

"Would I go back to Palestine? I don't know. I couldn't answer that until there is a Palestine. But I know that it took the Israelis two thousand years to return to the homeland. I doubt that it will take us that long."

PALESTINE HAS been inhabited for more than ten thousand years, initially with people related to the Neanderthals of Europe. It was not unified in ancient times under a single town, as happened in Egypt and Mesopotamia, but rather it was a collection of city-states and allied tribes of seminomadic pastoralists. Among them was the Jewish tribe, the Israelites, a well-armed and highly motivated group whose monotheistic faith and stern code of ethics set it apart from its neighbors.

Some anthropologists believe that the Jews, like the Arabs, had once been one of the wandering tribes of the Arabian Peninsula. According to the Old Testament, Moses led the Jews out of Egypt's Sinai Peninsula in search of Israel, but after forty years in the wilderness he and his followers were sentenced to death by God for doubting His word, and he died before crossing the Jordan River. Joshua, Moses' divinely commissioned successor, then led the Jews the rest of the way into the promised land of Judea and Samaria (today the Israeli-occupied West Bank of Jordan[1]). Joshua was also an astute military commander, and the Jews laid claim to the land by killing, capturing and expelling the inhabitants they found there, the Canaanites.[2] To paraphrase Joseph Stalin, God always favors the side with the better army.

The Israelites' claim to Palestine was based on the Lord's promise to Abraham of a Jewish state extending "from the river of Egypt [the Nile] unto the great river, the river Euphrates" [in Mesopotamia, or modern-day Iraq].[3] That religious and nationalistic attachment to what is known in Hebrew as *Eretz Israel* (Land of Israel)—a Jewish state in Palestine—would one day be the foundation of Zionism, a political movement originating in Europe in the late 1800s. (The Koran says that after making the promise to Abraham, God told His last prophet, Mohammed, that Muslims should not be ruled by nonbelievers, thus negating the Israelites' claim in the Arabs' view.)

After the conquest of the Canaanites, an independent Jewish kingdom flourished in Palestine and Judaism developed. But because Palestine was a crossroad on the East-West trade route and a corridor to Egypt, many conquerors came and went. The Jews were usually the ones who suffered. The Babylonians deported them in bondage to Babylonia; the Greeks inflicted the original holocaust on them in 171 B.C.; the Romans destroyed their Temple of Solomon, in Jerusalem, between A.D. 70 and 135 and, laying

---

[1] The lands of east and west Jordan were united politically and culturally in ancient times, and Britain's 1920 Palestine mandate from the Allies covered both sides of Jordan. Jordan constituted two thirds of Palestine. In 1921 Britain chopped Jordan off from Palestine and installed Abdullah, son of the ruler of Hejaz in Arabia, as emir of an autonomous Transjordan. The independent kingdom of Jordan was proclaimed in 1948. More than 60 percent of Jordan's population today are Palestinians, who all have Jordanian citizenship.

[2] Israel was occupied by a variety of peoples when Joshua arrived: Canaanites, Phoenicians, Hittites, Aramaeans, Ammonites, Moabites, Edomites.

[3] Besides present-day Israel, this area would seem to include Jordan, Lebanon, Egypt's Sinai Peninsula, most of Syria and Iraq and possibly parts of Turkey and Saudi Arabia. Few Israelis today support such ambitious territorial claims.

waste the land, slaughtered or carried away nearly a million Jews. The Diaspora—the settling of scattered Jewish colonies outside Palestine—had begun and the word henceforth would always be synonymous with persecution and homelessness.

Only a few thousand Jews remained when the Ottomans conquered Palestine in 1516 and started four centuries of Turkish rule. But the idea of an autonomous Jewish homeland never died. In 1896 Theodor Herzl, a journalist-playwright living in Vienna, argued eloquently on behalf of Zionism in his pamphlet *The Jews' State*. Most of the world's Jews then lived in czarist Russia (mainly in what is now Poland) and Germany. The movement to create a state based on democratic socialism gathered momentum, and the trickle of Jews returning to Palestine to establish agricultural settlements became a steady stream. By the time British forces captured Jerusalem from the Turks in 1917, the population of Palestine was 535,000 Muslims, 85,000 Jews and 70,000 Christians.

The fact that tradition—though not always historical authenticity—identifies so many sites in and near Jerusalem as the scene of events for all three religions helps explain why the Arabs and Israelis are so intractable today over the fate of Jerusalem and Palestine. For Jews, the Western (Wailing) Wall, the last vestige of the Temple of Solomon, is the most sacred spot on earth. For Christians, the Church of the Holy Sepulcher marks the spot where Jesus died, was buried and rose from the dead. For Muslims, the Dome of the Rock—or the Mosque of Omar—is the place from which Mohammed made his miraculous night journey to Heaven, and it was toward Jerusalem, not Mecca, that the Arabs first turned in prayer. But what Westerners tend to forget is that violence between the Jews and the Muslims was rare until the rise of Zionism, and that Jews suffered far less under Arab and Muslim rulers than under the more "advanced" Christian civilizations represented by Rome, the Byzantine Empire, the Crusaders and, later, Germany.

European governments felt guilt in the early twentieth century over the continuous maltreatment of Western Jews, but no one wanted to absorb them. Neither did the United States, which had strict limits on immigration. That left Palestine. The British, playing Arab and Jewish aspirations against each other to advance the World War I effort and to protect British colonial interests, told the Arabs in 1915 that Palestine would be theirs upon the defeat of the Turks, and then the next year secretly agreed with France and Russia to internationalize the land. In November 1917 Arthur Balfour, the British foreign minister, promised his government's support for the establishment in Palestine of a national home for the Jews on the understanding that "nothing shall be done which may prejudice the civil and religious rights of existing non-Jewish communities in Palestine. . . ." With this policy statement, Britain hoped to encourage Russia to stay in the war and persuade the United States to enter it. In addition, Britain knew that a friendly Jewish Palestine could be useful in keeping open the Suez Canal and the sea routes to India.

The Balfour Declaration was the Jews' deed of trust for Israel. Had the Arabs managed to organize themselves a decade or so earlier and present as convincing a case to the British as the Zionists did, there might never have been a Balfour Declaration. British officials in Palestine never even mentioned the Balfour Declaration until 1920 for fear of a violent Arab reaction.

Arabism—a political movement for a united Arab land—was gaining strength at the same time Zionism was, partly as a natural expression of nationalistic desires in opposition to Ottoman rule and partly in reaction to Zionism. But neither the Zionists nor the Arabists were entirely honest about what they sought. The former spoke of a homeland in Palestine but privately wanted Palestine as the sovereign state of Israel. The latter talked about an independent Arab state while wanting a monarchy that probably would have been despotic and disruptive to the West. Both were possessive, fearful, uncompromising.

"The reawakening of the Arab nation, and the growing Jewish efforts at rebuilding the ancient monarchy of Israel on a very large scale—these two movements are destined to fight each other continually until one of them triumphs over the other," wrote Naguib Azouri, a Christian Ottoman official, in 1915.

In the period between the two world wars, Palestinian Arabs did not, however, think of themselves as "a Palestinian people"; their national identity was more often linked to Syria or other Arab countries. Most were poor, backward and lethargic tenant farmers whose land often was owned by wealthy Arabs living in Cairo or Beirut or in European capitals. In contrast, the Jews worked with astonishing energy on their *kibbutzim* (communal farms) to reclaim the land from the desert and build a viable homeland. They thought of themselves as Jews first and as Hungarians or Poles or whatever second. They were heady with the dream of Zionism—a concept that had only limited Jewish support until the rise of Hitler—and were for the most part insensitive to the Arabs' own aspirations. Riotous clashes between the two groups left hundreds dead in 1920, 1921 and 1929. The Arabs denounced the British as intensely as they did the Zionists, thus pushing their two enemies closer together.

President Woodrow Wilson, who had supported the Balfour Declaration before its publication, sent a commission of inquiry to Palestine during the violence to determine the wishes of its inhabitants. The commission reported that the Arabs were anti-Zionist and that Zionist leaders contemplated the dispossession of the Arabs. A British commission attributed the riots to the Arabs' disappointment over independence and their fear of being dominated economically and politically by the Zionists. Another British commission reported in 1929, "The Arabs have come to see in the Jewish immigration not only a menace to their livelihood but a possible overlord of the future."

Nevertheless some Arabs and Jews did seek accommodation and peace. One promising opportunity was the formation of a united Arab-Jewish front against the weakening Ottoman rule. Arab leaders presented the suggestion to Zionist officials in Paris in 1913, but the latter rejected it, preferring instead to curry the favor of Turkish rulers by portraying Zionism as a barrier to Arab nationalism. Six years later the Arabs' and Jews' nationalistic movements recognized each other and pledged "the closest possible collaboration." A document was drawn up that envisaged a unitary Arab-Jewish state with freedom of religion and schools that taught both Arabic and Hebrew. Arab leaders and moderate Zionists approved the proposal, but an assembly of Palestine Jews rejected it as "ridiculous and dangerous."

Immigration and conflict increased. In 1935 Jewish immigration reached 61,000, and between 1936 and 1939 an Arab general strike and revolt left five thousand Arabs, twelve hundred Jews and five hundred British dead or wounded.[4] The Peel Commission announced that Britain's obligation to Jews and to Arabs was irreconcilable and recommended the partition of Palestine. By 1939 the Jewish population in Palestine had grown to 445,000, and Tel Aviv, with 150,000 inhabitants, had become the first all-Jewish city in the modern world. Britain said in a white paper that year that its pledge for a Jewish homeland had been fulfilled, and that indefinite Jewish immigration and the continued transfer of Arab land to Jews were contrary to the spirit of the League of Nations covenant. It said that future land transfers would be subject to Arab acquiescence and limited to certain areas in Palestine.

The Jews were shocked. The white paper ended the Anglo-Zionist entente, and the Zionists shifted their political efforts to the United States. A scheduled discussion of the white paper in the League of Nations was preempted by the outbreak of World War II.

---

[4] Jewish immigration reached an annual high of more than 225,000 shortly after Israel's independence in 1948. Immigration declined dramatically later, and in 1985 only 11,298 Jews—9,842 of them Ethiopians—moved to Israel, a drop of 41 percent from the previous year. The reduced number of settlers— due at least partly to Israel's troubled economy—combined with the Arabs' high birthrate, raised fears in Israel that the Jewish state one day could have an Arab majority.

Twenty-seven thousand Zionists and twelve thousand Arabs enlisted in the British forces to fight the Nazis. David Ben-Gurion, chairman of the Jewish Agency, said, "We must assist the British in the war as if there were no white paper and must resist the white paper as if there were no war."

Britain had had enough of Palestine after the war. It was losing troops there, violence between Jews and Arabs was worsening, the U.S. Congress was pressuring Whitehall to permit unlimited Jewish immigration. The Arab kings and heads of state met in Egypt in 1946 to reaffirm the Arab character of Palestine and passed a secret resolution threatening British and U.S. interests in the Middle East if Palestinian rights were disregarded. Britain did not want to become further embroiled in the Arab world, and it turned the question of Palestine over to the United Nations.

The U.N. plan to partition Palestine, with the majority of the land going to the Jewish minority, was a nonstarter and would have created a country with a crazy quilt of crisscrossing borders. Despite some reservations, though, the Jews accepted partition because half a loaf was better than no loaf; the Arabs rejected it because half a loaf was not as good as a whole loaf. That rejection today forms the basis for the unofficial Israeli policy that the Palestinians abrogated their right to a homeland and to being "a Palestinian people" by saying no to half of what had once been all theirs. The Israelis contend that the Palestinians already have a homeland—in Jordan.

Civil war broke out soon after the U.N. resolution. The Arab and Jewish armies mobilized and recruited volunteers, and both were responsible for shameful deeds. In addition to blowing up the King David Hotel, Menachem Begin's Irgun guerrillas, an outlawed gang of terrorists, raided the Palestinian village of Deir Yassin near Jerusalem in 1948, killing 254 men, women and children. A few days after the massacre, an Arab group ambushed a bus going to a medical center on Mount Scopus and killed seventy-five Jewish doctors, nurses and professors. The British did little to stop the violence, and on May 13, 1948, General Alan Cunningham, the British high commissioner, folded the Union Jack and left Palestine. The Jewish Agency Executive Committee declared the next day that the parts of Palestine under Jewish control were now the independent state of Israel.[5] The Zionists urged the Arabs of Israel "to preserve the ways of peace and play their part in the development of the state, on the basis of full and equal citizenship and due representation in its bodies and institutions." But distrust on both sides ran too deep for accommodation. On May 15 the armies of Syria, Lebanon, Iraq, Egypt and Transjordan attacked.

Israel's first prime minister, David Ben-Gurion, realized that security was more important than borders and that without security Israel could not emerge and perhaps could not even survive. In a policy that helps explain Israeli actions today, he said that Israel must always retaliate if attacked, to deter the Arabs as well as to teach them an "educational and moral" lesson. He wrote that Jews had come particularly "from countries where shedding Jewish blood was cheap, where others had the legitimate light to torture and beat them. . . . Here we must show them that their blood is not cheap; that there is a Jewish state and army that will not permit [oppressors] to do with them as they please; that their lives and properties have value; that they must walk erect and with pride. We must demonstrate to them . . . that they are now citizens of a sovereign state that is responsible for their lives and their security."[6]

The Arabs, thinking Israel would be an easy conquest, seriously

---

[5] The United States had conducted a strong lobbying effort in the United Nations on behalf of Israel's creation. Washington recognized Israel immediately, and Moscow—then as intensely pro-Israel as Washington—extended recognition four hours later. By the summer of 1949, Israel had been recognized by fifty governments and was a member of the United Nations. Israel had full diplomatic relations with seventy-seven countries in 1986 and unofficial relations with dozens more.

[6] This passage is quoted from a review by Paul Johnson in the *New York Times* of *Israel: The Partitioned State*, by Amos Perlmutter (New York: Charles Scribner's Sons, 1986).

underestimated the Jews' courage, dedication and military skill. They had numerical superiority, but they lost the 1948 war within eight months, and were forced to sign a series of armistices with Israel because they lacked not only political solidarity, military leadership and coordination but also a unifying cause—for their fight had been waged only marginally for the Palestinian people themselves. "King" Abdullah of Transjordan wanted to annex part of Palestine as a step toward realizing his dream of a Greater Syria. Ibn Saud of Saudi Arabia, who had promised to send forty thousand soldiers against Israel but committed only seven hundred, bitterly opposed Abdullah because Abdullah—whose father had lost Medina and Mecca to the Sauds a generation earlier—was from the competing Hashimite family of Mecca. Iraq thought that Arab unity was fine as long as it could be the key player—a role that both Egypt and Syria also wanted. As historian Arthur Goldschmidt, Jr., points out, Arab leaders threatened Israel with defeat and even extinction but what they were really doing was trying to outbluff one another. They wanted the glory and the spoils of victory without having to commit themselves to the Palestinians.

More than seven hundred thousand Arabs fled Palestine between December 1947 and January 1949 to settle in the safety of neighboring countries, often as refugees under the auspices of the United Nations.[7] The Jews had called their exile the Diaspora; the Palestinians called theirs *al-Nakba*—the Disaster.

"I didn't want to leave," a prominent Lebanese banker told me. "But some of my friends—Jewish friends, mind you—came by the house one night. These were people who used to come to dinner, and they said my life was in danger. One of them, I remember, said,

---

[7] By 1959 about half of the Palestinians who had lived in Palestine in 1947 were in refugee camps outside Palestine. Of the other half, roughly one fifth remained in Israel and four fifths were spread throughout the world as expatriates. The largest concentration of Palestinians outside the Middle East (130,000) lives in the United States. By comparison, a larger number of Israelis (170,000) have voluntarily left their homeland since 1948 and settled in the United States.

'Mohammed, we want your land but we do not want to kill you.' So I left the next morning. I took the family and went to Jordan and started over. What else could I do?"

Israel has maintained over the years that the exodus happened because Arab leaders, both inside and outside Palestine, ordered the masses to leave in order to clear the way for the invading armies. The Arabs contend that the flight resulted from a carefully orchestrated Jewish military campaign of expulsion that depopulated 250 villages and several major towns. A classified report prepared by the Israeli Defense Forces in 1948 and kept unpublished until 1986 supports, at least in part, the Arab position. It says upward of 70 percent of the Palestinians fled because of Jewish military action or because of related psychological factors. The report cites surprise attacks, protracted artillery barrages and the use of loudspeakers broadcasting threatening messages as elements that precipitated the Palestinians' departure.

Often an attack on one village would hasten the depopulation of other nearby villages, for the threat of violence was as strong a weapon as violence itself. "The evacuation of a certain village because of an attack by us prompted in its wake neighboring villages [to flee]," the report states.[8]

The truth probably lies midway between the two sides' claims and the exodus was the result of both Jewish militancy and Arab deceitfulness. But regardless, al-Nakba solved one of Israel's most pressing problems—how to get rid of Muslims and Christians in a Jewish state. Only sixty thousand remained after "the disaster," and none of those who left would ever be invited to return. "It was a miraculous clearing of the land," said Chaim Weizmann, Israel's first president, "the miraculous simplification of Israel's task."

The Palestinians found little acceptance in the clannish societies

---

[8] The report, dated June 30, 1948, is entitled *The Arab Exodus from Palestine in the Period 1/12/1947–1/6/48*. It was analyzed in a 1986 edition of *Middle Eastern Studies*, an academic quarterly published in London, by Benny Morris, diplomatic correspondent for the *Jerusalem Post*.

of other Arab countries. Nor did they voluntarily integrate, preferring to remain with their own people. Young men searched refugee camps for women from their own village to marry. The educated elite sought one another out. They knew that the West, the Israelis and even the Arabs had sold them out. They knew there was no need for the squalid refugee camps, for Arab governments had the resources to absorb and settle the Palestinians. But the Arabs were willing to let them languish under a United Nations flag as a symbol of the injustices the Arabs themselves felt they had suffered through the centuries at the hands of outsiders. The Palestinians came to understand they could count on no one but themselves, and in exile Palestinian nationalism was born. Intellectual arguments over whether the Palestinians were "a people" became irrelevant because the Palestinians *felt* that they were a people, a nation. Some modern Palestinians trace their people's claim to Palestine back to the Canaanites, Phoenicians and other pre-Jewish settlers. This is a tenuous link, as their heritage generally goes back to the Arab invaders of the seventh century. Their more valid claim is that after living continuously in Palestine for more than a thousand years, they were driven out or left because of foreign Jews seeking historical justice for the sins of non-Arabs. And in their homelessness, another echo of Zionism came floating back as Palestinians began speaking of *al-Awada*—the Return.

ON NEW Year's Day, 1965, a little thirty-four-year-old pear-shaped man with a stubble beard went from door to door through Beirut's newspaper offices, handing out a press release that he called "Military Communiqúe No. 1." No one had ever heard of the man or his organization, and most of the editors never printed his claim of launching a guerrilla attack to sabotage Israel's national water system. That was just as well, because the attack never took place. It was foiled at the last minute by the Lebanese secret police.

The five-foot-four man, who looked almost comical in baggy guerrilla fatigues and unpolished boots, a *kaffiyeh* headdress covering his bald pate, was Abdul Rahman Arafat al-Qudwa—Yasser Arafat—and his outfit was known as al-Fatah, a group he and a dozen friends had set up in Kuwait six years earlier, convinced that the Palestinians could rely on no outsiders to carry their banner.[9] Promising "a generation of revenge," Arafat wanted to unite the dozens of Palestinian societies and organizations scattered throughout the Middle East and to gain recognition through an armed struggle. That principle was reminiscent of the words Menachem Begin once wrote as a young man: "We fight, therefore we are."

Twelve months before Arafat's inauspicious introduction to the Beirut press, the Arab presidents and kings had accepted Gamal Abdel Nasser's invitation to meet at the Hilton Hotel in Cairo. Most of the world's attention at the summit focused on how the leaders would deter the Israelis from tapping the waters of the river Jordan to nourish their own parched land. (The Arabs couldn't decide what to do and never took firm action.) A more far-reaching event in the Hilton's conference room drew relatively little notice—the establishment of something called the Palestine Liberation Organization. The P.L.O. was to be an umbrella group for the disparate political factions of various Palestinian groups, some of which favored Marxism, others democracy; some were pro-Soviet, others nonaligned; some were dominated by Syria, others by Egypt; some sought confrontation with Israel, others accommodation; some wanted a sectarian state, others one that was secular.

The P.L.O.'s charter stated that the Palestinians had to fight to regain their homeland—with borders stipulated by the British mandate—and that they had a right to self-determination. It called for the abolition of Israel by saying that Jews of Palestinian origin could continue to live within the liberated country, a country that would

[9] Fatah is a reverse acronym for *Harakat Tahrir Fiiastin*, the Movement to Liberate Palestine.

be secular and democratic. Some Palestinians say that the P.L.O. was consciously modeled after the Jewish Agency, the organization that sponsored Jewish immigration into Palestine and coordinated the military actions of several Zionist guerrilla groups.

The P.L.O. started assembling an army drawn from refugees, but the organization largely represented a community of aging politicians who were more moderate than those who would follow, and its accomplishments were few. Of more significance in 1965 and 1966 was Arafat's Fatah, armed by Syria, which launched attacks on Israel from Jordan, causing serious civilian casualties in the Jewish state. In the wake of the Arabs' defeat in the 1967 war—a war that put a million Palestinians under Israeli occupation—the P.L.O. fell into disarray, and Arafat and Fatah gained control. The vehicle they chose to carry their case to the world was terrorism, and at that they became real pros. Their hijackings and killings earned headlines around the globe, and soon no one asked anymore who the Palestinians were. Everyone knew. They were "terrorists."

"As long as the world saw the Palestinians as no more than refugees standing in line for U.N. rations, it was not likely to respect them," Arafat said. "Now that the Palestinians carry rifles, the situation has changed."

That was true, but Arafat's comment underscored a tactical blunder in the P.L.O. game plan. From the beginning Arafat realized that he needed to influence opinion in Western Europe and North America if the Palestinian cause had any hope of succeeding. Perhaps, he reasoned, the New Left and the youths who were protesting the Vietnam war would embrace him as they had Ho Chi Minh, Che Guevara and other contemporary heroes. The problem was that the P.L.O.'s platform was based on a negative—the destruction of Israel, a country universally admired in the West. The goal itself became obscured in the rhetoric and bloodshed of accomplishing the negative. Notoriety and legitimacy were synonymous to the P.L.O. leadership. It was a serious miscalculation. The organization never caught the fancy of Western liberals as, say, the F.L.N. freedom fighters of Algeria did, and Arafat did little to convince the skeptics that the Palestinians' motivation was as noble as that of the Israelis.

However badly Arafat needed the services of a New York public relations firm, he was nonetheless a skilled politician. He relied on intimate, personal leadership, as all Arabs do, and was a master of double-talk, of being at once manipulative and concessionary, of stirring oratory, even though his Arabic was so bad that grammarians of classical Arabic cringed. If you asked him a personal question, he moved quickly to turn the conversation back to politics, and he made it impossible to separate the man from the myth. The P.L.O. says he was born in 1929 in Jerusalem; others cite Cairo or the Gaza Strip as his birthplace. Although Arafat played down his aristocratic heritage, his father was a wealthy merchant, who moved with his family between houses in Jerusalem, Cairo and Gaza, and his mother was a member of the politically powerful Husseini clan.

He studied engineering at Cairo University, was active in the underground Muslim Brotherhood movement, fought Israel in the 1956 war and later moved to Kuwait, where he worked briefly as a civil engineer for the Department of Public Works. It was the only normal job he ever held. He is a Sunni Muslim, though he does not practice devoutly, and he has never owned a car, a house or any material goods to speak of. Indeed, he has slept in a different location every night for years because of well-justified security concerns.

Under Arafat the P.L.O. became the world's best-known, best-armed, wealthiest guerrilla organization. Upward of $1 billion a year, from "taxes" and Arab contributions, swelled its treasury during the peak of the oil-rich years, and its funds were invested everywhere, from the stock exchange on New York's Wall Street (mostly in blue-chip securities) to the fortresslike banks on Beirut's Hamra Street. The P.L.O. purchased a five-story town house worth $3 million on Manhattan's Upper East Side for its U.N. mission and maintained offices in a hundred countries that cost $50 million annually. It paid its guerrillas sixty dollars a month, set up schools and hospitals, and offered Palestinians a complete range of social services, including welfare payments and widow's pensions. It operated courts in Lebanon with P.L.O. judges, prisons with P.L.O. guards, and research centers with P.L.O. academics. The P.L.O. in effect became a corporation, but its bickering leaders could agree on nothing besides the fact that there should be a Palestine. Eventually their role shifted from that of liberation guerrillas to that of corporate executives, and in the process organizational survival became more important to the leadership than the cause itself. After bouncing from country to country on borrowed jets for a decade, embracing any president or king who would give him a minute or two, sometimes telling his pilots to change destinations in mid-flight, Arafat, I think, would be woefully bored if he ever had to settle down as the head of state of a small, sleepy country in the desert.

Many Palestinians questioned the P.L.O.'s tactics and Arafat's leadership, but virtually none, whether moderate or radical, would divorce himself from the organization spiritually, for the P.L.O. had become the framework for the Palestinian people. It gave them, for the first time, an identity. It had fought for them, made the world aware of them, spoken for them when no one cared to listen. Whether the P.L.O. was the "sole legitimate representative" of the Palestinian people, as it claimed, was immaterial. No other Palestinian group ever assumed the responsibility of negotiating on behalf of the majority. Washington and Jerusalem chose to deal with the Palestinians by ignoring the P.L.O. as though it would just disappear one day, and President Reagan characterized the entire organization as a "gang of thugs." To deny the possibility of direct discussions with the P.L.O. is also to deny the possibility of ever solving the so-called Palestinian problem. Would the United States have ever extricated itself from the Vietnam war if it had refused to sit with the North Vietnamese in Paris, even though North Vietnam was killing Americans at the time and insisting that its hundreds of thousands of troops in South Vietnam did not exist?

"By not negotiating with the P.L.O. you're making the same mistake Britain did in India when it was an empire," Mustafa Amin, Egypt's venerated and pro-Western newspaper columnist, remarked to me. "The British refused to talk to Gandhi and they got Nehru. When you get a radical leader, you often look back on the man you could have talked to yesterday and discover that by comparison he was a moderate. It's also easier to reach an agreement with a popular, strong leader than with a weak, unpopular one who may be a dictator."

Arafat did become more flexible in the mid-1970s—though moderate would hardly be an appropriate word—by shifting his emphasis from confrontation to diplomacy. As a result, the P.L.O. gained some sort of diplomatic recognition from upward of one hundred countries. Arafat addressed the United Nations in his guerrilla fatigues and told the membership, "I come to you carrying an olive branch and a gun; do not let the olive branch drop." He was received by the Pope, and was often treated as a head of state in his frenetic travels. Countless officials outside the Arab world—and later some leaders in it—counseled him to recognize Israel's right to exist and accept the two U.N. Security Council resolutions, 242 and 338, that could form a basis for peace in the Middle East.[10] But

[10] Resolution 242, passed unanimously in 1967 and written with deliberate diplomatic ambiguity, calls for the return to the Arabs of Israeli-captured territory in return for each state's right to live in peace. The P.L.O. objects to it because it speaks of them only as refugees, citing the need for "a just settlement of the refugee problem." Resolution 338, passed after the 1973 Arab-Israeli war, calls for direct talks between Israel and the Arabs. It says the Arabs must recognize Israel's right to exist and Israel must recognize Palestinian claims to express themselves freely in a portion of their homeland.

if Arafat, as evidence suggests, really did want to move in that direction, a move that would have required renouncing the P.L.O. charter and accepting the fragmentation of the organization into radical and moderate camps, there were those who worked hard to ensure that he remained as immobilized as a hamster in a spinning cage, running at top speed and going nowhere.

Israel had no greater nightmare than that of Arafat suddenly accepting the two U.N. resolutions. How could the Israelis then refuse to negotiate with him? How could they continue to portray the P.L.O. as a terrorist organization? Whom would they strike back against when Palestinian groups other than Fatah carried out acts of political violence? How could the United States continue to honor the written promise Secretary of State Henry Kissinger gave Jerusalem in 1975 that Washington would ignore the existence of the P.L.O. as long as the P.L.O. ignored the existence of Israel? Psychologically Arafat the Terrorist was less threatening to Israel than Arafat the Peacemaker.

As the terrorist, Arafat could be clearly the enemy, a daily reminder to the Israelis of the evils challenging their sovereignty, even though the P.L.O. does not represent a genuine challenge to the existence of Israel any more than the Black Panthers or the Weathermen did to the United States in the 1960s. As the peacemaker, however, he could assume the image of statesman and draw legitimate international support. If he shaved and put on a coat and tie, he would probably even change the warped perception of the Western television-viewing public that all Palestinians are unkempt hooligans. And the Israelis would eventually be forced to confront a deep, haunting memory seldom spoken of—that they took the land of others just as surely as the Romans had taken theirs two thousand years earlier. Arafat has long maintained that the recognition of Israel is his last hole card, and he can't play it without getting something in return. I think he's wrong. If he doesn't put his hole card on the table, there will be no game left to play.

It is, of course, to Israel's advantage that the P.L.O.—and later, the

Palestinian Authority—remain in chaos and that Arafat be held responsible for all terrorism, even though most of it is committed not by Fatah but by extremist groups dedicated to wrecking the peace process. In terms of how the West perceives the role of the Arabs and the Israelis in the Middle East conflict, Arafat has been a godsend to Israel, just as Menachem Begin was a blessing to the Arabs. It is no wonder that the Israeli sniper who had Arafat targeted in the crosshairs of his rifle's telescopic sight during the P.L.O.'s evacuation from Beirut in 1982 never pulled the trigger.

What seems likely is that Israel will never let Arafat make peace, and neither will the radical elements of the P.L.O. Nor will the Arab countries that want to control and manipulate the Palestinians for their own purposes. And so Arafat has become an anachronism, a parody of himself, shuttling from capital to capital, trying to appease his enemies and flatter his friends, never quite committing himself, never making his strategy quite clear, often sounding as though he were in a time warp and the year was 1948. He has talked out of so many sides of his mouth for so long that he has become a captive of his own rhetoric; when he speaks now in words couched in ambiguity about the need for moderation, no one understands what he has said.

The real victims are the Palestinian people themselves. Their leaders have failed them, their Arab brethren have deserted them. For years the P.L.O. was willing to keep Palestinians in dismal refugee camps—where its constituency was strongest—because that symbol of homelessness was what gave the organization its power. The P.L.O.'s military campaign has been a disaster and the *intifadas*—the stone-throwing boys of Palestine versus the gun-wielding men of Israel—have served Arafat well in the international arena of public opinion but failed in the arena that really matters: Israel. Moderate Israelis who wanted to accommodate Palestinian aspirations felt betrayed, and as suicide bombers took the lives of scores of innocent Israelis, the attitudes of the entire nation hardened. In its new home in the Gaza Strip, Arafat's Palestinian

Authority lacked diplomatic daring and the apparent awareness that peace is not a unilateral process. Israel has suppressed the emergence of Palestinian leaders in the occupied West Bank, and moderate Palestinians who would have made worthy leaders have been murdered by radical Palestinians simply because they were willing to admit what the rest of the world has known for four decades — that Israel exists and will continue to exist. Still, a Palestinian state is within reach, and today few in Arafat's Fatah wing speak of destroying Israel. They speak instead of a homeland in *part of* Palestine. Yet the P.L.O. remains a step too short, too late, always overtaken by events, and the peace plan it eventually accepts is invariably the one that was offered last year.

FIVE MONTHS after the P.L.O. was forced from Beirut, a contingent of four hundred journalists descended on Algiers, the run-down capital of Algeria, for the sixteenth congress of the Palestine National Council, a sort of Palestinian parliament-in-exile. The city was bedecked with banners that declared, "The liberation of Palestine is every Muslim's duty," and no one mentioned that the congress's first meeting, in 1948, had been *in* Palestine (in Jerusalem). The Saudis announced on the eve of the conference that they were making their quarterly payment of $28 million to the P.L.O., and this welcome news produced a mood of good cheer and much talk of continued resistance, almost as though the ghost of the Beirut debacle was not lurking there, hearing every word. "We left Beirut with our arms and complete honor so our Lebanese brothers would not have to suffer anymore," Khaled Fahoum, the council chairman, told the applauding delegates, offering an interpretation of history that was not precisely as I remembered it.

An official publication distributed to us at the opening sessions explained that the council was among the most democratic political organizations in the world, "since its members are the representatives of various heavily armed desperado groups." But if the three-hundred-odd delegates to the congress were desperadoes—or terrorists, as Israel and the United States called them—they certainly did not reflect it in dress or speech. True, Arafat wore his traditional black-and-white headdress and his holster, and one woman lamented that she had to give up hijacking planes when she became pregnant, but the majority displayed all the characteristics, including an expanding waistline, of a middle-class existence. Arafat's brother, Fathi, a doctor, showed up on a flight from Rome carrying an attaché case and wearing an English-style sport cap and a tweed jacket. With only a few exceptions the men wore conservative Western business suits. There was a generous display of elegant fur coats among the women. The delegates, who lived in Europe, the United States and various Arab capitals—Israel wouldn't let any Palestinians from the West Bank attend—looked as a group about as revolutionary as an opening-night theater crowd in London.

What struck me about the council was that it was indeed far more democratic than any government in the Arab world. Only Israel's Knesset (parliament) would have surpassed it as an expression of consensus. The delegates represented a wide range of political beliefs, and decisions were made by the' majority. The sessions and the votes were open to the scrutiny of the international media. Arafat, the P.L.O. chairman, sat at the center of a long, crowded conference table, running the show like a ward boss, turning back challenges to his leadership, patching together deals among grumbling dissenters. But in the end, the Palestine National Congress, facing a crucial moment in the Palestinians' history, really couldn't decide what to do next, where to take the movement or how to rejuvenate the cause. Delegates had to fill the long hours with talk of summer victories that never were, of unity and independence, of time-worn promises and threats.

"Our armed struggle will go on," thundered George Habash, the P.L.O's aging and ailing Christian war-horse. He had hobbled to the podium with a cane, and aides dried his brow with handkerchiefs during his two-hour speech. Sitting there in the smoky conference hall two thousand miles from Jerusalem, listening to Habash and watching the delegates who hung on each word, I could not help remembering the White Russians, the anti-Communists who gathered in Paris after the 1917 Bolshevik Revolution, always thinking they were going home, always waiting for the collapse of Lenin's government.

The struggle did go on, but not quite as Habash had envisioned it. Despite spasms of violence, the war-weariness of the Israelis and the Palestinians started nudging both sides toward peace. Polls showed that the majority of Israelis favored accommodation with the Palestinians, even an independent Palestine. By the time I returned to the Arab world on an extended assignment in the mid-1990s, the hateful climate had changed and the seeds of peace were in the air.

Jordan and Israel had signed a peace treaty in 1994, ending a forty-six-year state of war. The year before that, in September 1993, the so-called Oslo accords had been concluded with a handshake between Yasser Arafat and Israeli prime minister Yitzhak Rabin on the south lawn of the White House. It was an historic moment. The Palestinians had recognized Israel's right to exist, and the Israelis had recognized the P.L.O. as the representative of the Palestinian people. As part of the peace process, Israel would hand over seven major West Bank towns to Palestinian authority. A final settlement would be reached within five years, it was agreed.

"We the soldiers who have returned from the battle stained with blood," Rabin said, "we who have fought against you, the Palestinians, we say to you today in a loud and clear voice: Enough of blood and tears! Enough!" Arafat did not match Rabin's rhetorical heights but he did remind his audience: "We will need more courage and determination to continue the course of building coexistence and peace between us. . . ."

But there were extremists on both sides unwilling to summon the courage and determination that peace required. Israel continued to humiliate the Palestinians, holding them in a form of economic colonialism while dithering over returning occupied land and continuing to build settlements. Arafat, as usual, played it both ways, talking of peace while refusing to clamp down on Hamas, whose radicals were intent on torpedoing the peace process. Their new weapon was human—young suicide bombers sent into Israel to blow up themselves up along with as many innocent civilians as possible.

Still, the two sides staggered toward peace. In May 2000, Israel ended its twenty-two-year occupation of southern Lebanon. Two months later, under the auspices of President Clinton at Camp David, Arafat and Israeli prime minister Ehud Barak spent two weeks negotiating a final peace deal. Barak offered almost everything Arafat had been demanding, except Jerusalem itself. Peace was within reach. Arafat said no: the offer was not good enough. Violence resumed. By September another one hundred and fifty Palestinians and Israelis had been killed. The toll mounted by the day, reaching more than nine hundred by November 2001.

DESERT DAZZLE

Gold leads into gold, then into restlessness, and finally into crushing misery.

—*Kahlil Gibran (1883–1931)*
Lebanese philosopher

ON A June morning in 1932, on a forsaken Persian Gulf island known as Bahrain, the Arab world had an encounter with destiny that would shape its future as surely as would the eventual extinction of Palestine. Bahrain was a tiny place, just one sixth the size of Yosemite National Park in California. There were some date palms and some clusters of little sandbrick homes inhabited by pearl divers and local traders, but mostly Bahrain was flat and hot and empty. The only prominent landmark was a hill that rose 445 feet and had the grand name of the Mountain of Smoke.

A team from Standard of California (Socal) had come to Bahrain the previous autumn and set up its equipment below the hill. For nine months the men's drills chewed deeper and deeper, through pockets of tar, boulders and limestone, and their only reward had been buckets of sweat and piles of stone and soil. They cursed the fates that had brought them to this infernal desert, and no wonder. The Persian Gulf shiekdoms were a medieval frontier in those days with few attractions except sand, heat and flies.

Bahrain had no paved roads, electricity, flush toilets or radios.

Doha, the capital of Qatar, was a fishing village whose literacy rate was zero. The palace of Abu Dhabi's ruler was made of mud. Oman was populated by tribes that settled their disputes with swords. Poverty was universal throughout the Gulf, and the few schools that did exist there taught only the boys—and taught them nothing beyond how to recite the Koran. The backwaters were among those other-worlds that seemed to five only in the pages of the *National Geographic*, and the ruling sheiks had no intention of having it otherwise; they let few people out of their fiefdoms and so few were allowed in that the early Western prospectors wore beards and Arab robes to avoid being unnecessarily conspicuous to the xenophobic nomads of the Gulf.

The sun was already high overhead, burning hot, at six o'clock on that June morning in 1932 when the Californians' steel bit pierced a layer of blue shale. There was a mighty rumble, and from the bowels of the earth, two thousand feet down, erupted a jet-black torrent that would change the course of history. The men had sunk the well called Jabal and Dukham No. 1 and brought home a treasure, Arabia's first barrel of oil.

Mohammed Khajah, a former pearl diver whose business empire now includes supermarkets and an air-conditioner factory, remembers that first strike with a certain sense of amusement. "We didn't think it was any big event at the time," the elderly millionaire said, sitting behind a cash register in his market. A shiny new Mercedes-Benz was parked outside. "Who needed oil? We didn't even have any cars on Bahrain then. We'd have been more excited if Socal had struck water."

But that strike began what would be the greatest bonanza the world had ever known. Oil would become to the Arab world what coal had been to Europe in the Industrial Revolution and gold had been to the United States in settling the West. It would transform a society, challenge a people's values, divide classes and nations on the basis of wealth, and lead to breathtaking growth and development in the Gulf states and Saudi Arabia.[1] It would also make the Gulf Arabs the poor rich—people with money but no skills—and one day would force them to ask themselves whether such sudden wealth was a blessing or a curse.

THE FIVE city-states along the Gulf—Bahrain, Kuwait, Oman, Qatar and the United Arab Emirates—have a combined population of 8.2 million and occupy a land area slightly smaller than that of California. On a per capita basis, they are the richest collection of neighbors in the world. Although Bahrain was once the site of a four-thousand-year-old trading civilization known as Dilman, and Oman was a land of seafarers whose territory stretched into East Africa in the seventeenth century, the region has little real history except that of wandering, warring Bedouin tribes, who traced their roots back to Persia (Iran) and the Arabian Peninsula.

Along with the Saudis, they call themselves Arabians—the real Arabs, a people born in and shaped by a desert that has produced few ideas except for the universality of religion. They are the founders of Islam and the protectors of the Arab mystique, and they seem more secure in their identity than other Arabs I have met elsewhere. "We have no illusions about who we are," Bahrain's minister of development, Youssef Shirawi, said. "We are Bedouin. We are tribal. We are Islamic. We are Arabians. We are backward." While Egyptians and Lebanese and others may ridicule them for being unpolished upstarts, they find pride and strength in their Bedouin heritage. An Arabian proverb, expressing the carrot-and-stick approach to tribal power in the desert, says, "Show your enemy your sword and your gold," and the rulers in the Gulf and on the penin-

[1] Iran and Iraq were the first states in the region to strike oil, in 1908 and 1927, respectively. After Bahrain's strike in 1932 came Saudi Arabia in 1936, Kuwait in 1938, Qatar in 1939, Abu Dhabi in 1958 and Oman in 1964. The world's first oil well, incidentally, was drilled in Pennsylvania in 1859.

sula do precisely that. As the guardians of the two major forces in the Arab world—Islam and petrodollars—they keep friends contented and enemies appeased with the same style of guile and wisdom that their ancestors had used to protect and survive in their huge tribal *dirahs*, or ranges.

Bedouin society was basically democratic in the old days. The authority of rulers rested on the consent of their fellow tribesmen and could be challenged at any time, Collective responsibility was an important force, and women played a vital role in the community, often taking part in consultations on major decisions. In addition to fetching water, milking the animals, raising the children and spinning yarn, women were expected to pitch and tend to the family's black hair tent—the House of Hair—which was divided inside into three sections: the men's quarters, the family room and the kitchen. Women often accompanied their tribes to the battlefield to cheer their warriors on.

In olden times the tribes and clans that proved themselves the toughest warriors were the ones who ended up being the rulers. The clans become dynasties, and the dynasties became the royal families of today's sheikdoms and emirates and monarchies. It is a politically incestuous state of affairs: as rulers of neighboring sheikdoms are often distant cousins, power changes hands only within members of the royal family, and fathers, sons and uncles fill all the top posts of government. The Sabah family, for instance, has ruled Kuwait since 1751, and Sabahs today occupy the governmental positions of prime minister, deputy prime minister, minister of foreign affairs, minister of interior, minister of defense, minister of oil, minister of information and minister of social affairs. The Sabahs' cousins, the Khalifas from the Otoub tribe, captured Bahrain from the Persians in 1783, and the Khalifas have governed the island ever since, The sultan of Oman took power by overthrowing his father in 1970, the emir of Qatar by disposing of a cousin in 1972. Most of the major families are related in Qatar, and it is said that if one

member of the royal Thani family gets a nosebleed, every other
nose in the country bleeds as well.

The Portuguese, Persians and Turks all occupied parts of the
Gulf states at various times, starting in the early 1500s, but the most
lasting foreign imprint was left by the British. They had come to
thwart growing French influence and to protect their trade routes
from Arab and European pirates who operated in the Gulf from the
seventeenth to nineteenth centuries. Needing protection, the small
vulnerable and impoverished desert kingdoms signed a series of
agreements and treaties with the British that would remain in effect
until 1971, when the once great maritime power withdrew its forces
to a new line "east of Suez."[2] What emerged along the Gulf was a
cluster of independent city-states, defined on tribal lines, that were
nations more in name than in spirit. As a unit, though, they and
Saudi Arabia constitute the most cohesive entity in the Arab world.
Endowed with 70 percent of the Middle East's known oil reserves,
their internal interests and external concerns are shared, and their
region is the only place in the Arab world where the concept of
political Arab unity bears any semblance to reality.[3]

Predictably enough, the Western companies that controlled the
Arabian oil industry in its early years of development were not generous. They kept most of the profits, doling out comparatively small
slices to the ruling sheiks. Socal's first concession with Saudi Arabia
in 1933 paid the sheik of Jeddah one dollar per *ton* of oil produced.
(Crude oil was then selling in the United States for fifty cents a *bar-*

[2] The earliest British accord in the Gulf was a treaty of friendship signed with
Oman in 1798. In 1853 Britain signed a "perpetual maritime truce" with the
sheikdoms that now make up the United Arab Emirates.
[3] Largely because of fears generated by Iran's announced desire to export its
Islamic revolution, the five Gulf states and Saudi Arabia established in 1981
the Gulf Cooperation Council to coordinate planning on political, social, economic and defense issues. Headquartered in Riyadh, the council has proved
far more effective than other Arab regional bodies that have been splintered by
political differences.

rel.) As often as not, the sheiks kept their cut as a personal treasury rather than putting it into national development and risking a change in their people's simple life-styles. Sheik Shakhbut ibn Sultan of Abu Dhabi used to store the money oil companies paid him under his bed until mice started nibbling away at it. He then put it into a bank but still refused to spend, saying, "I am a Bedou. All my people are Bedou. We are accustomed to living with a camel or a goat in the desert. If we spend the money, it is going to ruin my people, and they are not going to like it."

But change was coming. Britain converted its naval fleet from coal to oil after World War I; the United States was developing into a major industrial power; the world's thirst for oil would soon be insatiable. Prices edged upward. Westerners today usually hold the Arabs responsible for gouging the industrialized world with exorbitant prices for their petroleum, but that perception needs some correcting. First, it was the Western oil companies that initially did the gouging, not the Arabs. And second, it was the United States' non-Arab ally, Iran, that took the initial steps that made the wild increases of the 1970s possible.

Revolutionary Iranian nationals, campaigning under the banner of anti-imperialism, began agitating in 1951 to end Britain's control over the Anglo-Iranian Oil Company. The tension quickly spread to the Arabian Peninsula, where the Saudi ruler, Ibn Saud, learned that Aramco (the Arabian American Oil Company) was paying more in taxes to the United States than it was giving to Saudi Arabia in royalties. Rather than increasing its royalties and thus decreasing profits, Aramco agreed to pay Saudi Arabia a per-barrel tax, which the company could write off against its U.S. taxes. This deal doubled Saudi Arabia's income while costing the U.S. government $200 million in lost revenue. The Saudis were mollified. Political calm returned to the Middle East when the United States' Central Intelligence Agency helped overthrow the two-year premiership of Mohammed Mossadeq in Iran in 1953 and returned the pro-Western shah, Reza Pahlavi, to the throne. (The West had been instrumental in establishing the Pahlavi "dynasty" in the first place, in 1925.)

The shah was a weak and indecisive man who needed to exert his authority and show his independence from Washington. In 1957 he pushed through a new law that revolutionized the oil industry by making Iran at least a half partner in all future concessions with international oil companies. Nationalization of the industry spread from Iran to the Arabian Peninsula and the oil fields of North Africa. The Iranians and Arabs were at last realizing the political power of oil and were taking control of their own economic destinies.

The Arab-dominated OPEC cartel—the Organization of Petroleum Exporting Countries—tried to punish Israel's supporters in the 1967 Arab-Israeli war by cutting off sales to the West.[4] There was, though, an oil glut in the world then, and the boycott lasted only a week, costing Saudi Arabia $30 million and Kuwait $7 million. It was not until the next Arab-Israeli war, six years later, that OPEC managed to create economic chaos in the West. This time, with demand for oil growing and the West already talking about an energy crisis, OPEC combined production cuts with a quadrupling of prices. The push for huge price increases was led by the pro-American shah of Iran, who had to overcome Saudi Arabian demands for fiscal restraint. For the first time the so-called First World was being held hostage by the Third World, and editorial cartoons of "the ugly A-rab" in the American press all asked basically the same question: What right do these unsophisticated ingrates have to do *this* to *us*? The irony is that there never was a shortage of oil in the West. It was the *anticipation* of a shortage that caused the panic. (The world had an eighty-eight-day supply of oil in the panic of 1979, when OPEC prices jumped from $18 to $34 a barrel and there was a perceived petroleum shortage. In 1983, when prices fell because of an oil glut, the world had a ninety-three-day supply. A

---

[4] The seven Arab nations in the thirteen-member OPEC cartel are Algeria, Iraq, Kuwait, Libya, Qatar, Saudi Arabia and the United Arab Emirates. The non-Arab members are Ecuador, Gabon, Indonesia, Iran, Nigeria and Venezuela.

margin of just five days made the psychological difference between panic and composure in the West.)

In instituting their 1973 embargo, the Arabs seriously misjudged the West's reaction. *Al-Ahram*, Egypt's leading daily paper, said in urging the boycott that U.S. students, forced to study in unheated classrooms, would begin demonstrating on behalf of the Arabs against Israel, just as they had protested against the war in Vietnam. But the embargo only served to harden the attitude that the Arabs were the enemy. Part of the anti-Arab reaction was due, I think, to the fact that the West had become so used to manipulating and exploiting developing nations for its own political and economic gain that it simply could not comprehend a reversal of roles. Its multinational corporations and its arms salesmen reaped huge profits from the Third World. Its missionaries traipsed through the hinterlands, imposing their standards on peoples who were ignorant and susceptible. As the late Jomo Kenyatta, Kenya's founding father, once said, "When the missionaries arrived, the Africans had the land and the missionaries had the Bible. They taught us to pray with our eyes closed. When we opened them, they had the land and we had the Bible." The West's governments carved up undeveloped regions with artificial boundaries, fought superpower proxy wars on their turf, played one country off against another and supported repressive dictators for reasons that had nothing to do with the inhabitants' well-being. The oil embargo was the Third World's revenge. Had Brazil been able to do with its coffee or Ghana with its cocoa or Liberia with its rubber what the Arabs did with their oil, I suspect that each would not have hesitated for a moment before increasing prices and limiting production.

Between 1973 and 1979, the price of a forty-two-gallon barrel of oil exploded, going from less than $3 to as much as $39 on the spot market. With daily production of thirty-two million barrels, OPEC members were earning $8.7 billion a day, $2.62 billion a month, $3.1 trillion a year. The price they set was the price they got. The Arab oil producers were suddenly awash with more money than they could absorb. Everyone had hit the lottery and won first prize—a trunkful of blank checks. Life was a gold-plated fairy tale.

THE FLIGHT from Cairo or Beirut to the Gulf states takes only a couple of hours, and in that time the traveler is transported to what might as well be a different planet. He leaves behind a world of decay and dulled tones and steps into one of glitter and dazzle. On what used to be endless plots of barren desert, cities as modern as Dallas now reach skyward, shimmering oases of marble and glass. They purr with air conditioners and bristle with television antennas. There are indoor skating rinks, space-age hotels such as the $150 million, pyramid-shaped Sheraton in Doha and elegant restaurants that offer lobster from Maine, beef from Australia and cheeses from France. Multilevel shopping malls are stuffed with the latest fashions from Paris, electronic gadgets from Japan, video movies from the United States.

I had telexed several of the sheikdoms one August, saying I wanted to make my first visit to the Gulf. Their replies all said, with slight variations, "Suggest you delay trip until October when weather better." I proceeded anyway and met a young Bahraini millionaire on the Gulf Air flight from Egypt. "You don't get these vegetables in *Cairo*, do you?" he asked the hostess, picking at his salad as though he suspected that some terrible creature was hiding under the leaf of lettuce. "Goodness, no," she said. "We don't cater *anything* there." Thus assured, he started to eat. Fareed Khajah wore a Western business suit and apologized profusely when he spilled his third beer over me. He was pleased that I had so many questions about what life in the Gulf was like, and when I told him I wanted to meet people other than government officials, he offered to pick me up the next morning at my hotel.

As promised, at 10:00 A.M., he pulled up outside the Bahrain Hilton and honked. He stayed in his car, windows rolled up, air conditioner on. I had been waiting by the glass revolving door, reluctant to prematurely leave the lobby, where the Pakistani and Thai staff had stacked ice-cold towels on a table for heat-struck guests. Khajah motioned to me and I stepped outside. The 120-degree blast hit me like an executioner's sword, taking my breath away. My dark glasses steamed over instantly and became blinders. I felt for the door of Khajah's white convertible and stumbled in.

"Terrible, isn't it?" he said, putting down the receiver of his mobile phone. "These summers in the Gulf are the worst in the world." It was I who now wore the Western suit and who sweated. *He* wore the traditional loose-fitting, ankle-length white skirt (a *dishdasha*), and a square checked headcloth. I envied him; he looked cool and comfortable.

The Mercedes, the newest of his twenty-one cars, glided out of the hotel driveway and headed north along the Persian Gulf. The coastline was sprinkled with tar balls from an Iranian oil slick. We moved past tall office buildings, an elegant yacht club, American-run luxury hotels (Bahrain's first hotel wasn't built until 1969), drove through a sprawling industrial park with a power station and aluminum plant and, fifteen minutes later, reached the tip of the island and Khajah's factory. He had a thousand employees, contract workers from the Philippines, and their T-shirts bore the message WE DON'T JUST BLOW . . . WE COOL. Khajah and his two brothers made air conditioners. One of their biggest customers was Saudi Arabia, which had a population of only ten million but was the world's third largest market for air conditioners.

"We started in a back room, and for five years we worked from six in the morning until nine at night," Khajah said. He checked inventory as we walked through the factory. It was not air-conditioned, and the workers sweated profusely. "Even now, we're still here at eight at night. My father taught us that unless you work for something, you don't appreciate it, and I believe in that philosophy. I know Americans think Arabs are lazy. Well, all I can tell you is that many of us— maybe most of us—worked hard and honestly for what we have, and I think we'd have been successful whether we had oil or not."

I asked Khajah if he would take me to meet his father, whose supermarket was on the other side of Manama. No sooner had we gotten into his Mercedes than the mobile phone rang.

"Excuse me," he said. ". . . George? Good morning . . . It's broken? You'll die in this heat without it. Which unit is it, the 510 in the bedroom? OK, that sounds like you only need a new blower. We've got a replacement in the factory. I'll get it over to you this afternoon."

Khajah hung up. The caller, he said, was a member of the royal family. And in a small, personal place like Bahrain—indeed, in the Arab world as a whole—no one likes to go through channels to a middle man. Everyone goes right to the top. Even a common laborer ordering a $1.89 spare part doesn't expect a deal with a supply clerk. He wants to talk to the chief executive officer.

Traffic was heavy heading across town. Khajah pointed out a little boatyard where fishermen made *dhows*—one of the few sights to remind you that Manama is more then ten or eleven years old— and he slowed down by a traffic circle to show me the former mud-walled palace of the emir, now fenced off and abandoned, its gardens overgrown with weeds. There was talk of turning it into a museum. "My father remembers when you could have bought all of Bahrain for about five hundred dinars [$1,100]," Khajah said. "Everything was very slow and small then. He says you could take a walk and see only two things—the Gulf and the desert. Personally I think that would have been awfully boring. The action people my age have known is a lot more exciting."

TO MAKE room for the new, the old was bulldozed away in the Gulf states, and with it went much of the culture and many traditions. Yesterday never was and tomorrow was here already. Hospitals equipped with the latest technology, billion-dollar universities, grassy parks dotted with date palms, towering banks and sparkling airports with daily service to Asia, Europe and Australia attested to the pell-mell dash into the twenty-first century. Women who used to poke through the souks for spices now shopped for lingerie in department stores. Men whose fathers had known no world beyond their hair tents now thought nothing of making a business trip to London—perhaps even buying a plane to get there. And architects brought in from the West to rebuild the oil kingdoms were challenged with an unknown professional problem: how to maintain the sexual segregation of Bedouin tented existence by constructing public buildings and private villas that had separate areas—and sometimes even separate entrances—for women.

Driving through Dubai in the Emirates one day, my Pakistani cabdriver pointed to a modern eight-story building across the street. "That used to be our best hotel, a five-star hotel," he said. "But no one stays there anymore. It's too old."

"When was it built?" I asked.

"Oh, about five years ago, I think."

The 1970s was the Disposal Decade for the oil producers. Everyone had so much money that household furniture was often discarded and replaced every six or seven months; wardrobes were changed whenever a new line of designs arrived from Europe, and Cadillacs, Rolls-Royces and Mercedes-Benzes were simply junked in mint condition if they broke down or needed an oil change. The Boeing Company alone sold three hundred jets in the Gulf between 1961 and 1980, and this former backwater became the fastest-growing commercial air route in the world, handling twenty million passengers a year. King Fahd of Saudi Arabia hired the Los Angeles artist who had designed the floating space city in *Star Trek* to refurbish his Boeing 747 with gold-plated hardware, a three-story elevator, plastic chandeliers and ceiling mirrors, a medical operating theater, a bulletproof escalatorlike container to carry His Highness from the ground to the plane, and small dials in the two staterooms and the formal dining room that pointed toward Mecca.

Another member of the royal family spent nine hundred thousand dollars refitting a Boeing 707 for a tour of Europe but got bored with the idea of traveling and abandoned the jetliner on the tarmac of Britain's Luton Airport.

In Kuwait speculators set up a makeshift stock exchange in the lobby of a downtown parking garage. They called it Souk al-Manakh, literally, the "resting place for camels," because not too many years ago Bedouin had left their camels nearby when they came into town for supplies. The exchange listed three dozen non-Kuwaiti companies in the Persian Gulf that for the most part existed only on paper. There were, for instance, shares available in a tire company that never produced a tire and shares in a poultry firm that owned no hens. But with so much money around and no place to invest it domestically, traders started bidding up the prices of the companies' stock to insanely inflated levels. Playing the wild, unregulated market became the national pastime, and Arabs arrived from other capitals with suitcases full of money to cash in on the windfall.

In the space of a week, or even a day, prices of shares doubled, tripled, and kept right on flying. Students slipped out of class to get the latest quotations, and in the course of a day you'd pass dozens of pedestrians with portable phones, all on the line to their brokers. To cover their purchases, buyers postdated checks by a year or two, paying a premium of perhaps 300 percent more than the value of the stock on the assumption that it would be worth that much more by the time the check was presented for payments.

This made the sellers happy because they could sell the checks at a discount and buy more stock. And the buyers were happy as well because they got the stock at once and could mortgage it to buy more. Everyone in effect was a banker, and the currency was Monopoly money. A passport clerk named Jassim Mutawa suddenly found himself worth on paper $38 billion. An architect parlayed a fifty-thousand-dollar investment into $250 million in a year's time, and a merchant celebrated his good fortune at Souk al-Manakh by buying sixty Rolls-Royces and giving them away to friends.

"The whole thing was a dream, really a dream," the publisher of the *Kuwait Times*, Yousef Alyan, said with a delighted chuckle, recalling the day he sold some shares for four hundred thousand dollars that had cost him forty thousand a week earlier.

"You know, I had a friend who was ahead eight hundred million dinars [about $3 billion]. 'Do you know how much money that is?' I said. 'Look, why don't you just cash in? You couldn't spend all that in a thousand years if you tried.' He said, no, he wanted to hit a billion dinars. So he hung in and, of course, he lost it all. Today he's $52 million in debt. But he doesn't seem terribly worried. He says everything will work out."

The dream ended in mid-1982. Kuwait's proximity to the Iran-Iraq war was causing nervous investors to look for more secure markets abroad. A sudden shortage of liquidity sent panic-stricken traders to the bank to cash in postdated checks before they were due (which is legal in Kuwait). But debtors didn't have adequate funds to cover the twenty-eight thousand checks that had a paper value of $91 billion. The market collapsed, and with it went the fantasies of many men. Jassim Mutawa, the passport clerk, ended up $25 billion in debt; his bankruptcy petition is said to be the largest ever filed anywhere. But unlike Wall Street's crash in 1929, no one jumped out of windows and no one ended up selling apples on street corners. The government set up an emergency fund to bail out "small" investors with individual losses of less than $6.8 million, and there was the general feeling that in the long run no one would be too badly scorched. As one retired broker told me, "What's a few million among friends?"

In putting all this in perspective, it is worth noting, as F. Scott Fitzgerald did, that the rich are different from you and me. And, as Ernest Hemingway responded, "Yes, they have more money." The Kuwaitis had a per capita income of about $24,000 — roughly twice what it is in the United States and seventy-seven times that in Yemen, the poorest Arab country. For them the spectacular and the extravagant were the trademarks of development and maturity. Even middle-class homes had marbled driveways and a fleet of luxury cars outside. Everyone you met was the executive director of one company or another, and virtually every businessman had a phone in his car, a telex in his office and a few million in the bank. "You really had to make an effort *not* to get rich in the seventies," a salesman of construction equipment said.

On top of that, the huge surplus of funds enabled the Saudi and Gulf governments to establish cradle-to-grave welfare societies that made the Scandinavian countries look like skinflints. There were no taxes of any sort; every citizen was guaranteed a job and an education, and medical care was free; food was subsidized and gasoline cost twenty-five cents a gallon. Anyone could get a free plot of land, a ninety-thousand-dollar interest-free loan to build a home or a grant to start a business just by asking the ruler. University students in Riyadh received a three-hundred-dollar-a-month stipend, and married couples started their lives together with a government gift of seven thousand dollars. When Saudi Arabia's soccer team unexpectedly won a zonal elimination tournament in 1984 to earn a trip to the Olympics in Los Angeles, Crown Prince Abdullah showed his delight by giving each of the starters manila envelopes stuffed with fourteen thousand dollars in cash. The head of the soccer federation gave each player a bag of gold worth about ten thousand dollars; King Fahd chipped in with Rolex watches and plots of land worth one hundred thousand dollars apiece.

What the governments really accomplished with such largess was to buy off everyone. Religious leaders were bought off with grand new mosques and immense sums poured into Islamic affairs. The middle class and the Shiite minority were bought off with the generous perks of a welfare state, the military with an elitist, affluent status in society. (A Saudi private in the army earns twenty thousand dollars a year and receives a fully furnished house with eighteen-hundred square feet of space.) Royal families took hefty cuts of multimillion-dollar foreign contracts in the form of "commissions," but the pie was so big that everyone shared and everyone prospered. No group got left behind, and nothing ensures political stability better than prosperity across the board and rising expectations that are being fulfilled.

Arab oil revenues of $1 billion a month subsidized Iraq in its war against the Iranians, whose desire to export (Shiite) Islamic revolution threw jitters into every (Sunni) royal family from Kuwait to Riyadh. "The governments of the world should know that Islam cannot be defeated," Ayatollah Ruhollah Khomeini said in 1979, after returning to Iran from exile in Iraq and France. "Islam will be victorious in all the countries of the world, and Islam and the teachings of the Koran will prevail all over the world." The oil producers also showered countless millions on the Palestine Liberation Organization, not because of the cause itself but because they didn't want the P.L.O. causing trouble inside their own borders. They were as generous to their adversaries (for example, Syria) as they were to their friends, such as Tunisia. This was a new style of executing foreign policy. It was checkbook diplomacy, and the Fraternity of the Superrich hoped its benevolence would isolate the Gulf and the peninsula from the turmoil of the Arab world, thus making continued stability and development possible.[5]

And that development was stunning. Deepwater ports were dug, petrochemical plants, cement factories and fertilizer installations built. Industrial cities took form in the middle of nowhere. Freeways twisted across the desert; satellite communications reached out to the world; oil pipelines were buried in sand to protect them

[5] Actually only five of the eighteen Arab countries qualify for the Fraternity of the Superrich: Saudi Arabia, Kuwait, Qatar, the United Arab Emirates and Libya. The other oil producers—Bahrain, Oman, Algeria and Egypt—have limited reserves and comparatively modest incomes. Iraq has large reserves, but its revenues have been drained since 1980 by the war with Iran. The world's two largest producers of crude oil, incidentally, are the Soviet Union and the United States.

from terrorist attack. Saudi Arabia alone poured $500 billion into national development. During one seven-year span, a new school opened every three weeks in the kingdom, and in four years' time the Saudis increased their annual wheat harvest from four thousand tons to 1.3 million tons and became wheat exporters. (The government paid Saudi farmers $978 a ton for the wheat, about five times what it would have cost on the world market.) Bahrain developed into an international banking center that rivaled Hong Kong in regional importance. With Beirut in flames and Cairo deteriorating, Manama, the relaxed and pleasing capital of Bahrain, became the new headquarters for Westerners doing business in the Middle East.

Although blessed with one abundant resource, the oil producers had one great vulnerability: they lacked another resource the rest of the world takes for granted—water. Once they had shipped in drinking water from Iraq to supplement the meager supply of their springs and had talked seriously about towing in giant icebergs from Antarctica. Now billion-dollar water-desalination plants sprawled along the Persian Gulf coast, their control rooms protected by thick terrorist-proof steel doors. Saudi Arabia and the Gulf states became world pioneers in the new desalination process, and Bahrain became the highest per capita water consumer in the world, using 225 gallons a day compared with the international average of 57. Sprinklers worked constantly, and gardens bloomed in the parcels of sand while soft green lawns reached down the medians of divided highways. This is just how the prophet Mohammed said it should be: "Whoever bringeth the dead land to life . . . for him is reward therein."

Sheik Rashid ibn Said al-Maktum of Dubai got so excited over the transformation of his little sheikdom that he used to ride construction booms up the sides of buildings every morning to personally inspect the daily progress. The seven sheikdoms in the United Arab Emirates thrived as they outdid one another in ways that were grander, bigger and more expensive.[6] Dubai and Sharjah built sparkling international airports—ten miles apart. When Abu Dhabi constructed a 150,000-seat soccer stadium—big enough to hold most of the people in the emirate—Dubai countered with the world's largest dry dock. Abu Dhabi put up a glass-fronted bank that seemed to reach the clouds, and Dubai went one better, with a forty-story trade center.

The Gulf was a fun place. I loved my trips there, and often found myself looking for an excuse to transit through Bahrain. "You were just *in* Bahrain," my editors used to say over the phone from Los Angeles. "Why do you need to go back?" The first reason was very American; I wanted to consume. I always left Cairo with an empty duffel bag folded up in my suitcase, and in Bahrain's bountiful supermarkets I would stuff it with treasures that were not available at any price in Egypt: jars of chunky peanut butter, cans of baked beans, corned beef hash and crispy noodles, boxes of taco shells, bottles of maple syrup, packages of Monterey Jack cheese. Sometimes I even tucked in a bottle of my favorite whiskey, Canadian Club.

The second reason was more acceptable to my editors: the development of Bahrain was a compelling story. The Bahrainis are the poor cousins of the Gulf and they like to think they have more substance and less dazzle than some of their wealthier friends next door. Bahrain's population (600,000) is of such manageable size that the country has the appealing feel of a small American city. Everyone knows everyone else, and Sheik Isa ibn Salman al-Khalifa's cabinet ministers are accessible (a luxury Western journalists did not always have in the Arab world), forthright and

[6] The United Arab Emirates, known as the Trucial States before independence from Britain in 1971, comprise seven sheikdoms, each of which has a large degree of autonomy. They are Abu Dhabi, Dubai, Sharjah, Ras al-Khaimah, Ajman, Umm al-Qaiwain, Fujairah. They cover a land area about the size of Maine and have a combined population of one million.

articulate. They drive their own cars around town, shun bodyguards and escorts and live in family compounds, where two or three generations reside together in a dozen look-alike houses, built around a swimming pool and a health spa.

Sheik Isa—the eleventh in the line of Khalifas who have ruled Bahrain for more than two hundred years—held open house at 7:00 A.M. every other day in his office. Any citizen with anything to say about anything could drop in unannounced, even if he only wanted to complain about the shortage of downtown parking spaces. The emir was politely taken aback when I asked him if a head of state should spend so much time on mundane matters that in the West would be handled by a junior clerk at city hall.

"Of course," he replied. "We are a family here, a big family, and I want to know what my people's problems are. If something is wrong, I want to correct it."

Like Bahrain itself, the emir was small, standing not quite five feet. His presence conveyed both gentleness and unspoken power, and his eyes twinkled with elflike mischievousness. On weekends he opened his private beach to Western expatriates living in Bahrain, and would call out to them to join him on his patio for soft drinks and cake. His first question always was, "What do you think of Bahrain?" Once asked why he spent so much time at the beach, he answered, "I do it to exercise my neck, looking at all the pretty women around."

"Tell me, Aly," he said one evening to an Egyptian journalist who worked in Bahrain, "what's the latest joke from Cairo." Aly stammered and said it was a bit off-color. But the emir nodded; he would hear it anyway. Midway through he broke in with the punch line and said, "That's an old one. Got any others?"

Sheik Isa's style, like that of his country, was uncomplicated and unpretentious. He was religious but didn't find it necessary to advertise his convictions with constant references to God. I found it interesting that the richer the country and the faster the pace of development, the more pious its people professed to be. Bahrainis are the most laid-back of the Gulf people, the Saudis the most uptight. For the superrich, money and excellence become synonymous, and business becomes almost as important as religion. This was not as it had been, and in their cry "*Allah Akbar*" (God is great), I think I detected a silent appeal for assurance from Above that they had not strayed too far from the known road.

Much the same thing happened in the United States during the prosperity of the Coolidge years in the mid-1920s. Business was booming, profits were flying. The accumulation of wealth became a national obsession, and the highest compliment one could pay a clergyman or a college professor was to say he was a good businessman. It meant he was a doer, a dreamer, a builder. But Americans felt vaguely unsettled and sought confirmation that their emphasis on money was within the bounds of morality and Christianity. They did this by associating religion with business. Wherever entrepreneurs gathered, the name of God was invoked.

The National Association of Credit Men went to New York for its annual convention, and the Cathedral of Saint John the Divine held a special devotional service for the three thousand delegates. At each daily session a clergyman, a priest and a rabbi prayed for them. A group from the Associated Advertising Clubs convened in Philadelphia and heard a keynote address on "Spiritual Principles in Advertising." The Metropolitan Casualty Insurance Company issued a pamphlet to its employees declaring that "Moses was one of the greatest salesmen and real-estate promoters that ever lived." The pamphlet went on to describe Moses as a "Dominant, Fearless and Successful Personality in one of the most magnificent selling campaigns that history ever placed upon its pages."

And Bruce Barton sold Christianity to the American public in his book *The Man Nobody Knows*, published in 1925, by equating religion with commerce and calling Jesus "the founder of modern business." Jesus, Barton wrote, was "the most popular dinner guest in Jerusalem" and a great executive. "He picked up twelve men from the bottom ranks of business and forged them into an organization that conquered the world. . . . Nowhere is there such a startling example of executive success as the way in which that organization was brought together." His parables were "the most powerful advertisements of all time. . . . He would be a national advertiser today." *The Man Nobody Knows* was the best-selling nonfiction book in the United States for two straight years.

WHEN THE leaders of Saudi Arabia and the Gulf sheikdoms held a summit in Kuwait in 1984, there seemed to be as much time devoted to praying as to consulting. But the most intriguing aspect of watching six of the world's richest leaders in action was that, as they walked down the aisle to take their seats in the newly built conference hall, there seemed to be a direct relationship between the productivity of each leader's oil fields and his size. King Fahd of Saudi Arabia, puffy and jowled, came first, the largest of the men and the guardian of the world's biggest reserves. Last came Bahrain's pint-sized emir, Sheik Isa, who was then pumping just 42,000 barrels a day. Earlier in the day, Kuwait's national television had provided live coverage as each head of state's jetliner, usually a Boeing 707, rolled up to a red carpet at the international airport. Fahd arrived last in—appropriately enough—the biggest plane, a Boeing 747.

The Kuwaiti ruler, Sheik Jabbar al-Ahmed al-Sabah, had gone to great expense in trying to make sure the summit came off without a hitch. Even the journalists were whisked through customs, with officials stopping them only long enough to confiscate an occasional bottle of liquor that had found its way into some traveler's suitcase usually camouflaged among dirty clothes.[7] "Oh, oh," said a Pakistani

[7] Although many Westerners think that no alcohol is sold in the Arab world, only four countries—Kuwait, Saudi Arabia, Qatar, Libya—are dry. The others sell beer, wine and liquor, at least in the luxury hotels, although in some cases there are restrictions against Arabs (but not foreigners) purchasing them.

customs agent, taking one of those bottles from a journalist's suitcase and placing it under the counter, "that is forbidden. Very forbidden."

To provide suitable accommodations for the leaders and their huge entourages—Fahd's numbered 260—Sheik Jabbar simply confiscated clusters of private villas. As one Palestinian journalist working in Kuwait put it, "The government giveth and the government taketh away."

Almost overnight, the government refurbished entire villas, knocking down walls, ripping out antiquated bathrooms, laying new carpets, building extensions. The owner of the mansion where senior Saudi officials stayed was startled to return to his home one afternoon and find that an elevator had been installed. Fahd, he was told, did not like walking up stairs. To make sure everyone was able to complete his appointed rounds in comfort, a fleet of white Oldsmobile 98 sedans and a convoy of Greyhound-type buses were imported. Each bus had fourteen swivel seats, a fully equipped kitchen, carpeted floors and a small movie screen.

The monarchs roared off from the airport to their villas and to the conference center in cavalcades surrounded by sharpshooters standing in the backseats of roofless police cars. Land Rovers mounted with .50-caliber machine guns ringed the conference hall. Delicious buffets, enlivened by fruit-juice cocktails, graced the tables of hotels and villas throughout the day and night, and at the end of the conference Kuwait gave all twelve hundred people in attendance an attractive ballpoint pen and announced it was picking up all hotel tabs. There was mild grumbling; the previous year Qatar had given everyone a diamond watch and a leather attaché case.

THE LAVISH spending of the Kuwaitis, the Saudis and a handful of others obscures the fact that most Arabs are poor. The great majority eke out a meager existence as farmers and are fortunate to own a donkey, let alone a camel. For millions of rural Arabs, life is lived today much as it was a century ago, and the thought of boundless wealth is simply irrelevant to the hardships and drudgery of each day. In Morocco, Tunisia and Egypt, slight increases in the price of subsidized bread in the early 1980s led to riots that threatened the stability of the governments. In Algeria, thousands took to the streets to demonstrate against the slumlike quality of housing. Millions of Cairo residents consider themselves lucky to live in cold-water flats, where nine or ten family members share one room.

For the oil producers, these poor Arabs represented a valuable source of cheap labor. And the oil boom of the seventies created a new class and a pressure group in the Arab world—a civilian work force that reached from the classrooms of Oman to the oil fields of Libya. In its ranks were doctors, professors, clerks and laborers, and it was their brain and brawn that would build the new societies in the Persian Gulf area and on the Arabian Peninsula.

Like the Gold Rush miners, they were drawn to the oil countries by the promise of wealth and opportunity. They left their families behind and poured by the millions out of North Africa and Asia in pursuit of the dream their own lands could not provide. No matter what hour of the day I ended up at Cairo's international airport, the terminal was always swirling with hordes of bewildered Egyptian peasants, headed for the Gulf on three-year labor contracts. They watched with envy as the planes that would take them away disgorged returning laborers who lugged trunk-sized cardboard suitcases, secured with rope, and struggled at the baggage conveyor belt to collect their electric fans, shortwave radios, toys and television sets.

More than three million Egyptians were working outside their country in the mid-1980s. So were one million Sudanese, and more than a million Pakistanis, Indians, Sri Lankans, Filipinos, South Koreans, Bangladeshis, Mauritanians and Thais. The companies that supplied the manpower extolled the virtues of their wares, almost as if they were selling livestock. One newspaper advertisement in a Gulf paper suggested: "Consider Pakistani man-power for your project to ensure maximum production results." Another advised: "Bangladeshi workers are well known for their honesty, sincerity and hardworking qualities." A third referred to the "diligence and pleasant personality of the Thai worker." And an Asian employment agency distributed a glossy booklet in Arabic entitled, *Ten Commandments for Working with Thai People*. (Example: "Thou shall not shout.")

Without the foreigners, there would have been no miracles around the Persian Gulf. They were the doctors who staffed Saudi Arabia's space-age hospitals and the civil servants who kept Kuwait's government running smoothly. They were the policemen in Dubai, the waiters in Iraq, the schoolteachers in Oman, the hotel clerks in Bahrain. Most important, they were the common laborers, the people whose sweat transformed the old into the new. The influx of foreigners was so great that in the United Arab Emirates (population: one million) and Qatar (250,000) they outnumbered the locals four to one. You could drive through some of the sheikdoms in the Emirates and have a hard time even finding a local Arab. Everyone on the streets—cabdrivers, construction workers, shop-keepers, auto mechanics—was a foreigner. If you dropped a ciga-rette butt on the sidewalk, a uniformed Thai would materialize out of nowhere to sweep it up with his little broom and pan, then would disappear just as quickly.

The guest workers were treated as third-class citizens in the homogeneous Gulf and Saudi societies, even if they were profes-sionals, but the monetary rewards made the indignities tolerable. An Egyptian university professor, for instance, could expect to make about $62,500 during a thirty-year teaching career at home. In Kuwait he could earn $108,000 in four years. A peasant laborer could save enough in three years to buy a plot of land back home, build a modest house, maybe even start a small business. The $3 billion in remittances Egyptian expatriates sent home every year represented Egypt's largest source of foreign exchange, more than what the country earned from cotton, Suez-Canal revenues and tourism combined.

So the huge oil revenues affected more than just the oil-producing states. Their money flowed through Egypt, North Yemen, Tunisia and the poor countries, and transformed those societies as well. But the sword had a double edge: the immigration of village men to the oil fields brought psychological stresses to the families left behind, while the remittances and luxury goods the workers sent home created a new privileged class of rural elite. A new term was coined to describe the resultant changes in behavior patterns—the Dubai Syndrome.

Egyptian farmers, suddenly no longer poor, started eating canned fruit bought in the cities—the same fruit they used to grow—and stayed up so late watching television that they didn't get to their fields the next day until midmorning. The government responded by closing the two state-run television stations an hour earlier. Money was everywhere, and it shaped new values. Individualism became a greater force than nationalism; intellectualism became subservient to "cashism." Suddenly an illiterate maid could earn more than a schoolteacher; tenant farmers became landlords; the sons of donkey-cart drivers went off to college to study commerce.

The migration of peasant Arabs in and out of Saudi Arabia and the Gulf did not lead to a cross-fertilization of ideas or a wider worldly awareness, as travel and living abroad usually do. The migrants had remained isolated in the Arab world's most religiously conservative states. Their years there exposed them to money and a fundamental interpretation of Islam, not to the enrichment of culture, debate and human contact. In the host countries they were viewed as a necessary evil, economic mercenaries who were not in sync with the ways of desert Arabs. At home, as a newly monied class of illiterates, they represented a challenge to the established order of the village hierarchy, and this created a sense of disorientation in class-conscious societies.

Saad Ibrahim, an Egyptian sociologist, contends in his book *The New Arab Social System* that many of Egypt's social and economic defects are a result of the immigration to the oil fields and the comparative wealth it brought.[8] I found it curious, though, that to the best of my knowledge no one in the Gulf states or Saudi Arabia ever undertook any studies to determine the sociological impact of the oil boom on those societies; it was almost as if no one really wanted to know. But surely that impact went far beyond the façade of marble shopping centers. A generation was weaned on the notion that wealth and success had nothing to do with sweat and toil. Young men had only to take from their countries; they did not have to give. Everyone became an executive, but no one learned how to drive a nail or fix a faucet, and somewhere along the line an important step in the process of nation building was lost.

Reality had hit the Saudis by the time I returned to Riyadh in the 1990s. Saudi Arabia had overspent and overbuilt. Per capita income had actually dropped by more than $2,000 annually since the boom years, to $9,000. Life was a little less flashy, the expectations of the young were toned down. In one of the healthiest signs of national development I saw, Saudis were starting to fill menial jobs, even those as hotel bellhops and waiters.

It was easy to deride the Arab nouveaux riches for their conspicuous consumption and wild extravagances in the seventies and eighties, but I suspect history will judge them well. "I'd hate to think how we'd have handled such a windfall," a British diplomat in Saudi Arabia said. "Why, we'd still be sitting around in committees, twenty years later, arguing on how to spend it. These people had the good sense to let the future happen, and I think they got rather good value for money." Indeed, no area of the world ever faced the challenges of such abrupt, bountiful wealth, and none ever accomplished quite so much quite so fast.

[8] Ibrahim, a democracy activist, was arrested on trumped up charges of spreading false information and sentenced in May 2001 to seven years in prison.

National development was executed by serious and capable cabinet ministers, most of whom were dreadfully overworked because
the lower levels of bureaucracy were not noted for competence or
efficiency. They gave top priority to building an infrastructure—
roads, communications, power plants—and to developing secondary industries that would lessen their dependency on crude oil.
There was little altruism in their financial planning; their fortunes
were invested not in the economies of the Third World or in the
poverty pockets of Arab nations that desperately needed injections
of foreign exchange but in the West, where they were safest. Saudi
Arabia put $60 billion into U.S. government bonds; Kuwait set up
a $35 billion Fund for Future Generations and invested in forty-
one foreign countries. Billions more came off the top for social services—hospitals, universities, housing projects, education.

Qatar raised its literacy rate from zero to 40 percent in just over
two decades' time. Caravans moved across the Arabian Peninsula,
bringing teachers and mobile literacy classes to nomadic Bedouin.
Kuwait offered $180 to each adult who achieved an acceptable
level of literacy. Oman broke ground for its first university, and
Saudi Arabia's institutions of higher education filled up with ninety
thousand students; more than fifteen thousand others were enrolled
in colleges abroad. Eighty-six percent of Bahrain's children were
enrolled in school at the close of the Disposable Decade, even
though attendance was not mandatory and some traditional-minded
fathers refused to expose their daughters to an education.

"This ministry is the path to the future," Bahrain's minister of
education, Ali Fakhro, said early in 1985, as we sat in his office overlooking the Persian Gulf, and talked about what lay ahead. The
boom was ending and petroleum prices were starting to slide. "If we
fail here, then all the oil in the world won't mean a thing."

ELEVEN

THE LEGACY OF OIL

THE BAD thing about booms is that they never last. They don't lead to sustained economic growth, and they seldom leave a healthy cultural imprint on society. The riches are spent, the boom ends, people move on. Spain frittered away its gold and silver from the New World four hundred years ago in a binge of high living that weakened and disrupted the empire. Visit Brazil's jungle town of Manaus, and about the only reminder you'll find of the Amazon rubber boom is the old opera house where Caruso once sang. Drive through the Nevada desert from Reno to Las Vegas, and ghost towns stand in silent testimony to an era when silver was king. Would this, I wondered, one day be Saudi Arabia's fate? Would twenty-first-century travelers to the kingdom find abandoned industrial complexes and empty cities being reclaimed by the desert?

I applied for a visa to visit Saudi Arabia during my first month in Cairo. Eighteen months went by before I received word that my request had been approved. Part of the delay was due to the Saudis' care in screening all strangers before letting them into their country. But I also had difficulty communicating with the consular officer at the Saudi embassy. His unofficial office hours were from 11:00 A.M. to 1:00 P.M., four days a week, but that was the time, his secretary said, that he liked to fly the falcon he was training for a hunt in Morocco. So I would sit with a group of other men in a waiting room while the male receptionist appeased us with promises that the consular officer would soon arrive. An adjoining room was reserved for women. At some point the receptionist would confront reality and announce, "It seems he is not coming today. You may leave a message." I had given up hope of ever getting into Saudi Arabia and stopped going to the embassy to plead my case. Then my phone rang one day. It was the Saudi embassy. "Why haven't you picked up your visa?" the voice asked.

Saudi Arabia is as large as India, and flying over it, on the flight from Cairo, one is struck by the emptiness below. It is a land with no rivers and no permanent bodies of water. It contains one of the world's largest deserts, the Rub al-Kahli (Empty Quarter), and only half a dozen population centers of note. Its population density is nine persons per square mile (compared with 8,508 per square mile in Washington, D.C.). But buried down there in that vast wasteland is one quarter of the world's known oil reserves, a reservoir of riches that would not be depleted for at least two hundred years. I asked the man with the British accent in the seat next to me if he was going to Saudi Arabia on business. "No one goes for laughs," he noted, and our conversation ended there. Our plane was full. Every seat in the economy section was taken by Egyptian contract laborers, dressed in brown cotton robes and clutching their identity papers tightly in their laps. Up front in first class, Arab and Western businessmen sat reading the *International Herald-Tribune* and *Fortune* magazine. I noticed that many of them, including the Saudis, were quaffing impressive quantities of French wine and Johnnie Walker scotch. Although liquor was available in Saudi Arabia on the black market for about $150 a bottle, the eighty-lash penalty for drinking in public made abstinence a sensible choice, and the drinks the passengers now gulped down would be the "last call" until they eventually left the kingdom on an outward-bound flight.

The man next to me was right. Saudi Arabia wasn't a barrel of laughs. In comparison with the Saudis, England's sixteenth-century Puritans were a wild bunch. The Saudis might kick up their heels when they got to London or Geneva, but at home they were straight-faced and straitlaced. Their energies were devoted to family, religion and business, and nothing else got in the way. Saudi Arabia had no movie theaters, no concerts, symphonies, ballets, operas or nightclubs. Backgammon games, considered a corrupting influence, had been taken off the market shortly before I arrived, and chessmen had been confiscated by the authorities because of their resemblance to idols. Video-game parlors had been closed so that religious elders could study their effect on society. At prayer times, everything shut down for ten minutes while the whole world—or so it seemed—knelt on mats, facing Mecca to communicate with God: "Glory be to Thee, O God, and blessed be Thy name and exalted Thy majesty. There is no deity to be worshiped but Thee, I seek the protection of God against the accursed Satan. . . ." The times of prayer, which vary because they are determined by the hours of sunrise and sunset, were printed in each day's newspapers, and the ten million Saudis responded as one at the precise moment of worship. Government clerks abruptly halted work, cars pulled over to the curb, shopkeepers shooed customers out of their shops and bolted the doors. This happened three or four times a day.

It seemed peculiar to be traveling through large cities and see only men. The women were at home, veiled and sequestered, protected from the gazes of strange men. They were not allowed to drive, work in sexually integrated jobs or swim in hotel pools, and when they did venture forth onto the streets, they wrapped themselves in the funereal black cloths that covered all bare skin and left everything to the imagination. Polaroid's self-developing cameras were a smashing success in Saudi Arabia because for the first time men could take pictures of their wives unveiled in the privacy of their homes—something they wouldn't have done with 35-mm cameras because lab technicians could have viewed the women while making prints. This was a society where lust was considered disgusting and love was a forbidden subject. No poets wrote of love, no novelists wove plots around it, no singer romanticized it. The authorities removed liquor advertisements and pictures of women in vaguely seductive perfume ads from *Time* and *Newsweek* each week before distributing the magazines to newsstands. It was as though the trauma of change and the encroachment of evil things did not threaten if one pretended they did not exist. Words and prayers, the Saudis hoped, were enough to keep the past secure, and people responded to peer pressure by doing and saying exactly what was expected of them.

King Fahd's young son was interviewed on state television one night while I was in Riyadh. He was a true jet-setter, whose travels had taken him to the glamour spots of the globe. Where, he was asked, was his favorite place in the world to visit? "Mecca," he answered. His second choice was Medina, another of Islam's holy cities. And the third? "Disneyland," he said finally, sounding like the eleven-year-old boy he was.

Saudi Arabia, the birthplace of Islam and guardian of its two holiest sites, is a homogeneous community of conforming believers. It is the only country named after a family, and the four thousand or so Saudi princes run it like a closely held family business.[1] At the centers of power behind the king are his cabinet (commoners do hold ministerial positions, but key posts are reserved for royalty), the country's ten thousand religious elders, the seventy-five-thousand-man armed forces and the business community. There is interplay between all five blocs, and although the country has no constitution except the Koran, no suffrage and no legislative assembly, the king achieves consensus through consultations with the royal family and tribal leaders. It is this blend of desert democracy and firm authoritarianism that has enabled the Sauds to reign without interruption longer than any other dynasty in the Middle East.

---

[1] One principality, Liechtenstein, near Switzerland, is also named for a family.

The Saud family began gathering power in 1748, when Moham-med ibn Saud, a besieged tribal chief, and Mohammed ibn Wah-hab, a religious reformer, formed an alliance in Diriyah outside Riyadh.[2] Together, with the sword and the Koran, they extended their rule throughout central Arabia, at times even challenging the ruling Ottoman Turks. In 1902, at the age of twenty-one, one of Saud's descendants, Abdul Aziz ibn Saud—the man who one day would sit in summitry with President Franklin D. Roosevelt—used the battle cry "Come, O men of Riyadh, here I am Abdul Aziz ibn Abdul Rahman—of the House of Saud—your rightful ruler" to rally support and capture Riyadh from the competing Rashid family.

Ibn Saud was the very picture of the Arab warrior. He stood six foot four, weighed 230 pounds, and beneath his broad shoulders there was not an inch of fat. His voice was deep and he loved to bel-low. During one set of negotiations with the British over the estab-lishment of a boundary, he was heard to shout mild profanities in frustration. The British were measuring the border in miles, and he wanted it explained in terms of fast or slow camels.

After defeating the Rashids, Ibn Saud set forth on a series of con-quests that were to unite the warring tribes and squabbling sects of the Arabian Peninsula into a single nation, the world's twelfth largest, which in 1932 he declared to be the kingdom of Saudi Ara-bia with himself as king. Ibn Saud, who claimed that his three greatest pleasures in life were women, perfume and prayers, solidi-fied his dynasty by marrying at least 120 women from tribes through-out the peninsula, but kept within Koranic restraints by never maintaining more than four wives at a time. As soon as a wife bore him a son, he divorced her and sent her back to her village. There she remained as the emblem of one man's nationalistic and sexual

---

[2] Wahhab was a fundamentalist scholar who wanted to rid Islam of practices that had crept into it from other Middle Eastern religions—among them the veneration of saints, tombs, trees and wells. The Saudis, who are Sunni Mus-lims, follow that conservative doctrine today and are members of what is known as the Wahhabi sect.

appetite. "In my youth and manhood, I made a nation," an aging
Ibn Saud said. "Now in my declining years, I make men for its population." When he died in 1953, his legacy included forty-seven
sons and more daughters than anyone had bothered to count. More
important, he left his kingdom a legacy of stability, for today every
Saudi recognizes Ibn Saud as the father of modern-day Saudi Arabia and thus accepts the legitimacy, politically and religiously, of
the Sauds.

Saudi Arabia is essentially a secret kingdom. No one outside the
inner sanctums of power fully understands how the royal family
reaches decisions, and the Sauds make sure this remains so by keeping their considerable family quarrels to themselves and never
washing their laundry in public. Each Western embassy assigns one
of its diplomats to report on the royal family, but that thankless task
produces few insights and not much of significance. One family
watcher I talked to had spent a year trying to figure out which
prince lived in what house and had come up largely empty-handed.

The family accumulates wealth and lives in shamelessly lavish
fashion, but it has also given Saudi Arabia strong, steady leadership
through both the lean and the fat years. If a few princes seem a bit
outrageous in their pursuit of the good life abroad, they at least have
the good taste to remain impeccably pious at home. Actually, I
never found the behavior of the rebel princes particularly unusual.
All I had to do was think back to my days growing up in Boston and
remember which of my friends had become the most unruly when
they broke the bonds of parental control and went away to college.
They were always the ones from the strictest homes, who had been
forced to go to church every Sunday and had never been allowed to
touch even a beer in the presence of their parents.

At the core of the Sauds' durability is their ability to feel the pulse
of the Saudi people through the *majlis*—literally in Arabic the
"meeting" or the "sitting"—that puts royalty and commoners in
touch on a daily basis. They understand what the people want and
they have the money to provide it. By embracing Islam, they make

religion a unifying, stabilizing force rather than the disruptive one it had been in the shah of Iran's downfall in 1979. As long as it can keep communicating and spending, as long as its prerogatives don't clash with the interests of the middle class, the military and the religious conservatives, the House of Saud will stand on stone, not sand.

Journalists need approval from the Ministry of Information in Saudi Arabia to interview government officials, and my first request was to attend a majlis, similar to the one that Sheik Isa of Bahrain held in his office every other day. Three days later a government Mercedes-Benz with a Pakistani driver and a Kuwaiti public relations officer picked up my wife and me at the Hyatt Regency and drove us across town, along boulevards so new that they hadn't even been named yet, to the office of the governor of Riyadh. Feeling slightly misplaced, we took our seats in a room the size of a basketball court, joining a hundred or more men in robes and headdresses who waited there for an audience with the governor.

They held petitions in their hands, and their feet tapped out nervous patterns on the carpet. They sat in upright chairs arranged along the wall, amid the opulence of crystal chandeliers and dark drapes. Sometimes their lips moved silently, as though reciting a prayer.

The prince arrived at 11:00 A.M., entering the antechamber with brisk strides, his aides in obedient pursuit. He was a man of striking features: tall and lithe in his gold-fringed brown robe, an angular, Hollywood-handsome face with piercing eyes and a mouth that seemed ready to smile but did not. His subjects rose as one.

Prince Salman ibn Abdul Aziz is King Fahd's brother and the father of the young Saudi prince who in 1985 became the first Arab astronaut. He was educated by private tutors and had been appointed governor of Riyadh Province at the age of eighteen. In the twenty-seven years since then, he had held three or four majlises every day, often seeing as many as two thousand people a week. Every member of the royal family in positions of authority, from King Fahd on down, also holds majlises. This is the link between the ruled and the ruler. Every Saudi has direct access to his chieftain, no matter how trivial his grievance, just as he always did back in the times when tribes wandered across the peninsula.

The men who had waited for the prince stood before him now in a long line. Salman sat below a portrait of his father, the warrior-statesman Ibn Saud, and removed his glasses. He nodded for the first man to step forward. To his right stood a dozen aides, ready to be dispatched to various ministries, courts and offices to solve the petitioners' problems.

Many of those who approached kissed the prince's shoulder. If they tried to kiss his hand, he withdrew it brusquely, for all the Sauds remember the pictures—and the implications—of the shah of Iran's subjects kissing his feet. The Sauds are careful to separate themselves from any display of subservience and try to avoid erecting barriers, other than those defined by wealth, between the royal family and the people.

The problems Salman dealt with that day were minor: a family dispute, a complaint over inadequate housing, an imprisoned son, a request for money. Although he never overruled a court decision, he read each petition quickly, jotted a note on it for future action or sent an aide hurrying off to remedy the problem on the spot. "Salaam aleikum" (Go in peace), each man said as his brief audience ended.

In practical terms, the majlis is a service center, not a form of real democratic expression. It is a wasteful expenditure of time for kings and princes. Yet psychologically it is the foundation of the royal families' stability in Saudi Arabia and the Gulf states. The secret of their longevity is that they have made alliances with everybody, particularly the religious establishment, and have stitched society together through a constant process of group consensus. The Sauds have built the whole kingdom around Ibn Saud, using him like the center post in a circus tent. Although a group known as the Sudairi Seven—King Fahd and his six full brothers, whose mother was a

Sudairi—hold ultimate power, the monarchy is less than absolute because the system contains many checks and balances. Fahd, once a high-living prince, would be pleased if the Saudis loosened up a bit—he finds it necessary to escape to the privacy of his yacht, moored at a private island near Jeddah, so he can occasionally enjoy some of the normal pleasures of life. But he follows, rather than sets, the tone of Saudi society, and the moral conservatism and religious devotion one finds in Saudi Arabia pretty much reflect the will of the people, something the Sauds keep in touch with through the majlises and the fact that the royal clan's four thousand princes are spread throughout all society, from the army to the ministries, from the desert towns to the cities.

SAUDI ARABIA seemed a strange place to be talking about tough times. Teenagers roared through the city streets in spanking-new Buicks and Pontiacs, ignoring signs that said, *Dear drivers: Your life is precious for your family and your country. Protect it.* Saudi families whiled away the weekends at the national pastime—shopping—in glistening malls replete with fifteen-thousand-dollar fur coats, diamond-studded watches and American-style soda fountains that served hot-fudge sundaes. American businessmen sat with their Saudi counterparts in the piano bars of plush hotels, sipping orange fizzes and pineapple delights, discussing deals of Rockefellerian magnitude. The electronic pagers in their pockets beeped like a chorus of crickets across the lounges, and Indian waiters hurried over, portable telephones in hand.

But by 1986 times had indeed turned tough—at least by the standards of the boom years—and Saudi Arabia and the Gulf states were coming to grips with a new reality: oil, like any other mineral, was a resource of limited value, governed by the laws of supply and demand.

The worldwide demand for oil had been growing at a rate of 7.6 percent annually in the 1970s when prices spiraled skyward. As

energy bills mounted, a global recession set in and the industrialized nations were forced to respond to what President Jimmy Carter
called "the moral equivalent of war." National policies encouraging
conservation were adopted. Alternative sources of energy were utilized. Non-OPEC production was increased, particularly in Alaska,
Mexico and Europe's North Sea. Huge stockpiles of petroleum
grew in Japan, Europe and the United States. And the public's attitude toward the use of energy changed. Thermostats were turned
down, cars were driven less, speed limits were reduced, commercial
jetliners lightened their flying weight—even removing plastic covers from magazines and scraping paint from fuselages—and began
using computers to find the most fuel-efficient altitudes for flight.
They saved millions of dollars and millions of gallons by keeping
their engines shut down during delays at the gate, restructuring
routes, adding more seats and reducing speed. On a five-hundred-
mile flight, for instance, pilots found they could cut fuel consumption 7 percent by flying at 500 mph instead of at 520 mph.

At the Department of Defense, U.S. naval ships were modified to
reduce drag in the water, and an aggressive barnacle-cleaning pro-
gram was ordered. On the highways truckers installed air-deflector
screens above their cabs to reduce wind resistance. The result was
up to an 11 percent savings in fuel. American-made cars that averaged 13.1 miles per gallon in 1974 were getting 17.3 miles by 1984,
and in the span of that decade, according to the American Petroleum Institute, Americans cut their energy consumption by 23 percent. At the same time, the annual growth in the world's demand
for oil had shrunk to just over 1 percent.

All this led to an international oil glut and to diminished reliance
on OPEC production. The United States' reliance on oil imports
tumbled to 4.3 million barrels a day—half of what it had been
in 1977—and much of those requirements were met by newly
expanded sources in Mexico and Britain; the United States' reliance on Saudi Arabia and the Persian Gulf fell to only 2.5 percent
of its total oil imports. In March 1983 OPEC responded to the

downturn by making its first price cut in history, slashing five dollars from the benchmark price of thirty-four dollars per barrel. Saudi Arabia, the cartel's giant, tried to regulate the flow of oil by closing and opening its taps to match global demands and conditions, just as the U.S. federal government regulates the supply of dollars on the market. But OPEC members had economic commitments from the wild spending days of the seventies' boom and were often unwilling to abide by limited production quotas. Prices kept falling, and by 1986, for the first time in a decade, had skidded into the nine-dollar-a-barrel range before starting to edge back upward. OPEC's fixed benchmark price became irrelevant, the price that mattered was the one established by supply and demand on the international spot market. Oil became a problem for marketers, not consumers, and OPEC became a cartel that could not control its own members, let alone the global pricing structure. Its share of world exports tumbled from 63 percent in 1979 to 38 percent in 1986, and the group in effect abandoned its attempts to curb production, thus ensuring an even greater glut. It was every man for himself.

The glut and the falling prices were a boon to the consuming nations. They saved the industrialized West an estimated $100 billion a year, cooled inflation, pushed interest rates down and stimulated investment. Every time a gallon of oil dropped one cent in price, U.S. commercial airlines collectively saved $120 million. There was, however, a flip side to the coin. Low, unstable prices also encouraged consumption and discouraged production in the developed world. They made it forget that oil was a limited resource. No one talked about finding alternative sources of energy anymore, of saving energy by turning off lights and driving less at slower speeds. Without courageous leadership in Washington, Tokyo and the capitals of Europe, the future seems apparent: sometime the glut will end, prices will rise, the oil producers will regain control over the world economy and there will be another energy crisis.

Although other developing countries would consider themselves blessed to have Saudi Arabia's "problems," the reeling economies on the peninsula and in the Gulf are no frivolous matter. In three years' time, the kingdom's income dropped from $103 billion to under $42 billion. Kuwait's fell by half, to $9 billion. Budgets were slashed, development projects put on hold, social expenditures reduced, real estate prices cut by as much as half, personal spending habits adjusted.

"I used to give away ten or fifteen BMWs a year to friends," a Kuwaiti businessman said in 1986. "Now I've stopped that, and rather than buying my wife a new car this year, I've given her the '85 Cadillac."

The construction cranes, which had become so common across every skyline that the machine was referred to as the national bird of Arabia, suddenly stood as lifeless as skeletons. Today they are a reminder of vulnerability instead of prosperity. The shopping centers are almost morguelike in their quietness and with their empty shops. One $200 million mall on Jeddah's seafront boulevard suspended construction in 1986, when financing ran out and its owners began scurrying around for cash. "It's up to God now," said a spokesman for the firm.

It was, I thought, to the Arabs' credit that they didn't blame their economic downturn on anyone. This was a reaction different from what I had encountered elsewhere in the Third World, where developing nations tend to hold external forces responsible for all their woes, and usually see a Western conspiracy behind every ominous shadow. I remember a Tanzanian university professor once telling me that the drop in coffee prices was part of a plot by American housewives against his socialistic country. My rebuttal that an abundant South American crop that season was the reason for lower prices and that U.S. shoppers spent little time thinking about Tanzania—if they even knew where Tanzania was—fell on deaf ears. But the Arabs took the price collapse quietly in stride, without threatening, cajoling or assigning guilt to anything but their own avarice and the fateful twists of the international economic order. It had been an exciting ride, and they greeted the twilight of their boom almost with a sense of relief, exhausted, needing some quiet moments to catch their breath and evaluate what had happened.

"The time has come for us to rethink our life-styles, to remember who and what we are," said Abdul Thani, deputy director of Qatar's Industrial Development Technical Center.

IN MANY ways the overnight transformation of Saudi Arabia was no less astonishing an achievement than the taming of the American West or the building of the Panama Canal. Proud they were, but the Saudis were not heady with the intoxication of victory. No toasts were raised to the pounding of the last golden spike.

They knew that they had gained their triumph and won their wealth without striving. No sweat had been shed in conquering their land. Their skin was smooth and their hands bore no calluses. The oil had been a gift—a gift from God, many said—and to put its proceeds to work, the Saudis had summoned the army of two million foreigners and paid them well to plan, consult, construct, maintain and toil in the blistering sun. It seems that this is Saudi Arabia's greatest liability: no one has learned how to turn the nuts or tighten the screws, and there will soon come a day when everyone can no longer be an executive.

The rulers of the superrich countries *bought*, and did not necessarily earn, a place of significance for themselves in the world. Yet the political impact of the boom has not been profound. Oil did not give the Arabs the leverage they expected with the West; it did not provide them with the power to force concessions from Israel or to achieve a settlement of the Arab-Israeli conflict; it did not make them immune from terrorism at home—religious Saudi fanatics took over the Grand Mosque in Mecca in 1979, and terrorists linked with Iran attacked the U.S. embassy in Kuwait in 1984—and it did not lead to the emergence of the Arab bloc as a world power, as had been envisioned in the 1970s. It did not even make Saudi Arabia a real power broker within the Arab community, where, like most other regions, influence is determined by military—not financial, intellectual or moral—strength.

But the Saudis never wanted to lead. That was a role Washington and other capitals tried to thrust Saudia Arabia into, and it was contrary to the character of this country that had stayed out of the five Arab-Israeli wars and wants more than anything to simply be left alone. Saudi Arabia is more comfortable building a consensus than pioneering a policy. It works, if goaded, behind the scenes, not on center stage, and it does not take risks. Caution is the hallmark of every political decision, for Saudi Arabia remains a vincible country, a desert kingdom with a small population, a one-"crop" economy, an old-fashioned political system and an enemy dressed in the robes of religious rectitude just across the Gulf.

An American oilman who had lived in Saudi Arabia for years recalled a night in June 1967, when a Saudi friend stopped by his home to say good-bye.

"I'm going to the war," the Saudi said. "I leave in the morning." There were handshakes, embraces and words of farewell.

A week later the American was taken aback to see his friend at a party in Ridyadh. He asked what had happened.

"My brother went," the Saudi said. "I had some business to tend to."

As it was, the Six-Day Arab-Israeli war of 1967 was over anyway by the time the two Saudi brigades reached Jordan. But the Saudi's decision to stay home said, I thought, a good deal about Saudi Arabia's priorities. The Saudis want to be conciliators, not confronters, but they are quick to reject suggestions that their unwillingness to fill Western-perceived roles or to emulate the West is tantamount to being fainthearted or backward. To those Westerners who come to Saudi Arabia and are apt to criticize everything from the restricted role of women to the brutal punishment of criminals, the Saudis have a quick and plausible response: This is our way, and it works for us; what needs to be changed will be changed, but at our own pace; do not judge us harshly because our ways are not your ways.

"We took some things from the West just to prove we are civilized, and that's foolish," said Hend Khuthaiha, the female vice dean at the Women's Study Center at King Saud University. "The West may be more advanced in areas like science, but I have never believed for a minute that your culture is more civilized than ours.

"You know, we go to the United States and see playgrounds and say, 'Oh, we need playgrounds, too.' So we build swings for five thousand dollars and our children don't use them. Swings aren't part of our culture. We would rather spend our time with our families than be on a playground with strangers."

The Saudis had two ways to go when oil prices quadrupled in the 1970s. One was to opt for cautious, slow development in order to maintain the society's balance and not disrupt the social structure. The other was for rapid development and all the uncertainties that went with it. They chose the latter, and, I thought, did remarkably well in maintaining their equilibrium. Their political institutions survived the boom intact; their cities remained virtually without crime; their identity had not been altered by Western influences.

But the real test lay ahead. Coping with the mundane problems of a normal society would be less exhilarating—and more challenging—than building, building, building. Sharing slices of a smaller fiscal pie with people who had come to expect so much so easily would hold inherent political dangers. So would reducing the tribute the Saudis paid to the P.L.O., Syria and others for the privilege of not being provoked. Sending home the foreign workers at the rate of sixty thousand a month, as Saudi Arabia was doing in 1986, would curtail the efficiency and range of services—and would produce social and economic strains on the countries to which the laborers returned. Would the Saudis really be willing to make sacrifices in the name of austerity and not throw away cars because the ashtrays were full? Would King Fahd still insist on traveling through his country with a retinue of eighteen hundred? Would the kingdom, despite its attempts to diversify, continue to be a slave to oil? Would it continue to spend its wealth and produce so little?

A single company, Aramco, wholly owned by the Saudi government since 1980, produces 97 percent of the country's oil, which in turn accounts for 89 percent of government revenues. Aramco, the world's largest oil company, is located in Dhahran, a sprawling, nondescript desert city on the Persian Gulf. A government driver and escort officer met me at the Dhahran international airport and drove me to my hotel. I was surprised, though not displeased, when they both sat down uninvited to join me, on my tab, for a buffet lunch at the hotel that cost $35 per person. That was, I later learned, a Saudi custom that went back to the days of Ibn Saud; anyone in the palace at mealtime—ministers, princes, businessmen, servants, drivers—is understood to have an invitation to join the king for lunch, and it is not unusual for the royal staff to set tables for a thousand drop-in guests. Saudi hospitality is boundless, and when a government official tried to pay my bill for three costly days at the Oberoi Hotel in Dhahran, I had difficulty convincing him that American newspapers did not allow their correspondents to accept gifts or monetary favors from any government, even their own. Baffled, he politely relented with the observation "That's certainly a strange custom."

The Ministry of Information had arranged for me to interview, in Dhahran, Aramco's president, Ali Naimi, who in 1984 had become the company's first Saudi chief executive, a position that had been held by Americans during the previous half century. Naimi was a slight, bespectacled man, not yet fifty, with a wide smile and an easy manner. He had been apprehensive of my visit, but relaxed when I told him I wanted to talk about his road to the presidency, not the downturn in oil prices. His story was that of Saudi Arabia itself, and whenever I doubted the permanency of the kingdom's progress in later months, I had only to think of Naimi and the other Saudis like him I had met to turn aside my skepticism. The distance they had covered in but a second's run was enough to make me believe that it boded well for the future and the kingdom would be spared from ever becoming a relic such as Manaus, abandoned in the wilderness.

For his first seven years, Naimi was a child of the desert, wandering with his mother's Bedouin tribe across the endless expanses. He tended sheep and, he said, found little time for mischief—or for dreams that any other life lay beyond the dunes.

When he was eleven, he took a job as an office boy at Aramco, filling a vacancy created by the death of his seventeen-year-old brother, Abdullah. Naimi supposed Abdullah had died of pneumonia, but back then, in 1956, death was so common among Saudi youth that no one paid much attention to the cause.

Young Ali did well at Aramco. He became a clerk, learned typing and shorthand, earned a company scholarship to study in Beirut. Later, when he decided to switch from administration to geology, an Aramco personnel officer interviewing him asked why. "Because I want to be president of the company," he replied.

"I meant it facetiously, of course," Naimi recalled, putting down his cup of Arabic coffee to savor the memory. "I didn't even realize then that almost all of Aramco's presidents and chairmen of the board had been geologists. But the gentleman interviewing me thought my reason was as good as any, and he let me make the change."

Naimi went on to get a degree in geology from Lehigh University in Pennsylvania and a master's from Stanford in California. He worked his way up the corporate ladder and never quite lost his awe of what was happening to him and to his country. He was, he knew, of the last Bedouin generation.

"My mother is seventy-seven and lives with me," he said. "She can't read or write, but she understands what I am doing and she is proud. It's just unfortunate that she grew up in an era when education was simply nonexistent for Saudis, because she is a very intelligent woman."

His mother's tribe is settled now and its nomads are no more. At most, only a few hundred thousand Bedouin still cling to the old ways in Saudi Arabia. The others, like the people of Naimi's mother, have taken advantage of government land grants and irrigation projects to settle down or have moved to cities, where they have been assimilated into urban society. Their children will have better lives than the parents ever dared dream of and will probably never know the camel as anything but the symbol of a dying era's restless freedom.

"Today's generation is different from mine," Naimi said. "We really had to eke out a living. That's something my children will never have to worry about."

ARAMCO'S ADMINISTRATIVE offices are in a compound, surrounded by low walls, fences and manned entry gates. Its employees live in another compound nearby. In fact, all of Saudi Arabia seems to be one giant cluster of compounds. Wealthy Saudis live in family compounds, their privacy ensured by ten-foot-high cement walls. Foreign businessmen live in company compounds, where a dozen or so homes are built around a community swimming pool and barbecue pit. Contract laborers live in compounds of dormitory barracks. Foreign teachers have their compounds, as do foreign doctors and nurses, foreign oilmen and foreign contractors.

Saudi Arabia even moved the eight thousand foreign diplomats and their dependents out of Jeddah, the traditional home of the royal family. For them the Saudis built a two-hundred-acre diplomatic compound, fifteen minutes from Riyadh, to accommodate all embassies and official residences. The new, self-contained diplomatic quarter has so many amenities—a fourteen-story international school, a huge sports facility, a posh social club, shopping centers—that one could live comfortably inside its perimeter and never have to venture forth into the ultraconservative Saudi world. Which is exactly the point. By keeping outsiders separate, if not isolated, the Saudis can exercise control over unwanted foreign influences—among them alcohol, gambling, pornography and drugs—that could penetrate and endanger the purity of their society. And by maintaining a low-profile presence, the foreigners are less apt to become resented by the Saudi public and the religious establishment as a noisy, nosy nuisance.

The day after I interviewed Ali Naimi, Aramco's public relations officer in Dhahran, Ahmed Lughod, invited me to lunch at his house. I took a taxi to the compound gate, where the security man let me telephone Lughod. He arrived a few minutes later in his Oldsmobile, and we drove down Elm Street and turned left on Rolling Hills Boulevard. It was the best of winter days in the desert, warm and cloudless, and, because it was Friday, the heart of the Islamic weekend, offices and stores were closed. Many of Lughod's American neighbors were in their gardens, relaxing on lawn chairs, or were digging in patches of flowers.

The ranch-style homes we passed stood on tree-lined streets. American cars were parked out front. On a stretch of lawn, two boys wearing Houston Astro T-shirts played catch with a baseball. On another a blond man wearing shorts and holding a cup of coffee waved a hello as Lughod drove by, slowed at an intersection and yielded to a shiny new Greyhound bus.

I felt as though I was in a Texas suburb that had been plopped in the middle of the Arabian desert. The compound, the largest for Americans in Saudi Arabia, contains the homes of many of Aramco's forty-seven hundred U.S. employees and, like the diplomatic quarter, is brimful of amenities. Residents have an eighteen-hole sand golf course, with green mats placed on the putting greens, and a score of tennis courts that are always vacant when the summer heat strikes. They have a 640-seat cinema that shows recent releases (a luxury Saudis can sample only on home video in their theaterless kingdom) and a modern supermarket stocked with Sara Lee coffee cakes and Oscar Mayer wieners.

The compound is really a world within a world, and although Christian church services are not allowed, government officials traditionally allow the Americans more discretionary leeway inside the complex than the Saudis themselves enjoy outside it as long as society's restrictions are not flouted too recklessly. The concessions date back to the days when the oil companies operated as a virtual independent government within Saudi Arabia. In this land of permanent prohibition, for example, making bathtub wine surreptitiously became a favorite pastime of the expatriates. All the necessary ingredients are readily available in any Saudi supermarket. When one American I knew moved past the checkout counter with twelve large cans of grape juice, a bag of sugar, hoses and funnels, the Pakistani clerk helpfully observed, "You forgot the yeast." The wine, it should be noted, does not age gracefully and needs to be drunk quickly. Inside the compound, foreign women do not have to cover their arms, back and legs; some drive cars, others work in jobs at Aramco that put them in contact with men. All these freedoms are denied them once they move beyond the security of the compound walls.

"You know, I love it here," said Lughod, an American of Palestinian heritage who had lived in Dhahran for nearly thirty years. We pulled into his driveway and stopped in front of the two-car garage. "It's like California, a very comfortable life. Yet"—he paused, reflecting a trace of sadness—"people still find things to complain about. It's amazing."

Some of the Americans in the Lughods' neighborhood were third-generation Aramco employees who had followed their grandfathers and fathers to the Arabian oil fields. For them Saudi Arabia held no culture shock at all. But for many of the seventy-five thousand Americans in Saudi Arabia—who represent the largest U.S. community in the Middle East—life in the kingdom is a difficult adjustment with few diversions and too many restrictions. Their complaints, however, are softened by company enticements that often include a 25 percent hardship allowance for working in Saudi Arabia, two months' leave a year, an annual paid trip back home, free private school education for children and subsidized housing.

"Every time I go back to Saudi after an 'out' I go through a period of terrible depression," an American engineer said. "I sleep nine or ten hours a night, I don't want to see anyone, I invariably come down with some stomach bug. I feel like I hate the Saudis, which I don't at all. Needless to say, my work goes to hell until I pull out of it."

A generation ago the engineer might have been dismissed as a neurotic. But psychiatrists now recognize culture shock as a medical phenomenon with dramatic, if temporary, emotional and physical symptoms. Among them are obsessive concern with cleanliness, depression, compulsive eating and drinking, excessive sleeping, irritability, lack of self-confidence, fits of weeping, nausea. It is not unusual for toilet-trained children to regress and for well-adjusted adults to become chronic complainers. Culture shock—a psychological disorientation that upsets one's equilibrium—can even strike someone settling into London or Paris but is apt to be most severe when all the familiar props of one's environment are knocked out from under a person, as they are in the Arab world.

Psychiatrists have determined that culture shock has five distinct stages: exhilaration upon initially encountering a new environment; then bewilderment and confusion, and glamorization of home or a previous foreign posting; then discouragement as one withdraws from the alien culture, moves closer to the expatriate community and comes to view the host nationals as "them"; then gradual recovery marked by an understanding and perhaps an appreciation of the host country and its people; and finally, a return to normal.

"For whatever reason, Americans really are liked in Saudi Arabia, and we're treated well, almost as a privileged class," an American banker said. "This surprises a lot of people. Some even find it confusing. In the States we don't read much about the Arab point of view. We just hear about Israel's. So Americans come over here thinking they're going to be disliked. They may even come with an anti-Arab attitude. Then after three to six months, there's a complete reversal. They find out they like the Saudis they're working with. I mean, the Saudis on this level probably have a master's from the University of Southern California or some such place. These are bright people who have been around. And this kind of startles an American if he's a newcomer."

THE SAUDIS have plenty of reasons to worry about security. Israeli jets regularly flew up and down the Gulf of Aqaba within sight of Saudi Arabia, and in 1981, apparently wanting to test the Arabs' response, Israeli planes conducted a series of low-level mock-bombing attacks on Saudi Arabia's northwestern base at Tabuk. Oil pipelines running for hundreds of miles across the desert are vulnerable to terrorist attack, and the wells themselves, spread over thousands of square miles, would be virtually indefensible in the face of a determined enemy. On Saudi Arabia's southern flank is Yemen, to the west Egypt, to the east Iraq and Iran—all hotbeds of fundamentalism. Military analysts say that Saudi Arabia would have only fourteen seconds' warning time to scramble its jets if enemy planes were to cross the Fahd Line, an imaginary line drawn about ten miles inside Iran, just north of the Persian Gulf coast. At home the royal family has just as many worries and frets that every little sneeze may mask an expression of discontent among the Shiites, the soldiers or the religious elders.

Two American presidents, Carter and Reagan, pledged to defend the Arabian oil fields against outside aggression, and a third, George Bush, went to war to keep the commitment when Iraq invaded Kuwait in 1990 and threatened to push on to Saudi Arabia. The Saudis know their future, economically and militarily, is inextrica-

bly linked to the West, and however timid they are to speak out publicly in defense of Israel's right to exist or America's war on terrorism, they are not likely to do much to threaten that relationship. If
one wanted to imagine what real tumult in the Arab would be like
and what havoc an unfriendly government in Riyadh could raise
with Western interests, one need only envision a Saudi Arabia in
the hands of Iraq's Saddam Hussein or Afghanistan's Taliban.

About five minutes after the kingdom was seized by extremists,
the royal families in the Saudi-dominated Persian Gulf sheikdoms
would topple like houses of cards, and the eastern flank of the Arab
world would become a mecca of opposition to the West, to Israel, to
moderation within the Islamic community, to sensible oil-pricing
policies.

The U.S. Congress understands the stakes—but sometimes not
the Saudi Arabian psyche. "Your military attachés come to us," a
Saudi diplomat in Washington told me, "and say, 'You need such
and such American weapons to defend yourself.' So we order
them—and mind you, we're paying cash, not asking for gifts—and
you humiliate us in the corridors of Congress, debating our trust-
worthiness, then turning us down with lame excuses that the
weapons might be used against Israel or might fall into the hands of
terrorists." Actually, with the billions of dollars of armaments the
United States has poured into the Arabian Peninsula and the Arab
Gulf states, neither has ever happened. Washington's blinders-on
view is that Israel is an outpost besieged by a "bunch of Arabs" and
that anyone who doesn't want to join the Washington-Jerusalem
axis is a recalcitrant, and possibly an enemy. However politically
appealing that platform may be for U.S. officials at election time, it
ultimately fails because if the United States continues to lose its
influence in the Middle East by shunning Arabs whose friendship
it had once cultivated, if Saudi Arabia cannot defend itself and the
tide of Khomeinism spills through Arabia and flows on to Jordan,
Israel's security—and its *existence* unless the United States is willing
to go to war—could be threatened as never before.

With or without genuine American support, however, Saudi Arabia is in a good position to cope with the pressures of the post-boom era. Economically it can withstand a protracted oil-price war better than any other producer; it costs the Saudis only three dollars per barrel to extract their black gold—compared with upward of nine dollars a barrel in the North Sea—and with known reserves exceeding 261 billion barrels (one quarter of the world's supply), Saudi Arabia remains wildly wealthy by any standard. Politically the House of Saud does not seem a probable victim for the type of internally motivated, vengeful extremism that swept aside the Pahlavis in Iran. Its dynasty, unlike the shah's, has historical legitimacy and does not rest on the shoulders of one man. The Sauds have made their alliance with the *ulema*, the religious establishment, and their piousness hardly leaves room for complaints that Saudi Arabia has strayed too far from the dictates of the Koran.

But Saudi Arabia could change—at least in terms of policies even if the system itself remained intact—if Crown Prince Abdullah succeeds the ailing King Fahd. Abdullah is the black sheep of the royal family. He does not want to be identified with the West, particularly the United States, and he seeks better relations with the hard-line Arab states, such as Syria. He is an ambitious man, more pious and more of an Arab nationalist than Fahd, and a Saudi Arabia with Abdullah as king would be far less responsive to Washington's interests than the present monarchy has been.

The stability of Saudi Arabia and the Gulf states may be determined in the long run by the very element the royal families created through their dispersal of oil money—the middle class. Throughout the Disposable Decade everyone lived beyond his means, and tomorrow was always better than today. There will be displeasure as the fairy tale fades, displeasure that will require adjustments and reeducation. The House of Saud and the Gulf dynasties will have to fine-tune their arcane and burdensome decision-making processes that straddle the line between tradition and modernization, and that have given money but not power to the burgeoning middle class. The boom years created change that feels strangely artificial because, beneath the façade of marble and glass, few political reforms were undertaken. The middle class, having known education, prosperity and the passion of unfettered expectations, will set the tone and pace in the Retrenchment Decade as the oil producers try to consolidate their gains from the boom. Its children, having traveled the world and seen the fruits of democracy abroad, will not gracefully accept forever a tightly controlled society whose freedoms are limited and whose opportunities for significant political change are few. They will make the demands to which the rulers must respond if the House of Saud is to survive the twenty-first century.

TWELVE

SOME MEN AT THE TOP

THE WEALTH of Saudi Arabia and the Persian Gulf states created a class of oil barons. To protect their investment they needed national stability, and to do this they had to screen out the convulsions of the Middle East. So they in turn created—or at least encouraged and subsidized—a praetorian guard, a network of others willing to confront Israel, take risks in Lebanon and with the Palestinians, control the Shiite fundamentalists, and play the Russians off against the Americans. Foremost among these proxy warriors was Hafez Assad, the president of Syria, whose country's coffers were enriched with $1 billion a year in tribute from the oil barons.

Like many Arab leaders, Assad seemed to have a split political personality. He was a tough military man with the urbanity of a barrister and the charm of a snake-oil salesman. His conservative business suits were correctly tailored, and with his close-cropped hair, trim moustache and ramrod-straight posture, it was somehow difficult to imagine him in traditional Arab dress, bent in prayer, though his fingers constantly worked over a set of amber prayer beads; he did not drink and had not had a smoke since he quit, cold-turkey, his five-pack-a-day cigarette habit. He had tied his fortunes to the Soviet Union in the days of the Cold War, yet would have cast the Russians aside the moment they no longer served his purpose. He invoked the name of God when it fit his needs but was guided by political expediency more than by any Higher Power. He spoke of the dignity and well-being of the Syrian people—and watched over them with five intelligence agencies. Anyone who got out of line needed to take the precaution of first making out his will.

Amnesty International identified sixty-five forms of torture used on Syrian political prisoners, and the U.S. State Department lists Syria as one of five countries in the world that sponsor international terrorism. Assad did not seem much concerned with such allegations. In 1980, after a presidential guard tried to kill him with a hand grenade, seven hundred inmates in Tadmur Prison were massacred. In 1982, when some Sunni fundamentalists from the Muslim Brotherhood started causing trouble in Hama, Syria's fifth largest city, Assad dispatched his brother, Rifaat, and eight thousand Syrian troops to quell the uprising. In a two-week artillery bombardment that leveled large parts of Hama, they flushed out and killed the fundamentalists, as well as about twenty thousand civilians. (During the siege, wall posters in Damascus' Sheraton Hotel continued to advise tourists to "Visit Scenic Hama.") And it was Assad, many diplomats believe, who at least tacitly approved the suicide bomber's mission that killed two hundred forty-one U.S. marines in Beirut in 1983.

With all this, a first-time visitor to Syria might expect to find a chamber of horrors and a den of anti-Americanism run by a bogeyman. Not so, at least not superficially, and not for those who steer clear of politics.

Damascus, continuously inhabited since at least the third millennium B.C., is a relaxed and lovely city, its wide boulevards shaded by cypresses and eucalypti, its parks and private gardens full of bubbling fountains. The supple lines of Islamic architecture sweep across the city, casting shadows over the crowded sidewalk cafés, and in the first neon-glow of night, Damascus comes alive as no other Middle East capital does. Over glasses of scotch and Lebanese wine, Syrians and foreigners alike while away evenings in fine restaurants and greet the morrow in nightclubs featuring cabarets and the Arab world's only topless dancers. No wonder

Damascus is a favorite mecca of Middle East–based Westerners for whom meeting a Syrian is synonymous with being invited to a Syrian home for dinner. The only ones made speechless by the Syrians' sybaritic penchant for enjoying themselves are the Iranian pilgrims who arrive by the planeful to visit a Shiite shrine on the outskirts of Damascus and must lower their gaze as they walk past theaters showing movies such as Charlton Heston's *The War Lord*, by vendors hawking lottery tickets and postcards of blond girls in bikinis, by posters advertising the buxom beauty of a California belly dancer named Tamara.

I, like the Iranians, was intrigued by how oblivious the Syrians seemed to be to the same pressures that made other Arabs cower. Part of the reason lies in the history of Syria itself. Once the capital of the Omayyad Empire that stretched from Spain to India in the seventh and eighth centuries, Damascus was historically a seat of learning, the home of poets, philosophers and writers, and Syria's cultural and artistic contributions to the world rivaled those of Mesopotamia and Egypt. Saladin, the Arabs' twelfth-century hero, used Damascus as a base to fight the Crusaders, and it was from Damascus that he ruled an empire reaching from Cairo to Baghdad that represented one of the Arabs' proudest eras. The Syrians, then, grew up with an identity, a sense of having had a history, a pride in the value of independent-mindedness. Just as important, Syria, like Lebanon, was always secular. Aramaic, the language of Jesus, is still spoken in two villages, and about 13 percent of Syria's nine million people are Christian. There are also three thousand Jews left in Syria, who represent an important merchant class. They are the remnants of a much larger community depleted over the past four decades by Arab persecution and the attraction of a Jewish state.

And part of the reason Syria moves to its own beat is that Assad had no qualms about crushing any form of opposition or simply liquidating religious radicals and other pests. Assad, a former air force commander and minister of defense who seized power in a bloodless coup in 1970, and his inner circle of power brokers were members of the Alawite minority, a Shiite subsect not known for its religious fervor.[1] Topless dancers and forbidden pleasures were Assad's spiteful way of telling his Arab neighbors—and his own people— that he didn't give a damn what they thought; he was his own boss and he had the power behind him to prove it. Under Assad, Syria built a 450,000-man military machine, used terrorism as an instrument of foreign policy, took control of the radical wing of the Palestine Liberation Organization and, by becoming the dominant alien power in Lebanon, gained manipulative influence over the seething restless Shiite masses of the Levant that other governments fear.[2] When the Saudis appeared at Assad's door bearing gifts, it was they who bowed and scraped. Not the other way around.

In the West, Assad was depicted as the spoiler, the one who torpedoed peace plans, settlements in Lebanon and reconciliation among the P.L.O. factions. But however offensive he may have been to the United States and Israel, Assad was among the cleverest politicians in the Arab world and was known as a man who honored his word. The goals he pursued were definable, constant and, from a Syrian point of view, logical. He wanted for Syria everything that the Saudis didn't want for Saudi Arabia. He wanted his country to be the pivotal and preeminent Arab kingpin, just as Egypt was in the 1960s. He wanted to be the man in the Levant without whose

[1] The Alawites are an esoteric Islamic sect that often sided with the Christians against the Sunni Muslims in the Crusader wars. Like the Druze and the Shiites, they felt economically and politically oppressed by the Sunnis, and in Syria, where they represent about 10 percent of the population, they rose to power through the military. They have tried to overcome the suspicions of other Muslims by pressing hard for Arabist causes. But the Alawites enjoy some un-Islamic customs, such as drinking wine at religious ceremonies, and are dismissed by many conservative Muslims for not being sufficiently pious. Syria's population is primarily Sunni.
[2] The Levant is a geographical and political term for the countries along or near the eastern shores of the Mediterranean, an area the British called the Near East. They include Syria, Israel, Lebanon, Jordan, Iraq, Cyprus and Turkey. The word comes from a French participle referring to the rising of the sun (in the east); in British slang "levant" means to welsh on a debt.

cooperation neither war nor peace was possible. He wanted to be the dark shadow over Israel, which annexed Syria's six-hundred-square-mile Golan Heights in 1981, an action that both the Soviet Union and the United States condemned. And with infinite patience, ruthless brutality and crafty political savvy, Assad put his blocks into place, one by one.

His survival, like that of most Arab leaders, was due to the army's continued loyalty and an effective intelligence apparatus. The threat to that survival came primarily from the Islamic fundamentalists, who consider the Alawite-dominated rule heretical and reject the basic secular values of Assad's omnipotent Ba'ath party.[3] But Assad took a country that was considered ungovernable, a country crippled by an epidemic of coups d'état after gaining its independence from France in 1946, and made it both governable and stable, at whatever price. By the time of his death in June 2000, he had ruled for thirty years, longer than any modern Syrian leader. One can only suppose that the son who replaced him, Bashar al-Assad, intends to rule just as long. A colonel in the Syrian Army, Assad was so young (thirty-four) that the constitution had to be amended to remove the forty-year-old minimum-age requirement for the presidency. Just to make sure his ascendancy was on the up-and-up, the government announced that an amazing 97 percent of the electorate had endorsed him as the sixteenth president of the Syrian Arab Republic. The elder Assad's durability underscored an aspect of the Arab world that escapes many Westerners: the Arab

[3] The Ba'ath (meaning renaissance in Arabic) party was founded in Damascus in 1947 by the group's philosophical leader, Michel Aflaq, a Syrian Christian. Its platform is based on Arab nationalism and socialism, and envisions a "unified, democratic, socialist Arab nation," reaching from Saudi Arabia to Morocco, under a single leadership. Once a clandestine party, its early support came from students, intellectuals and professionals, but its base has been broadened to attract followers of all faiths in Syria, Iraq, Jordan and Lebanon. Both Syria and Iraq are ruled by competing wings of the Ba'ath party. Damascus and Baghdad both claim exclusive legitimacy of the Ba'ath movement, thus denying the party any central, unified command authority.

world has enjoyed surprising stability over the past two decades; it is arguably the most politically stable region in the Third World.

The grand old man of Arab politics, Habib Bourguiba, was president of Tunisia from 1956, when France gave his country its independence, to 1987. Hussein ibn Talal became king of Jordan in 1953 at the age of sixteen and ruled until his death in 1999. King Hassan II succeeded his father, Mohammed V, in 1961 and is seventeenth in a family dynasty of Alawites who have reigned in Morocco for more than three hundred years. He died in 1999. Moammar Kadafi has been in power in Libya since 1969. Egypt and Algeria have both had peaceful successions upon the death of a president.

With few exceptions, the Arab world today is run by monarchs and generals. Their power is centralized and their rule is highly personalized, usually built around an ego cult that they themselves have created. Turn on the six o'clock television news in almost any Arab country, and the announcer drones on for the first two or three minutes describing in the most mundane detail how the head of state passed his day. When Israel invaded Lebanon in 1982, Tunisia's Bourguiba suddenly found himself the victim of his own personality cult. Wanting the latest news of the war, he turned on the evening news broadcast by the state-run television station. For four minutes he watched pictures of himself swimming laps in his pool while the anchorman delivered a commentary on the excellent state of the president's health. Fuming, Bourguiba phoned the station director and bellowed, "Enough! Get me Lebanon!" There was a momentary blackout while technicians made the transfer. Then Bourguiba was gone, replaced by satellite-delivered war news from Lebanon.

The tragedy of the Arabs' brand of authoritarian leadership is that it doesn't leave much room for democracy. Freedom of expression is a privilege, not a right. Kuwait, for instance, prided itself on having a feisty, fifty-seat parliament, but only the fifty-seven thousand male Kuwaitis who can trace their roots in the country back to 1921 were allowed to vote in parliamentary elections. When Kuwait's emir worried that debate was getting a bit too lively in 1986, he simply dissolved the national assembly and sent all its members home. "Democracy is shaking," he declared. President Hosni Mubarak of Egypt, an air force general, is more committed than most to the concept of intellectual freedom, yet Egypt has been in a state of martial law since Anwar Sadat's assassination in 1981, and local journalists in Cairo (and elsewhere in the Arab world) practice the most destructive form of censorship—self-censorship—rather than risk the consequences of governmental ire. Even Assad and Moammar Kadafi of Libya lace their speeches with references to the importance of the democratic process. Yet at best the various consultative councils in the Arab world can do little more than propose and recommend. The monarchs and the generals do the deciding. The result is twofold: intellectuals, feeling stymied and frustrated, have left the Middle East by the thousands to escape creative suffocation and start new lives abroad; and religious fundamentalists, capitalizing on the emotional weariness of a silenced people, have been able to stir and stimulate the masses with their messages of radical change.

FABLED BAGHDAD is a cheerless place. It is gray and solemn, a sort of Moscow without Marxism. People walk with a shuffle and seldom smile. They speak very cautiously, for President Saddam Hussein's undercover agents, like those of Assad in Syria, are everywhere. The agents tap hotel phones, follow strangers in the streets, monitor university classes under the guise of being students. No foreign publications, such as *Time* or *Newsweek*, are allowed into Iraq, and Iraqis are not permitted to own a typewriter, a machine the government fears could be used to churn out propaganda.

There is only one way to do things in Iraq—Saddam Hussein's way. A stocky, steely-eyed man of peasant origins, Hussein ensures that iconoclasts do not stay free to gloat or proselytize. When he shuffled his cabinet in 1979, a brief government announcement said only that the six ministers who fell from favor had been killed by the guns of—and in the presence of—the eighteen surviving ministers. Al Capone would have felt right at home with such company.

None but the deaf or blind could be unaware of Hussein's extraordinary presence. Go anywhere in Baghdad, and there he is. His huge portraits, framed in ornate gilt, watch over the Iraqis from public squares, storefronts and hotel lobbies. His picture is on the windows of taxis, on the sides of buses, on the front page of state-run newspapers. In 1983 fifty-nine of the sixty-four books published by the Information Ministry were collections of presidential speeches. Hussein's aides wear gold watches with his portrait on the dial, and in the war museum attached to the Tomb of the Unknown Soldier, there are no less than 101 pictures of Hussein. He appears, smiling or stone-faced serious, in Western business suits, in traditional Arab garb, in military uniforms, Like an actor, he has an image to fit every occasion, an expression to mirror every mood.

After checking into my hotel, the first thing I used to do upon arrival in this bleak and dispirited country was to go to a travel agent and inquire about the availability of homeward-bound flights. But on the Wednesday I got to Baghdad every shop was shuttered, and the city was closed down, as lifeless as a ghost town. Hussein, I learned after considerable puzzlement, had declared a holiday for himself, and a good part of Baghdad had gone to the rally to express its support for the president.

Schoolchildren had been bused in from the countryside, government employees had marched in from their offices, factory workers had been loaded into flatbed trucks and driven by soldiers to the demonstration. The orderly throngs surged out of the plazas and through the canyons of look-alike buildings, and their throaty cheers echoed across Haifa Street to the banks of the Tigris River—"Saddam! Saddam! Saddam Hussein!" A government escort officer stood on the outskirts of the rally, smiling. "You see," he said, "this is why we don't have to hold elections in Iraq. You are witnessing a referendum for the president."

I watched the obedient masses shouting their slogans. It was not easy to catch any sense of Iraq's splendid past. Once, though, perhaps five thousand years earlier, when all property belonged to the gods, this was the Mesopotamia of the Old Testament, and the world's most advanced civilization flourished along the banks of the Tigris and Euphrates rivers. Here was where the Sumerians became the first cereal agriculturists and developed the first form of writing based on phonogrammic as well as pictorial symbols. They made the first wheeled chariot, and discovered that tin and copper smelted together produced bronze, a new, more durable metal useful in making weapons.

Mesopotamia—"the land between the rivers"—was the granary of the Near East then, full of date orchards and lush green fields where farmers grazed thousands upon thousands of sheep. This, some say, was the site of the Garden of Eden. Singing boatmen in fishing canoes plied their way through giant reeds that laced the network of man-made irrigation canals. City-states prospered, and Babylon became a symbol of grace and style whose image lingers to this day. King Hammurabi, nearly twenty-five hundred years before the birth of Islam, devised the world's most comprehensive legal code here, dealing with everything from rent to divorce to labor conditions. It was intended, he said, "to cause justice to prevail in the country, to destroy the wicked and the evil, that the strong may not oppress the weak."

Babylon—with its famed Hanging Gardens, one of the Seven Wonders of the Ancient World—fell to the Persian imperialists in 539 B.C. and became a Persian colony.[4] The idyllic days were soon filled with decay and rebellion. The Mesopotamian languages dis-

[4] The name Persia in modern times referred merely to the province of Fars. The country's name was changed in 1935 to Iran, denoting the whole plateau between Afghanistan and Turkey. Iran's 42.5 million people speak Farsi, not Arabic, and are members of the Shiite sect.

appeared; the Persians diverted established trade routes away from Babylon; the dams and dikes that controlled the waters of the Tigris and Euphrates fell into disrepair. The Babylonians rose up against their rulers, protesting immense taxes to be paid in silver and the requirement that they feed the Persian royal court for four months every year. Their attempts to oust the Persians failed, and the leaders of their rebellions were tortured to death. Great repression followed. Not until 331 B.C., when Persian forces stationed in Babylon surrendered to Alexander the Great, did Iraq free itself from its hated neighbor. All Babylonia hailed the Greek as its liberator.[5] Nine centuries later, in A.D. 634, long after the great cities of Mesopotamia had crumbled and been buried under the rivers' silt, eighteen thousand Arab tribesmen, led by the religious general Khalid ibn al-Walid, burst out of the Arabian Peninsula on the mission that would carry Islam all the way to Spain. Iraq, then comprising mostly Christian tribes, was quickly conquered, and Baghdad rose, like Damascus, to become an intellectual center of God's people, producing jurists, scientists, poets and philosophers. For nearly five hundred years, until the mid-thirteenth century, much of the civilized world was ruled from Baghdad. Such was the golden legacy that Saddam Hussein inherited in 1979, when he rose to uncontested power in an in-house shuffling of the palace guard.

Hussein walked with brisk, deliberate strides into the conference room of his military headquarters. He had decided to hold the first press conference ever for American journalists, and about two dozen of us had received visas to Iraq for the occasion. We sat around a long horseshoe-shaped table and Hussein took his seat on the raised platform, fifty feet away, surrounded by aides and bodyguards. He wore green army fatigues, a beret, spit-shined

---

[5] Alexander respected Babylonian traditions and accepted the people's worship of their chief god, Marduk. He developed grandiose schemes to restore Babylon's grandeur, which included making it one of the two seats of his empire. But his plans were never carried out, for Alexander died in 323 at the age of thirty-two, probably of malaria contracted in Babylon.

boots; a Soviet pistol was on his hip. His face was round, and the first traces of a jowl were taking form under his chin. He had a shock of black hair, heavy eyebrows and a dark, full moustache. He parted his lips as though to smile in greeting, but his expression remained one of glowering sternness and no smile came. My first thought was, I would not like to have this man interrogate me alone in a room.

A journalist cleared his throat and asked about relations with Washington. Hussein waved the question aside. "First," he said, "I want to know what criticisms you have heard about Iraq. About what the world thinks of Iraq." There was a moment of uncomfortable silence. Well, one of my colleagues volunteered, some people say the president was considerably less popular than the presidential cult might indicate. Then a second added that there was the issue of Iraq being a police state. And, said a third, there was talk that opposition figures in Iraq simply disappeared in the night, and he rattled off a list of six Iraqi figures who had not been heard from for some time.

It was probable that no such candid exchange had ever before been held with the Butcher of Baghdad, as Hussein's enemies called him, and the room fell so quiet that I could hear the nervous breathing of the information minister, Latif Jasim. Hussein's aides sat in stunned silence. The deputy prime minister dropped his pencil. One bodyguard turned his glance toward the far wall, as though just the act of looking at the nefarious inquisitors might cast an evil spell on him. But Hussein handled each accusation calmly, showing no discernible emotion and always referring to himself in the third person. "Saddam Hussein believes that . . ." he would say. Of the "disappearances," he said, only one official, former Minister of Health Riad Ibrahim, had been executed. Everyone else was alive and well, although specifics of their well-being seemed to escape him.

Against this backdrop of excesses, it may sound contradictory to speak of Hussein's positive contributions to Iraq. But they were not insignificant in a country that had become known for political lunacy and instability. Iraq experienced twenty-two revolutions or coups d'état between 1920 and 1979. It had been one of the wild-eyed radical Arab states and one of the Soviet Union's first partners in the Arab world. It worked actively to promote instability in the Persian Gulf (which Iraq calls the Arab Gulf), even trying to invade Kuwait in the mid-1970s. It gave hijackers a red-carpet welcome, treated terrorists like international dignitaries, and led the movement to expel Egypt from the Arab League after Anwar Sadat made peace with Israel. For years you couldn't pick up a newspaper in Baghdad without reading about the satanic policies of the United States and the need to destroy Israel.

Under Hussein an egalitarian society evolved where one saw neither abject poverty nor flaunted wealth. Official corruption in his regime, diplomats said, was unheard of. The literacy rate rose to 70 percent, the villages were electrified. Hussein, a Sunni Muslim governing a Shiite majority, did not let the mullahs meddle in politics, but kept peace with religious elders critical of his secular Ba'athist policies by spending $200 million refurbishing the country's mosques. Political instability became a curse of the past, and Iraq's immense oil reserves—second only to those of Saudi Arabia—ushered in an era of prosperity. Money brought moderation, as it has everywhere in the Arab world except Libya, and Hussein started sounding almost right-wing, telling an American congressman, Stephen J. Solarz, "No Arab leader has now in his policies the so-called destruction of Israel or wiping it out of existence."

So things were going pretty well for Iraq in September 1980, when Saddam Hussein made the gravest miscalculation in the Middle East since the Arab armies attacked the fledgling state of Israel. Iran was churning with revolutionary disorder in 1980, threatening to swallow up the Sunni-led oil sheikdoms around the Persian Gulf and goading Iraq with propaganda, organized subversion and occasional cross-border bombardments. On September 19 a senior delegation from the Gulf states gathered in Baghdad at

Hussein's invitation to consider how best to contain the Ayatollah Ruhollah Khomeini and his Shiite revolution.[6] Hussein showed up for luncheon at 4:00 P.M., three hours late. He apologized for his delay, saying he had been in a secret meeting with his generals. Then he dropped a bombshell on his guests: he had, he said, decided what to do about Khomeini—he was going to war against Iran.

"I told him, 'Don't do it; don't go to war,'" a cabinet minister recalled. "I told him, 'They've got forty-two million people and you've got fourteen million. You'll just get ground down and fall under the influence of whatever foreign power is supplying you with arms.' But he was very insistent. He thought Iraq could win the war in a few weeks and finish off Khomeini."

Three days later the unholy war began. Iraqi forces swept across the 875-mile-long Iran-Iraq border and tore through crumbling Iranian lines, grabbing and occupying four hundred square miles of southwestern Iran. Hussein's timing seemed superb. The once mighty Iranian military machine had been crippled by the shah's overthrow the year before. Ten thousand of his former officers had been imprisoned or dismissed. Hundreds of American-made planes and tanks had been grounded by a lack of spare parts the United States was no longer willing to supply. There was no reason to believe any country would come to Khomeini's aid, and Hussein was confident that his army—considered the most professional in the Middle East after Israel's and Jordan's—could conduct a swift surgical operation and be home with Khomeini's head within the month.

As it turned out, Hussein's generals had given him very bad advice. The invasion enabled Khomeini to rally his people in a nationalistic cause, diverting attention from domestic problems and helping to institutionalize the Iranian revolution. "The purest

---

[6] The Persians started as Sunni Muslims and did not embrace Shiism until the fifteenth century.

joy in Islam," Khomeini explained, "is to kill and be killed for God," and hundreds of thousands of young, untrained Iranians answered his call, rushing to the front clutching the Koran. President Assad—anxious to unseat Hussein and take total control of the Ba'ath movement—closed down Iraq's oil pipeline to Tripoli, Libya, via Syria. North Korea, Eastern Europe and Libya poured weapons into Iran. Israel provided the Iranian military with covert technical assistance and channeled American-made weapons and spare parts to the ayatollah, figuring Iraq remained a more serious threat to long-term Jewish interests than Iran. According to reports, the Reagan administration secretly sent three shipments of military spare parts to Iran to gain the freedom of three Americans held hostage in Lebanon by pro-Iranian militiamen. France and the Soviet Union sold guns to Iran (as well as Iraq), recognizing, as the United States did, that Iran's size, wealth and location made it the strategic prize. The superpowers remained officially neutral, but clearly no one was uncomfortable with the notion that this was a useful war as long as it didn't spread; after all, two unsavory characters, Hussein and Khomeini, were locked in a death struggle that kept them both on the sidelines of international mischief-making. Henry A. Kissinger expressed the prevailing sentiment most succinctly: "The ultimate American interest in the war [is] that both sides should lose."

The war, militarily stalemated for the most part since Iraq's initial advances and subsequent retreat from Iran, had by 1986 become the longest major conflict in modern Middle East history and the most costly engagement between two countries anywhere since World War II. Casualties soared past one million dead and wounded as both sides' cities came under bombardment. Iraq used mustard and nerve gases on its enemy. Iran sent pubescent schoolboys to walk through minefields; they were torn apart by the explosions—five thousand children died clearing one minefield alone in 1982—and tanks followed on the cleared pathways. Almost every family in Iraq and Iran was touched by death, yet in Baghdad I had trouble finding anyone who remembered how the war had started or why it was being fought. The Iraqis knew what they were fighting *against* but were not sure what they were fighting *for*. All they understood for sure was that this was a war between two men more than one between two nations, and that it was not likely to end as long as both Hussein and Khomeini remained in power.

This was also a war between Muslims that brought all the competing forces of Islam to bear on one battlefield. It confirmed, I thought, suspicions that even if Israel was removed from the Middle East equation, peace would not suddenly descend on the fractured world of the Arabs. Here in the marshy plains of southern Iraq and the hilly killing fields farther north was the clash of sects (Shiites and Sunnis, who have contested for thirteen hundred years the line of succession from Mohammed), of visions (Iran's sectarian theocracy and Iraq's modern secularism), of inter-Arab rivalries (with the so-called radicals supporting Iran and the professed moderates backing Iraq), of two iron-willed personalities trying to settle old scores. Khomeini dismissed Hussein as a heretic and said the Gulf war was not one for territory; it was a war "between Islam and blasphemy." Hussein responded that Khomeini was nothing more than "a shah in a turban" and promised that "true faith will beat humbug."

The enmity between the Iraqi and Iranian leadership has its roots in ancient history as well as in modern border disputes.[7] Until 1975, Iraq controlled both banks of Shatt-al-Arab—the River of the Arabs—at the southern Iraqi port city of Basra. Here the Tigris and Euphrates rivers meet to form a 120-mile-long estuary to the Persian Gulf. During negotiations in Algiers that year, Iraq granted Iran sovereignty over the eastern bank of Shatt-al-Arab, and

[7] Iraq and Iran temporarily buried their traditional enmity in 1937 by signing the Saadabad pact with Turkey and Afghanistan that joined the four nations in a nonaggression treaty. The motivation was not pan-Arabism—indeed Iraq was the only Arab nation of the four signatories; it was a preoccupation with the potential threat of the Soviet Union.

in exchange Iran agreed to end its support of anti-government Kurdish rebels operating in Iraq. As part of the understanding, Shah Mohammed Reza Pahlavi insisted on an unwritten codicil: Khomeini, Iran's religious leader who had lived for thirteen years in the Iraqi Shiite holy city of An Najaf, had to end his political activities. But Khomeini refused, and Hussein—Iraq's strongman, though not yet its president—ordered him exiled in 1978. "He ate Iraqi bread and drank water from the Euphrates, but he was ungrateful," said Hussein. He bundled the old man off to Kuwait. The last thing Kuwait wanted was a rabble-rousing ayatollah in its midst, and authorities there denied him a visa, causing Khomeini to leave for Paris in a highly agitated state. He was one of seven hundred thousand Shiites thrown out of Iraq over fifteen years' time, and when he returned triumphantly home to Iran the next year, following the shah's overthrow, he thirsted for revenge.

A few days after Hussein's press conference, Iran suffered particularly heavy casualties in unsuccessful human-wave attacks on the Iraqis' defensive lines around Basra. "There will be a bus leaving for the front tomorrow to show you our victories," a government official told us. It seemed peculiar getting on a bus at 4:00 A.M. for the war zone, as though we were tourists heading out for a day's sightseeing, but we were anxious to see what had happened, and we grumbled as our escort officer had to leave the bus to roust one of the journalists who had overslept, delaying our departure from the Baghdad hotel for thirty minutes. The journalist had been one of the best-known American correspondents covering the Middle East twenty years ago. Somewhere along the line he had fallen from grace with his editors and had moved on to a smaller daily paper, and now, almost seventy and still traveling the war circuit, he stumbled into the bus, stuffing his shirt into his pants and mumbling apologies. Dazed with sleeplessness, he looked disoriented, feeling his way toward a seat and, finding it occupied, having to move to the rear to claim another. Jesus, I wondered, was that the fate that awaited us as foreign correspondents? Would I wake up to the pounding on my door in Baghdad one morning when I was seventy, falling out of bed in darkness, to catch a bus to the front of some futile and awful war?

The journey to Basra took five hours. Huge convoys of tanks and trucks loaded with soldiers and artillery guns rolled with us toward the front, and speeding the other way—headed for the Vale of Peace burial grounds in An Najaf—were orange taxis with coffins lashed to their roof racks. I would have traded my portable typewriter for a cup of coffee and a doughnut, but the flatlands we passed through were empty and devoid of roadside restaurants, and we did not stop until we reached a compound surrounded with barbed wire outside Basra.

"Here you will see that the demon Khomeini is fighting this war with children," our government guide announced. Inside the compound Iraqi officers brought out a dozen Iranian "soldiers" who appeared to be no more than undernourished waifs. Most were thirteen or fourteen years old and had not yet started to shave. They sat cross-legged on the ground, sullen and scared and hollow-eyed, having no idea why a group of English-speaking strangers without uniforms or guns had shown up to ask them questions.

The boys were illiterate peasants. They said they had received two weeks' military training before being sent to the front, but had never fired a rifle in practice. Some had been prodded into making suicidal attacks by fake maps that showed the holy Shiite cities of An Najaf and Karbala located a hundred yards or so across the Iraqi border—a location that missed the mark by about two hundred miles. Several had arrived at the front carrying their own coffins, for they all shared a singular belief: there could be no greater glory than to die as martyrs for what Khomeini had said was a *jihad* (holy war).

But the battlefield I found was watched over by no god. On the chaotic Iranian side, viewed through binoculars, turbaned mullahs bounced along on brightly colored motor scooters among the youthful *bisij* (revolutionary guards) and the teenage children they used as fodder. They exhorted them with prayers and shouts of "Down with America!" Each combatant received a plastic key to heaven to be worn about his neck, and then they were sent on their way, across open fields of Iraqi fire, an army of believers marching to its glorious destiny. The regular army supported the volunteers with artillery, fired from safely behind the lines, and did not move up until the way had been cleared.

Most of the Iranian dead had been removed from the swampy plains by the time we got to Basra, and the war zone had fallen quiet except for the thunder of Iraqi artillery. Iraq, though, had never been able to capitalize on its overwhelming superiority in artillery, tanks and planes, and had been largely content to fight a defensive war. Its pilots bombed—not very accurately—from high altitudes that offered none of the dangers of deadly low-level runs, and its infantry commanders showed little aggressiveness. What's more, its troops, unlike Iran's, took offense at the idea of dying and fought mainly from an elaborate catacomb of trenches and earthen parapets reminiscent of World War I battlefields. Their timidity and lack of motivation were not going to produce victory, nor was Iran's suicidal bloodletting likely to accomplish conquest.

The stakes were high for the world in the Iran-Iraq war. If Khomeini had won and a wildfire of Shiite fundamentalism spread through the region, Iran could control Arabia's oil fields. It is a script the United States and Western Europe would have used military force to prevent. But ironically the struggle between Iran and Iraq had little real significance for anyone but the belligerents, despite dire predictions to the contrary when it began. Iraq's attacks on ships in the Persian Gulf did not stop oil tankers from calling at Iran's oil-exporting facility on Kharg Island, and Iran did not make good on its threat to retaliate by closing the Strait of Hormuz off the Omani coast. Khomeini was not able to export his Islamic revolution anywhere but to lawless Lebanon, and Hussein's economy did not disintegrate, thanks to the backing of his former enemies—the Arab oil producers, who underwrote his war campaign, and Egypt, which supplied weapons and 1.3 million workers to offset the drain of war-bound Iraqi men taken from civilian jobs. And the Gulf states learned to live with threats that their support of Iraq made them vulnerable to Iranian-sponsored terrorism by increasing security precautions. Kuwait, for instance, made it illegal for women to drive cars while veiled. The reason: male terrorists could disguise themselves as veiled women and have an easier time penetrating public areas on suicide missions.

By 1986, Hussein would have taken any kind of settlement that let him escape with his honor and his skin. Khomeini wouldn't let him have it; he still had a lot of people he could waste and was willing to stand firm, demanding nothing less than Hussein's abdication. Had the industrialized powers been willing to invoke military and commercial sanctions against Iraq and Iran, the war would have withered away in a matter of months. But the narrow focus of perceived American and Soviet interests in the Third World stoked the flames of confrontation, and the United States, for one, gained considerably from the war.

Capitalizing on the Arabs' fear of Khomeinism, U.S. administrations were able to speed the militarization of Arabia with huge arms sales and at the same time expand U.S. military influence in the region. Deals were struck around the Gulf and on the peninsula that gave the United States access to Arab military facilities in an emergency, and even Saudi Arabia found it advantageous to begin collaborating with U.S. intelligence agencies. The same countries that had caused economic panic in the United States with their oil-price increases a decade earlier now have covertly turned to the United States to protect their oil fields if a worst-case scenario comes true.

The war with Iran ended in August 1988, when Iraq accepted a U.N. resolution for a cease-fire. But Hussein was not ready for peace. Two years to the month later, his tanks rolled into Kuwait to begin an Iraqi occupation of its oil-rich neighbor. Precisely what Hussein had in mind was never clear, though it was presumably the control of Arabian oil wealth, possibly including Saudi Arabia's. His dreams of grandeur were short-lived. In five weeks of air attacks and 100 hours of ground combat, a U.S.-led coalition that included military support from most Arab governments freed Kuwait and drove the Iraqis back across the border in the winter of 1991.

Hussein's army, the world's fourth largest, offered little resistance and was pulverized. More than 175,000 Iraqi troops surrendered; an estimated 85,000 were killed. Hussein declared victory. And a lot of foolish Arabs cheered, believing he had stood down the Great Satan. Hussein, however, had clearly led the former Mesopotamia back to the Dark Ages. Two of Hussein's sons-in-law, who held high positions in the military, defected to Jordan in 1995 and criticized the Butcher of Baghdad. Hussein invited them back to patch things up and had them killed. The U.N. embargo instituted after the Persian Gulf War ended commercial air service to Baghdad and cut Iraq's legal oil sales. Hunger was widespread and children died because of a lack of medicine. The country's per capita income had been cut in half by the year 2000, to $1,200. Only one thing survived the aftermath of the Gulf war intact—the splendor of the life-style enjoyed by Hussein and his closest loyalists.

LEO DUROCHER could have been talking about the Middle East when he said, "Nice guys finish last." This is a region where the respect a leader garners is based on toughness, not innovation, where compromise is equated with weakness. With few exceptions, nice guys don't make it to the top, and if they do and if they want to stay there they have to remold their images by creating what is often a mythology of stern rigidity and omniscient authority. Opposition is tolerated only so long as it acquiesces to the generals and monarchs, and remains respectably close to the party line. Originality of thought and independence of action are not qualities associated with Arab leadership. Nor is the electoral process a characteristic of Arab politics. The populace has nothing to say about who holds ultimate power and guides the nation's destiny. The leaders are there because their fathers were there, or because an inner circle of power brokers put them there. And once they are there, they remain at the helm until they die or are overthrown.

THE HAFEZ Assads and the Saddam Husseins represent the extreme in their ironfisted attitudes toward power. But thirty-five hundred miles west of Baghdad, on the Atlantic flank of the Islamic and Arabic world, one finds another brand of leadership that is closer to the mainstream. The protagonist here was King Hassan II—former jet-setting playboy and political magician *extraordinaire*. He referred to the Moroccans as "my children," and he ran his kingdom with an unquestioned authority that was firm but not brutal. He had the charm and arrogance of a man born to rule, and when he kept Queen Elizabeth waiting for fifteen minutes before receiving her during her visit to Morocco in 1981, his aides were quick to dismiss the Queen's annoyance. "The King could never have kept the Queen or anybody else waiting, because the King cannot be late," explained the minister of court.

Morocco, a French protectorate until its independence in 1956, is the anchor of Western interests in North Africa, and I think I felt more inherently at home there than I did in any Arab country. While the vision of most Arab countries is directed inward, Morocco looked outward, beyond the Atlantic to the United States and across the Strait of Gibraltar at the mouth of the Mediterranean to Europe, just twelve miles away. Hassan's heart was in the East but his mind was in the West, and the framework of his policies was more Occidental than Oriental. He did not trap himself in Third World bluster or Arab and African causes in which he did not believe, and this independence of mind and action gave him more maneuverability than most of his peers enjoyed. He was conservative, pro-Western, anti-Communist, old-fashioned, a sort of Ronald Reagan of the Arabs.

Hassan was one of the few Third World leaders I can think of who gave, rather than sold, his country's friendship to the United States and the West. He took pride in the fact that Morocco— under his great-great-great-great-great-grandfather, Sultan Moham-med III—had been the first country in the world to recognize the United States of America (in 1777) and that the still-active U.S.-Moroccan Treaty of Friendship (signed in 1778) represents the longest uninterrupted accord in American history. Hassan let the Voice of America build a $175 million radio transmitter in Tangier. He gave U.S. planes and ships temporary use of Moroccan military facilities at no cost in the event of a Middle East crisis, and he per-mitted unlimited port calls by U.S. vessels, including those with nuclear arms. It was Hassan who arranged secret meetings between Egyptians and Israelis that led to Anwar Sadat's dramatic visit to Je-rusalem in 1977, and Hassan who led the fight to reinstate Egypt's membership in 1984 in the Organization of the Islamic Confer-ence, a global, Arab-dominated group that had expelled Egypt for making peace with Israel.

Washington in turn was giving Morocco $100 million per year into the 1990s in economic and military assistance, about $4 per Moroccan. (By comparison, Israel was receiving $625 per person, Egypt $54 per person.) Looking for more support, Hassan sent his prime minister to Washington to plead Morocco's case. He received a cordial welcome from Reagan administration officials and re-turned home empty-handed, but no threats emanated from the palace that the brush-off would result in any policy alterations. "There's a feeling here that Moroccan friendship is taken some-what for granted by the United States," one of the members of the prime minister's delegation to Washington told me, "but to tell you the truth, Washington probably *can* take us for granted. We have traditionally looked to the West, and that's not going to change because we do or don't get money from someone."

If I had to choose one aspect of Hassan's life that reflected his Western orientation, it would be the king's passion for golf. That may sound peculiar, but an Arab monarch who likes to chip out of bunkers with a nine-iron is unique. With the exception of President Mubarak, a squash enthusiast, I never knew another Arab leader who exercised, let alone partook in sports. King Fahd of Saudi Arabia, who had the elevators installed in his private jet and his Kuwait residence, doesn't even like to *walk*. Once Arabs leave their schoolboy soccer fields behind, they seem to become sedentary, and it is rare that one sees a jogger or tennis player or someone exerting himself physically by choice. The Arabs are spectators, not participants. Quiet hobbies enjoyed in the West—reading, painting, stamp-collecting, or just tinkering—are largely alien pastimes in the Arab world, where leaders devote their energies to discussions, prayers and family life. But Hassan was a doer, and he always moved just fast enough to outdistance the doomsayers predicting the imminent demise of his dynasty.

When his father, Mohammed V, died suddenly in 1961 after minor surgery, Prince Hassan ascended the throne as a thirty-two-year-old bachelor who had spent more time worrying about his wardrobe than about attending to his royal duties.[8] He flew his own plane, frequented European nightclubs and liked fast cars, spirited horses and vivacious women, though not necessarily in that order. Skeptics and supporters alike figured his kingly life span would be about three months. But presto, new image! "The man you know as Prince Moulay Hassan no longer exists," Hassan told his countrymen upon becoming king.

Hassan never had to eat those words. He became a master of populist politics and one of the Arabs' most skilled statesmen. He disbursed patronage and played various groups and parties off against

---

[8] One might take issue with this statement, for Hassan, at the age of twenty-six, had been involved in negotiations with France that led to Morocco's independence in 1956. France had exiled Sultan Mohammed and his family, including Prince Hassan, to Corsica, and then to Madagascar, in 1953 to defuse Morocco's independence aspirations. But terrorism and rioting against the French increased, and the royal family was allowed to return in 1955.

one another, letting none get too weak or too strong. His internal security force was trained by the Israelis—yes, *Israelis*—and was one of the most efficient in the region, without being unduly repressive. His credentials as Morocco's religious leader were so impeccable that even the fundamentalists were envious: King Hassan was a direct descendant of the Prophet Mohammed, and he had the genealogical charts going back thirty-seven generations to prove it. This lineage, combined with a family dynasty that reaches back seventeen generations, gave Hassan's rule a legitimacy that few Arab leaders could match. Perhaps that accounts for the risks he was willing to take and the confidence he displayed. Or perhaps he took the risks because his location at the far end of the Maghreb put a lot of miles between Morocco and the flash points of the Middle East.[9]

Whatever the reason, he did not suffer from the insecurity complex that afflicted some of his contemporaries. While other heads of state found it safest to say nothing at all about Khomeini, Hassan loved to lambaste the ayatollah in speeches and would even take on the legend of Gamal Abdel Nasser from time to time, saying the late Egyptian president spent too much time trying to impoverish the rich instead of enriching the poor. And while others offer end-

[9] The Maghreb, an Arabic word for "west," consists of the former French colonies of Morocco, Algeria and Tunisia, a region twice the size of Alaska with a population of nearly 70 million, almost all of whom are Sunni Muslims. (Some scholars include Libya and Mauritania in the grouping for political purposes.) Various attempts to develop unity within the Maghreb over the past thirty years have largely failed because of the differences between the countries: Morocco is monarchial and Atlantic-oriented, Algeria confrontational and outspoken, Tunisia moderate and quiet. A Maghreb Permanent Consultative Committee, which includes Mauritania but not Libya, was set up in the 1960s but seldom meets and has accomplished little. The preamble to Morocco's constitution defines Moroccan identity as being, in order, Maghreb, Arabic, Islamic and African. Hassan shocked his countrymen—and angered Washington—in 1984 by agreeing to form a loosely defined union with Libya. But as with most Arab alliances, there was less to the treaty than met the eye, and Hassan canceled it in 1986 after Moammar Kadafi castigated him for meeting with Prime Minister Shimon Peres of Israel.

less words of support to the Palestinians, Hassan has stepped back a foot or two from that problem and was one of the few Arab heads of state to invite his country's Jews to come back home from Israel. Few did, but Morocco still has the largest (20,000) and most accepted Jewish community in the Arab world, and this gave the king some clout in Israel, where half a million people of Moroccan descent represent the biggest bloc of Arab Jews. Hassan's spirited but deferential 306-seat parliament was also extraordinary by Arab standards in that its membership included one Jew and two Communists. The king knew precisely what he was doing, though, in allowing those members to be seated: the Jew was his link to Israel's Moroccan constituency, and the Communists were his conduit to Algeria, whose leftist government backed a guerrilla movement fighting Morocco for control of the Western Sahara.

Spain occupied the Sahara, a phosphate-rich chunk of desert abutting Morocco's southern border, in 1884, largely to provide security for its Canary Islands colony. The territory had no streams, little rain, a nomadic population and, by actual Spanish count, seven hundred palm trees, seventy-six thousand camels and eighteen hundred asses. By 1975, in the dying days of Generalissimo Franco's regime, Spain wanted out, but discussions on the colony's future got bogged down, with Morocco and Mauritania both claiming sovereignty and Algeria wanting to muscle in on the negotiations. To press Morocco's claims, Hassan put together an unarmed army of 350,000 volunteer civilians in less than three weeks and sent it on a Green March to the Sahara. (Green was the color of Mohammed and is thus the color of peace.) The Spaniards were dumbfounded by the spectacle, but they got the point. Hassan halted the march at a bridge spanning a dry riverbed on the outskirts of Layoun, the Sahara's only substantial population center, and three days later he replaced his civilian volunteers with soldiers. Spain responded by cutting Algeria out of the talks, ceding the northern two thirds to Morocco and the southern third to Mauritania, and going home, Hassan's bold stroke won him the acclaim of his countrymen, some of whom named their children born during that nationalist triumph not Mohammed or Salah or Abdullah but Green March.

Mauritania later dropped its claim, and Morocco found itself fighting a nasty little war alone against Algerian-backed Muslim guerrillas in the Colorado-sized Sahara. The Polisario, as the rebel movement is known, wants to create Africa's fifty-second independent state for the 75,000 native Saharans. It would call the country the Saharan Arab Democratic Republic.[10] Hassan countered with a ridiculous idea: he would build a sand wall around the population centers and the phosphate-mining region, thus yielding the worthless desert to the guerrillas and protecting everything that mattered inside the berm. Military analysts scoffed and called the wall Hassan's Folly. But folly it was not. By 1986 the ten-foot-high wall, laced with mines, machine-gun positions and electronic devices, stretched for 950 miles through the Sahara and had rendered the Polisario largely ineffective. Moroccans by the thousands heeded Hassan's call to move into the Sahara as frontier settlers and fulfill their patriotic obligation. To reward them, the king spent a fortune developing the forlorn backwater with mosques, hospitals, schools, housing and a huge soccer stadium. He had pulled another rabbit out of the hat, turning a desert war in a godforsaken wasteland that could have been his political undoing into a national rallying point supported by every Moroccan.

There was just one hotel in Layoun when I last visited, the thirty-

---

[10] Polisario is an acronym for Popular Front for the Liberation of Saguia el Hamra and Rio de Oro, the Spanish names for the two regions of the Sahara. The movement was formed in 1968 by young Saharan intellectuals living in Spain and claimed in 1986 to have ten thousand men under arms. They operate out of Tindouf, a base just inside Algeria. The Arab League, not wanting another conflict on its hands, considered the war an African problem and paid little attention to it. The Organization of African Unity admitted the Polisario as a member in 1982, causing Morocco to withdraw from the body. Hassan, who had packed the Sahara with his loyalist settlers, said he was willing to settle the whole affair with an internationally supervised referendum, an offer the Polisario has not accepted.

five-room Paradores, built in the last years of Spanish rule. When the Spaniards hurried home in 1975, they took everything with them, even the animals from the two-acre zoo. All that remained as a reminder of ninety-one years of European rule in the Sahara were some forts, shantytowns and an airport. The Paradores was spotlessly clean, admirably run and almost never full, and sitting alone one evening on its veranda, amid the Sahara's numbing isolation and an endless silence broken only by the rustle of palm leaves and the nighttime stirring of the wind, I felt as though I had reached the end of the earth.

The empty cages of the miniature zoo I had seen earlier in the day were full of sand, their steel bars rusted. Donkeys plodded through the streets, hauling carts loaded with cooking-gas containers, and men dozed in dark closet-sized shacks that served as butcher shops and vegetable stands. It seemed strange that so many men had chosen such a desolate, useless place to fight in and die for.

My plane to Casablanca had been canceled by a sandstorm, and I fell into conversation with a young man named Douri Ahmed, who worked at the hotel as a driver, handyman, waiter, mechanic and desk clerk. We sat on the veranda, sheltered by palms bending to and fro. The cactus plants around us were covered, like everything else, with layers of powder-fine sand, and a cement spillway nearby, designed as a decorative trough to carry water through the courtyard, was stone-dry, as I guess it had been for a long time. Douri said he had first seen the Sahara as a volunteer on the Green March and had returned to Layoun six years later when King Hassan asked for settlers. I asked him why he had come back. "Because I am a patriot," he said.

Douri wore a wide-brimmed leather hat that resembled a Stetson. He took it off to show me, saying it was his most cherished possession, and I told him it was very handsome and would like to have one myself. The Sahara, he said, was very difficult, but he did not regret his decision to come, for the place and its people slowly grew on you.

"We have a proverb here," he said, "and the proverb is this: 'When you come to the Sahara, you cry; when you leave, you cry even more.' The people, you see, are very amazing in the Sahara. They are very direct, and they speak honestly about things. Their doors are always open for a glass of tea, even if the man of the house is out. We have complete confidence in our women.

"The only problem with living in Layoun is that it is hard for a young man like me to find a wife. There are women here, yes, pretty women, but usually they stay inside and their fathers insist that you must be rich to marry them.

"First, you must have carpets, a lot of carpets. On the first day of the marriage celebration you have to be able to afford two goats for slaughtering. On the second day, you slaughter a camel, and that is very expensive. And then there is gold. You must give the father a lot of gold before you can marry his daughter. Why, in my village in the north, I could find someone to marry for a hundred dirhams [one hundred dollars] and a couple of words. But here, no. So you can see this is a very big problem for me."

I commiserated with him, and he seemed thankful to have found an understanding ear. The next morning was clear and crisp, a good day for flying, and as I was leaving my room at the Paradores to check out, there was a knock at my door. "This is for you," my young friend said, holding his hat out to me with both hands. I told him I appreciated his kindness but couldn't possibly accept the gift. He insisted and I knew I had to relent, for to reject Arab hospitality is to insult the giver. A few hours later I left the Western Sahara for Casablanca, wearing Douri Ahmed's prized leather hat.

THE SAHARA had done something else beneficial for King Hassan II besides winning the undying admiration of people like Douri. It had kept his 170,000-man army occupied supporting a national cause, and in the Third World there is nothing more dangerous than an idle army with no useful purpose to serve. Every Arab leader, in fact, serves at the discretion of his military, and men such as Hassan walk a tightrope trying to keep their senior officers content, their ambitious junior officers rewarded and their foot soldiers obedient. The generals and colonels seldom offer a viable or imaginative alternative to the regimes they depose because their concerns are focused primarily on the perpetuation of their own power. Hassan had twice been challenged by his military; each time he escaped through his own wily daring and the grace of either God or good luck.

For his forty-second birthday in July 1971, Hassan invited a thousand guests, including the entire ambassadorial corps, to a day of golf and banquets at his oceanside palace in Skhirat, one of seven palatial retreats he owns. Midway through the sit-down luncheon, fourteen hundred cadets stormed the grounds, firing wildly at the guests. They were led by a rebel officer whom Hassan had slapped in public after the officer had taken his troops on an unnecessarily grueling training march. Hassan dashed away unharmed during the frenzied shooting that killed 450 people, including the chief justice and the Belgian ambassador. He took refuge in a nearby apartment and, after the rebel commander had been shot dead by loyalist soldiers, emerged three hours later in the company of a sergeant and several younger soldiers.

"Long live Hassan the Second!" chanted the troops still milling about the palace grounds. Hassan shouted a call to prayer, and the rebels put down their arms and knelt, facing Mecca. The revolt was over. Hassan responded by ordering the execution of nine of the country's fifteen generals and retiring the other six.

Hardly had he recovered from that scrape than, thirteen months later, death came courting again. Hassan was flying home from France in his Boeing 727. Suddenly off the right wing three American-made F-5 jets appeared, one of them flown by the king's most senior air force general. They cut loose on the king's jetliner, knocking out an engine and peppering the cabin with bullets. As they were returning for a second strafing run, Hassan grabbed the air-to-air radio and, pretending to be the pilot, said, "The tyrant is dead. Don't hurt anyone else." The dissident airmen veered off, the king landed safely and the conspirators were soon flushed out. "I must never place my trust in anyone," the king later confided to an ambassador. After that he rarely flew anywhere in Morocco, preferring to travel by road in cavalcades that often included more than two hundred cars and fifty motorcycles, and just as rarely did he sleep in the same bed two nights in a row.

Hassan, I thought, was particularly intriguing because he was an anachronism—a king who lived in splendor among the impoverished masses while royalty was on the decline elsewhere in the world—and because his country was the classic example of a Third World nation struggling to go nowhere. Indeed, after the shah's overthrow in Iran, the U.S. Central Intelligence Agency predicted in a secret report that Hassan would be the next American ally to fall, probably within six months. It did not seem an unreasonable assessment. Morocco's literacy rate of 24 percent and its per capita income of eight hundred dollars were among the lowest in the Middle East, its unemployment and birth rates among the highest. Official corruption was rampant, the gap between rich and poor was immense, the foreign debt was creeping past $11 billion, and with an economy based on phosphate and vegetables, not oil, there wasn't much hope of hitting a national sweepstakes as the Saudis and Kuwaitis had. According to the World Bank, 40 percent of Morocco's twenty-two million people lived below the poverty line.

On top of that, Hassan's regal life-style was enough to raise the eyebrows of even high-living Saudi princes. He shuttled between his palaces with an entourage of five thousand, letting his sinus problems and the climate dictate where he lived from one season to the next. His real estate holdings were extensive, and he maintained a large harem; his wife, Lalla Latifa, who was never seen in public, was "the mother of the royal children," not a first lady. He staged celebrations for himself, and to ensure that the events had sufficient glitter, he hired American public relations firms to pay movie stars and other luminaries to be in attendance as honored guests.

The production he put on when his eldest daughter married the son of his information minister in 1984 would have done justice to a Cecil B. De Mille spectacular. But here is where Hassan again showed the power of populist politics. Rather than making it just a family affair, the king flew in peasant couples, 250 in all, from each of the provinces to exchange vows at the same time. Five days of tribal dancing, processions of camels and around-the-clock buffets attracted tens of thousands of Moroccans, rich and poor, to Fez. Thus what could have been a resented display of royal extravagance became a joyous holiday that united the nation in celebration.

King Hassan's death in July 1999 resulted in a predictably smooth transition of power. His eldest son replaced him, and the new king, Mohammed VI, said he would rule as his father had. A cease-fire had taken hold by then in the Western Sahara, although Morocco continued to postpone a referendum there on self-determination. The standard of living in Morocco had improved since I last saw the kingdom, with per capita income having increased fourfold, to $3,200 a year. Perhaps most important, Morocco remained a sensible, stable place, far from the storms that blew through so much of the Arab world.

IT IS, I think, the legitimacy of Hassan's dynasty and religious heritage—and the manner in which he used both to personal advantage—that gave him longevity and popular support. Arabs tolerate, even expect, a degree of corruption and a certain amount of opulent living from their leaders. They expect their generals and kings to be above them, like tribal chieftains, and they do not look favorably on a head of state who conveys the image of the common man, as did, say, Jimmy Carter during his administration. Since there is no democratic tradition in the modern Arab world, the desires of the people are usually of secondary importance on a head of state's agenda. The masses can be pacified with doles and gifts. I found it curious, for instance, that Moroccans apparently placed more significance in Hassan's role as a religious and political leader who could stoke nationalistic sentiments in time of crisis than they did in the fact that under him their standard of living was deteriorating.

King Hassan's eldest son, Sidi Mohammed, a bachelor with a master's degree in political science and an advocate of women's rights, came to the throne on the day of his father's death in 1999. His reign got off to a promising start. Ruling as King Mohammed VI, he freed eight thousand prisoners and fired the all-powerful minister for interior, Driss Basri, saying he wanted Morocco to be a state of law, not a state of fear. He promised to pursue his father's course of making Morocco a tolerant society.

Despite the political stability the Arab world has known for more than a generation, the foundation of its regimes' credibility is built on sand. They have ignored the world's most powerful political force—man's inherent yearning to have freedom of choice, freedom of thought, freedom of action. In Latin America, Africa, Asia and the Caribbean, the 1980s and 1990s witnessed the building of a democratic momentum and in the process disposed of demagogues and dictators.

Only the Arab world—which doesn't even have a single elected mayor—has remained immune from serious democratic experiments. The reasons for this are tied to both culture and tradition, but they do not mean that the Arab has any less desire to make himself heard than the American or the Filipino or anyone else. Nor do they mean that he will accept indefinitely the manipulation of leaders whose causes are not necessarily his causes. The educational explosion in the Middle East, the growth of the middle class and the burgeoning number of young Arabs traveling abroad will lead to the asking of questions, the making of comparisons and the demanding of a role in shaping national destinies. And this in turn could lead one day to a democratic revolution. It would be a revolution that has its roots in the human spirit, not in allegiance to a superpower, not in religion, not in weary rhetoric about confronting Israel and unifying the Arab nation. Such a prospect is a terrifying one to many of today's insecure Arab leaders, but the results of such radical change would be no less socially dramatic than those of the revolution that swept through Iran on the wings of Islam.

THIRTEEN

A JOURNEY'S END

IT TOOK time and patience, but eventually Cairo really did feel like home. The noise, the congestion and the decay hardly rattled me at all anymore. After three years, I had passed through the stages of culture shock and settled comfortably on the plateau where an alien land no longer felt foreign. What at first had appeared so mysterious—Islam, the roots of the Arab-Israeli conflict, even the Arabs themselves—had become such a commonplace part of my daily life that the enigmas had given way to what seemed, from time to time at least, lucid and intelligible.

Mr. Darwish, the fix-it man, kept repairing my toilet and the toilet kept breaking, and that no longer bothered me. I realized it was *never* going to function properly. At first, through the rhythm of habit, I had worked on Fridays, the Muslim holy day when everything in Cairo but my office was closed, and had taken Sundays off. Despite my resistance, a new schedule coinciding with Arab practices slowly evolved; Friday eventually seemed such a normal day-off that I was always briefly puzzled when, unthinkingly, I would place a business call to the United States on Sunday and find that no one was there. I became so used to waking up each morning before sunrise to the call to prayer that when I would go to Europe on vacation, the silence was unnerving and, in the confusion of half-sleep, I would lie awake awaiting the muezzin's reminder that "God is great. I testify that there is no god but one God. . . ."

The more I traveled through the Middle East, the more I came to appreciate Egypt—the home of one of every four Arabs. For all its forgotten glory and crippling economic problems, Egypt is very special. It is multilayered, and the more you peel away, the more there is to discover. More films are made in Cairo, more books published, more political ideas debated than in the rest of the Arab world combined. The intelligentsia represents an influential class founded on honest intellectual achievement. Unlike many of its wealthy friends, impoverished Egypt has the courage to lead, the willingness to break ranks and act with an independent mind. For that very reason, most Arab governments resent Egypt and are content to keep Egypt ostracized for having made a separate peace with Israel. They want no head rising too far above the crowd. But without Egypt the Arab nation is impotent. The Arabs are mistaken in believing they have strength in numbers and unity in their search for unanimity. What they need is a bold and rational voice that speaks for the whole and, lacking one, it is apparent that they need Egypt more than Egypt needs them.

Anwar Sadat had led the Egyptians across the Suez Canal in 1973 and into peace with Israel in 1979, yet few Arabs today judge Sadat as I believe history will—as a great leader who seized a moment of opportunity. While the American public adopted Sadat as a Western folk hero—the first Arab ever accorded such status— the Egyptians vilified him as a man motivated by ego. They resented his taking a place on the world stage when pressing domestic economic and social problems seemed largely ignored. They hated him for having an opulent life-style befitting a pharaoh, and disliked his wife, Jihan, for speaking out on women's problems and birth control and political issues. Psychologically the Egyptians were not prepared for a liberated woman whose thoughts were freed from the manacles of past traditions. Nor psychologically were they prepared for peace with Israel. It was not that they wanted war more than peace; it was that they heard nothing in their leader's words and saw little in Israel's actions to indicate that the Jewish state was not still the Arabs' enemy. (Nor did Israel see anything to indicate that the Arabs weren't still its enemy.) Sadly, Sadat did not understand that he had lost touch with the heartbeat of the Middle East, and he died in 1981, the victim of fanatical Islamic assassins, wearing a Gilbert and Sullivan–style uniform and believing he was popular.

Not many Arabs would agree, but I think the Camp David Accords (in 1978) that laid the foundation for the Egyptian-Israeli peace treaty represented one of the most promising milestones the Middle East had passed in thirty years. True, it was fatally flawed because it assigned roles to the Palestinians and to King Hussein of Jordan (Hussein's grandfather, Abdullah, had been crowned king of all Palestine in 1948) without consulting them or ensuring their participation. But it was a starting point. It ended a generation of war between the region's two most powerful armies, and it addressed, however unsatisfactorily, the Palestinian issue. From that beginning, a wider settlement could have taken form had not both the Arabs and the Israelis let the opportunity slip like sand through their fingers. The Arabs torpedoed the treaty by expelling Egypt from the Arab League and condemning direct negotiations with Israel. Israel shot it down by continuing to build Jewish settlements in the occupied Arab territories and by invading Lebanon in the summer of 1982. Neither side could agree on how to deal with the Palestinians. And in the failure of Camp David was born the fifth Arab-Israeli war.

Although leaders for both sides recognize that there can be no military solution to the Middle East's problems, neither has a constituency willing to make the concessions necessary for peace. The Levant has become the Belfast of the Middle East, a place where the chivalry of compromise has been overtaken by the posturing of belligerence. Two peoples whose cultural and national identities are steeped in religion have learned only how to talk *at* each other, not *to* each other. Each uses the narrow focus of religion to confirm the position of righteousness. What one side considers an expression of nationalism the other side dismisses as an act of terrorism. What is courage to one is cowardice to the other.

Harold H. Saunders, an architect of the Camp David Accords and formerly the U.S. government's top Middle East expert, summed up the psychological barriers that make peace so elusive when he addressed a group of young Egyptian diplomats in Cairo in 1985.

"I think," he said, "there is something deep-rooted in the Israelis that says, 'We were persecuted. We lost our homes. We were displaced, and now we are living in the homes of those we displaced and farming their land.' It would be a lot easier in human terms if the Israelis could simply forget those people.

"If the Israelis have a claim to the land given to them by the right of God, how can they recognize the claim of the Palestinians to the same land? I think the fear begins right there. If somehow the two peoples could acknowledge that they were both deeply hurt by history and could meet on some common ground, I think you would begin to have a human basis for starting toward a solution."

The Palestinians' plight is the major irritant in the Middle East, the one issue that galvanizes, polarizes and inflames. The choice seems fairly simple—to destroy the Palestinians or to give them a homeland in the Israeli-occupied West Bank of Jordan. Nothing less will diminish international terrorism and enable Israel to get on with the business of developing as a normal nation. The first solution is unacceptable to almost everyone—even to the vast majority of Jews—and the second one is implausible as long as the Palestinians themselves remain divided between war-makers and peace-makers and are willing to let suicide bombers articulate policy.

Granted, solving the Palestinian question is not going to eradicate all the Arabs' problems. It would not bring democracy, end poverty or heal the wounds of division in the Arab world. What if Israel were to evaporate overnight? Would that calm the rough seas of Arabia? What if there *never had been* an Israel? Bloodshed would have been avoided, to be sure, but the Arab world would, I think, still have been the confused, defensive and divided place it is today—a world striving for a role in the global community and for a historical identity, its authoritarian leadership unresponsive to the masses, its spirit torn by the juxtaposition of tradition and temptation. If anything, Israel has been a unifying factor for the Arabs, just as South Africa was for black Africa. Israel offers the Arabs a rallying point. It gives them a convenient peg on which to hang blame for everything that has gone wrong. If Israel had not been there to consume their energies, the Arabs might well have turned their attention to forcefully settling the many intra-Arab disputes over borders and sovereignty that reach from the Arabian Peninsula to the mountains of the Levant to the far deserts of the Maghreb.

In my travels I used to ask people what the Middle East would be like in a generation's time. What legacy were they bequeathing their children? The question invariably led to a moment of silence, and the answer always hinged on one of the two things that had cast the Arabs so suddenly into the consciousness of the world—oil and the presence of Israel.

"There are only two choices," Chedli Klibi, the Arab League's secretary-general, said when I asked him the question. "Either Arab peace efforts are met on the Israeli side, and supported by Western Europe and the United States, or Israel continues to reject all peace settlements and continues its policies of expansionism and force. If the first choice happens, peace can prevail and people can devote their efforts to national progress. If it is the second choice, then I can only envision darkness, for Israel as well as for the Arabs. Lebanon has given us a taste of that dark future."

Surely, though, the culpability cuts both ways. The Arabs did not confront the realities of the nineties because they remain hostage to the myths of the fifties. Their governments cannot bring themselves to accept publicly the permanence of Israel because they do not dare commit the heresy of admitting that Arab unity is a charade. Too often they deal with their world not as it is but as they *wished* it were. They can't back down because they have a vital stake in opposing Israel: their own credibility. If they relent, then what have the last fifty years been all about?

As I prepared to leave the Middle East, I had a disturbing realization. During nearly four years there I had traveled over one hundred thousand miles, been in all eighteen Arab countries and covered wars in Lebanon and Iraq, negotiations between the Egyptians and Israelis, and peace plans put forward by the United States, France, Egypt, Saudi Arabia and the Arab League. I had seen Western peacekeeping forces in Lebanon come and go, petrodollars in the Gulf states rise and fall, religious extremism and terrorism spread. Yet in all that time little had been resolved.

The Palestinians remained in limbo, a homeland within sight but not within grasp. Islamic and Jewish extremists continued their slow march toward political power based on platforms of intolerance, inflexibility and racism between Jew and Arab. Terrorism became institutionalized, an anvil for misanthropes who knew no other tool to weaken the strong and strengthen the weak. The Arab-Israeli dispute remained on dead center, making the term "peace process" a misnomer because the word "process" implies movement. The Israelis grew stronger militarily, weaker economically, and moved dangerously close to a colonial-style dependency on the United States. The Arabs grew stronger economically and weaker in commonality of purpose, and distanced themselves from the United States without straying too perilously far because the West still had much they wanted and needed. The United States, perplexed and perhaps bored with the complexities and intransigence of the Arab world, retired backstage. A great weariness gripped everyone. The Arabs' concerns shifted inward, toward domestic problems and an attitude of secularism.

"The Arab world is facing a civil war in which everyone has

exhausted his ammunition," Mohammed Heikal, an Egyptian political commentator and one of Gamal Abdel Nasser's most trusted advisers, told me. "There are those who have money and those who have ideas, but both are bankrupt. There is a realization that after the euphoria of the fifties, sixties and seventies, what we have is not what we wanted, that we need a different approach."

The cocky exuberance the Arabs enjoyed at the height of the oil boom engendered an atmosphere that gave them newfound clout. It was in that mood that the United Nations passed a resolution equating Zionism with racism, that the Palestine Liberation Organization legitimized itself by winning an invitation in 1974, through the efforts of the Communist and Afro-Asian blocs, for Yasser Arafat to address the U.N. General Assembly, the first representative of a nongovernmental organization ever to do so. That potency was short-lived, and it was symbolic of the Arabs' changing fortunes that when Arafat tried to get an invitation to address the General Assembly in 1985, he was turned down cold. The so-called Arab world had ceased to exist as a political "world"; it had become but a cluster of nations, like those in Latin America or Southeast Asia, forming its private alliances, consumed more by what divides than by what unites. Its power had peaked.

So the decade of the nineties became one of disillusionment and reexamination for the Arabs because their dreams from that oil era have not brought them the promised victories. The Arabs did not emerge as a new power bloc, and oil did not produce political eminence. Nor did oil bring Arab unity; in fact, it had precisely the opposite effect by dividing the Arabs into two clubs, the haves (with oil) and the have-nots (without oil). Zionism was neither derailed nor destroyed. The Islamic revival was notable primarily for producing a medieval ayatollah in Iran and a group of militant extremists who hijacked their religion and carried out evil in the name of Allah. The new class of instant millionaires created by oil had no distinguishing characteristics beyond the possession of money and goods. And Lebanon, once the pride of Arabs everywhere, was dropped from the World Bank's list of developed nations and reclassified as an underdeveloped nation.

If the Palestinians were in limbo in the era of declining oil prices, so, for entirely different reasons, were two other groups in the Arab nations—the intellectuals and the Jews. The days of the former were difficult; those of the later were numbered.

Intellectuals by the thousands have left their Arab homelands for Europe and the United States over the past thirty years, searching for the freedom of expression that nurtures creativity. It is a freedom largely denied them by their own heavy-handed governments, and their departure has robbed the Middle East of some of its best brains and most cogent voices. For all the changes of the seventies, the Arab nations of the eighties remained backward—politically, economically and socially—and it is from that backwardness that the politically alienated intellectuals have fled.

In Cairo, where the population explosion is creating a peasant society, reading is considered by the masses to be a specialized activity—justified if pursued for religious or practical purposes but essentially antisocial. In the oil-producing Gulf states intellectualism suffered as societies became consumer-oriented and artists and writers opted for entrepreneurial endeavors promising wealth. Saudi Arabian publications attracted top Arab writers with generous fees, but buying literary talent for political purposes had some creative limitations: every article had to extol the virtues of the Saudi royal family and none could criticize any country in the Persian Gulf or question any aspect of Islam. Almost everywhere Arab thinkers were expected to conform, to be interpreters for the ruler or ruling party. A sizable intelligentsia still exists in the Middle East and, in countries such as Egypt, fulfills an important role, but it has little significance in shaping society, challenging governmental policy or charting new courses through unknown waters.

The other group whose ranks have been depleted—the Jews—started leaving after World War II as a result of the growth of Zionism and the fear of Arab persecution. In the five decades since the birth of Israel, the Jewish population in Arab lands has shrunk from 850,000 to 40,000, about half of whom live in Morocco. The number of Jews in Egypt has fallen from 150,000 to 250, in Iraq from 150,000 to 400. Libya had only 9 Jews left in 1986. In most countries they had represented a class of professionals, merchants and financiers, and their exodus, in the early stages at least, left a hole in the economies of the Arab world.

Although the Arab-Israeli wars of 1956, 1967 and 1973 all led to an emigration of Jews, the most panicked flight occurred in the late 1940s. As pressure mounted for a Jewish homeland, rioters in North Yemen killed eighty-two Jews and wrecked 106 of the 170 Jewish-owned shops in San'a and the other cities. Iraq made adherence to Zionism, along with Nazism and Communism, a capital offense. Algeria revoked the Jews' citizenship. Egypt imprisoned Jews by the hundreds. Bands of youths sacked the synagogues in Tunisia.

"That chapter of persecution is behind us now," said Rabbi Reuben Roubennaji as he prepared to conduct services for seventeen worshipers in Iraq's only operating synagogue, a shabby little structure in Baghdad. "The numbers have stabilized. No one leaves anymore. For a long time in Iraq, we couldn't sell our property and we couldn't get into business. Now those restrictions are gone. We are completely free to worship. The government protects that right for us."

Because the Jews no longer represent a threat to anyone, the same is true throughout most of the Arab nations today. The Jews remain as a tiny, easily forgotten Arabic-speaking minority within the Muslim majority. Most are elderly, unskilled, poor and apolitical. Few have been to a wedding or a bar mitzvah for years. Except in Iraq and Morocco, their rabbis and kosher butchers have long since left. It is only funerals that bring the dying Jewish community together these days.

In the first half of the century, in what some still fondly remember as the golden age of Egypt's Jews, Cairo had twenty-seven synagogues, a Yiddish theater and three Jewish cemeteries. Today two of the cemeteries are part of the squatter-filled City of the Dead

and only the ninety-four-year-old Chaar Hachamain synagogue—
still resplendent if a bit worn—remains open. Several Egyptian
policemen in frowsy uniforms stand duty in a relaxed manner
outside.

I walked down Adley Street and entered the synagogue through
its alleyway entrance. The ceiling inside was high and domed and
the stained-glass windows from Italy sparkled in the afternoon sun-
shine. The marbled pillars were still shiny. The dark wooden benches
could accommodate one thousand worshipers, but unless a few
tourists showed up unexpectedly on Saturdays, the lay religious
leader, Mourad Gabbai, could seldom put together even the ten
men required to hold a formal service.

Gabbai, a retired government engineer approaching eighty, was
puttering about when I walked in and was happy to have someone
to show through his beloved temple. I asked him what the future of
Egypt's Jewish community was.

"The future?" he repeated, looking out at the empty synagogue.
"Why, there is no future. The Jews will just die out one day. Then
maybe the government will turn this into a museum. It's God's
will."

A funny thing. The Arab governments always seemed largely
intolerant to me, while the Arab people as individuals seemed basically tolerant. It is a contradiction that I could only explain by the
fact that the governments and the people are usually on two different wavelengths. Neither is an accurate reflection of the other, and
given their druthers, most of the 243 million Arabs would choose a
more open, democratic form of government than what they have
inherited. If they eventually do get the right to choose, and their
political systems become as democratic as their religion, which has
no clerical hierarchy, the seat of Arab intellectualism—now located
in London, Paris and the United States—would likely return to its
inherent home. The threat of fundamentalism turning into fanaticism would subside as a result, and the Middle East would become
a healthier place.

But I don't see much evidence that today's Arab rulers are prepared to make room for questioning voices or ready to make peace with one another. Almost certainly the jealousies and the rivalry for leadership will continue, the power vacuum will grow larger, and being an Arab leader will be a very risky business. What seems to be happening in the Middle East is that everyone is setting everyone else up to be a loser.

There can be no Arab winners as long as some governments remain convinced that violence can produce political results. Nor can there be any Jewish winners as long as Israeli governments believe that their right to security and self-respect is greater than others'. Nor can the United States be anything but an eventual loser as long as its elected officials are locked into the mind-set of viewing the Middle East from the simplest of perspectives: one side is inherently good, the other basically evil, and it isn't particularly necessary to understand who the Arabs are and what Islam is, because anyone not guided by Western logic is an unreliable ally anyway. What this leads to is a perversion of democracy, for the Middle East is the only area where Americans do not debate policy. Washington's handling of relations with Latin America, South Africa, the nations of the former Soviet Union, Southeast Asia and Europe all produce lively discussions and disagreements that range through the chambers of Congress and the conference rooms of think tanks, universities and publishing empires. The deliberations and the agitation often stimulate policy shifts that are beneficial to all concerned. But on the Middle East there is only silence. Any U.S. official discerned at election time as being pro-Arab—even if that only means seeking a balanced formula for the region—knows he is a marked man. It is no coincidence that the handful of prominent Americans who speak out today in support of Arab interests all have the word "former" placed before the title of senator or congressman.

By closing the door to debate, the United States is, I think, maneuvering itself into a situation where it is in danger of losing the whole Middle East. It overstates the roles countries such as Saudi

Arabia and Jordan can or will play, then condemns them and cuts off arms sales because they refuse to act against their own self-interests. The grass-roots animosity between Arabs and Americans is growing on both sides of the ocean for no reason other than ignorance, and most Americans do not understand that this tension often rests in the failures of its own government. It is reckless for Washington to throw away a relationship that the Arabs want to preserve, but the day is approaching when the United States and Israel might stand together and alone against the Arabs, and I can think of no more unhealthy scenario—for the Israelis, the Arabs or the Americans. It would deny the Israelis the true independence they seek, the Arabs the fairness they demand, and the Americans the oil and the friendships they surely need. It would nudge the Middle East another step closer to war, which in turn could result in a backlash in the United States, first against the Arab American community, then the American Jewish community. In the end, even the Israelis could turn against the United States, resentful that they are militarily, economically and spiritually indebted to and totally dependent on a foreign power, which, like any protector, would make demands that the ward is not prepared to meet.

Despite the Arabs' puzzlement over U.S. Middle East policies—and it *is* puzzlement because they genuinely can't understand why Washington does what it does—I was amazed in my travels how little anti-Americanism I encountered. In fact, except in Beirut and among those who lived in its shadow, there was none. The people I met wanted to be friends with the United States, and feeling rebuffed, they reacted with both hurt and anger. But never once did they make me feel less than comfortable as an individual American. And seldom was I not aware of the tremendous cultural imprint the United States has stamped on the world. Arriving at the Tripoli airport in Libya the first time, I stepped off the plane with considerable trepidation, wishing my passport bore some nationality other than American. The government escort officer sent to meet me took my passport wordlessly, opened to the first page and saw that my birthplace was listed as Boston. "Hey, wow!" he said. "You must be a Celtics fan. Didn't Larry Bird do a number on the Lakers last year!" I was bowled over. Here I was in Kadafi's damnable fiefdom and the first person I meet, young Mr. Mabrouk (meaning "congratulations" in Arabic), is a graduate of Bird's alma mater, Indiana State, who wants to talk about the National Basketball Association's championship series.

In Algiers, when there was not a hotel room to be found for any price, a taxi driver took me home to his third-floor walk-up apartment, put a blanket and pillow on the kitchen floor and gave me lodging for the night. We shared no common language, but I will never forget the beauty of our wordless communications. In Bahrain a young government clerk brought me home to meet his parents, brothers and sisters because, he said, it would be a shame if I left his country without understanding the closeness of families. Everywhere, so many doors were opened to me, so many tables were set with bountiful dinners, that I would have been hard pressed to reciprocate the gifts of hospitality and friendship even if my time and expense account had been unlimited.

MY LAST journey in the labyrinth of Arabia took me to the Sudan to cover the army's overthrow of President Jaafar Numeiri, who had fallen under the sway of religious extremists. Beset by economic and social problems he could not solve, he was turning his country into an Islamic republic and, as mentioned before, had adopted such a brutal interpretation of the Sharia (Islamic law) that public amputations and executions had become a weekly ritual. In the process, he had become wildly unpopular. The middle class—doctors, lawyers, teachers, merchants—took to the streets to demand that the army get rid of Sudan's president of sixteen years. Never before had an Arab head of state been toppled by the actions and expressions of the middle class. There was not another Arab leader who failed to take notice.

I left Khartoum and went home to Cairo to write a long series on the Arabs and their fortunes, which my editors in Los Angeles appropriately headlined, ARAB POWER ON THE WANE DESPITE OIL — WHAT WENT WRONG? They told me my successor as the *Times'* Cairo bureau chief had been chosen and I could make arrangements to leave. Part of me wanted to stay, for only in the last year or so had I felt truly at ease with my environment. But the other part was weary and knew it was time to go. Sandy and I bought tickets on TWA flight 847 to Rome, called the packers and organized our own farewell party.

We drove into the desert with thirty friends. At a stable near the Great Pyramids of Giza we rented fifteen camels and fifteen Arabian horses and set out across the dunes in the last light of sunset. A few miles away the owner of the stable had set up a tent, covered the sand with a half-dozen carpets and prepared a lavish spread of lamb kabobs, spiced dips for raw vegetables and barbecued chicken. An ice chest full of Egyptian beer was in the tent. The night turned chilly, the sky became black as coal, and we stayed late in our desert retreat. The isolation was splendid—silence and desert all about us, and on the distant horizon the tops of the three pyramids, golden in the illumination of floodlights, soared above the hills of sand. What we saw, what we were a part of that evening, had been all but unchanged for five thousand years. *Five thousand years.* The thought of returning home to the freeways of Los Angeles was jarring.

Sandy had to leave Cairo several days earlier than planned because of a business commitment, so we canceled our June 14 reservations on TWA 847—the ill-fated flight that would be hijacked by Lebanese terrorists and taken to Beirut. Sandy flew directly back to New York, and I stayed behind for a few days while the movers packed up our apartment overlooking the Nile. They wrapped the furniture in cardboard, found a special box for the leather hat Douri Ahmed had given me in the Western Sahara and, with a curious glance, tossed some spent shell casings I had saved from Lebanon into a manila envelope. The pile of cartons in the living room grew high, the books disappeared from the shelves, the pictures from the wall. Our warm, cheerful home suddenly felt soulless and forlorn. Nearly four years of memories had been relegated to temporary burial in cardboard boxes.

Gamal Rasmi, my friend who had danced away his bachelor days at the Playboy Disco, drove me to the airport the next afternoon to catch the Ethiopian Airlines flight to Athens. He and Manal had married, she had given him a son, and they seemed happy. "You will be back," Gamal said to me as we loaded my two battered suitcases into the trunk of his Peugeot. "Anyone who has drunk the waters of the Nile returns to Egypt. It happens to everyone, you know." I said I knew.

It was the holy month of Ramadan and the streets were quiet. Almost everyone was inside, waiting to break the daily fast as soon as the muftis declared that the first trace of the moon had been sighted. The drive to the airport is usually a nightmarish journey in honking bumper-to-bumper traffic, but on this day it took no time at all. Gamal pulled up to the curb at the international terminal. I had made this trip so many times before, always headed out onto the road for two or three weeks, always knowing that at the end of the journey I would be coming home to Cairo. The fact that I now had only a one-way ticket in my jacket pocket somehow disoriented me, as though I had been uprooted and cast adrift.

Gamal usually shook my hand good-bye when I left for a trip. This time he put his arms around me and kissed me on both cheeks. It was an Arab embrace that can mean either hello or farewell. "*Salaam aleikum,*" he said. Go in peace.

I picked up my two bags and headed toward the terminal. I had intended to pause by the open doors to wave good-bye, but I never did. The suitcases were too heavy to set down and then to pick up again and balance. So I walked straight into the terminal without looking back.

A STATISTICAL PROFILE

COUNTRY	CAPITAL	LAST COLONIAL POWER	INDEPENDENCE	POPULATION MILLIONS	PER CAPITA INCOME $	$$$ EARNER	PEOPLE PER SQ. MI.	LITERACY RATE %
Afghanistan	Kabul	–	–	25.9	800	agriculture	104	32
Algeria	Algiers	France	1962	31.1	1,550	oil	34	62
Bahrain	Manama	Britain	1971	0.6	13,100	oil	3	85
Egypt	Cairo	Britain	1922	68.4	1,290	exported labor	177	51
Iran	Tehran	–	–	65.6	1,650	oil	103	79
Iraq	Baghdad	Britain	1948	22.6	1,200	oil	134	58
Israel	Tel Aviv	–	1948	5.8	16,180	aid/industry	730	96
Jordan	Amman	Britain	1946	5.0	3,500	agriculture	145	87
Kuwait	Kuwait	Britain	1961	2.0	22,700	oil	286	79
Lebanon	Beirut	France	1943	3.6	4,500	agriculture	895	92
Libya	Tripoli	Italy	1951	5.1	6,700	oil	8	76
Morocco	Rabat	France	1956	30.1	3,200	phosphate	175	44
Oman	Muscat	Britain	1951	2.5	7,900	oil	31	59
Qatar	Doha	Britain	1971	0.7	17,100	oil	169	79
Saudi Arabia	Riyadh	–	–	22.0	9,000	oil	29	63
Sudan	Khartoum	Britain	1956	35.0	930	cotton	36	46
Syria	Damascus	France	1946	16.3	2,500	cotton	228	79
Tunisia	Tunis	France	1956	9.6	5,200	oil	152	67
United Arab Emirates	Abu Dhabi	Britain	1971	2.4	17,400	oil	74	79
Yemen	San'a	Britain/Turkey	1967	17.5	740	coffee/cotton	86	43

ACKNOWLEDGMENTS

THERE ARE so many people to whom I owe thanks for making this book possible, but none stands higher on the list than my wife, Sandy Northrop. Her love, support and companionship were given generously from the evening we first stepped off the plane in Cairo to the day the last page of my manuscript was written in Los Angeles. Sandy traveled with me on many of my journeys. Her photographs graced my stories in the *Los Angeles Times* and her editor's pencil did wonders reworking disparate sections of the manuscript into what I hope is a comprehensible presentation. Best of all, our years in the Middle East were a time of sharing, and in the process, we learned, grew, had fun, made friends and gathered memories we will cherish for a lifetime.

I owe particular debts of gratitude to the Alicia Patterson Foundation and my editors at the *Times*. The foundation's year-long fellowship provided me with the financial resources and the time I needed to continue my research and writing after I left the Middle East. And my colleagues at the *Times*—especially William F. Thomas, the editor, and Alvin Shuster, the foreign editor—provided the opportunities and the support that kept me challenged and always on the move. The chain of command on any newspaper stretches through many levels, and none was more important to me than the dozen or so members of our foreign-desk staff in Los Angeles, whose own travels have taken them on various assignments to the far corners of the world. They are the editors who shape, focus, correct and tone the daily stories from the field, and although their names are unknown to most readers, they are the strength on which bylines are built. To each whose voice was at the end of the line when I would call from Riyadh, Casablanca, San'a or wherever, I say thank you.

Although I drew on many references during the nearly five years it took to research and write this book, the primary source of my information was simply my own eyes and ears. What is here is what I saw, what I felt or what I heard and believed to be true. Tewfic Mishlawi, a respected Middle East political analyst now on the staff of the Center for Foreign Journalists in Reston, Virginia, was kind enough to read my entire manuscript for content and accuracy. His help and suggestions were invaluable. Thank you, Tewfic; it is nice to have you safely out of Beirut at last. Others who read sections of the manuscript or who gave freely of their time and knowledge include John Rodenbeck and Ann Kerr of the American University in Cairo; Brian Jenkins, an expert on terrorism at the Rand Corporation in Santa Monica, California; Ali Darwish, an Egyptian writer; Ali Mahmoud, the Associated Press's bureau chief in Bahrain; George Irani of the University of Southern California; Ambassador Joseph V. Reed, Jr., of the U.S. Mission to the United Nations; Dr. Omar Alfi, former director of the Islamic Center in Los Angeles; Dr. Hassan Hathout of the University of Kuwait; and Ishan Hijazi of Beirut, publisher of the *Middle East Reporter*, whose encyclopedic knowledge of the region has been a treasure shared by journalists, diplomats and authors for more than a decade.

I am also indebted to my colleagues at the *Los Angeles Times* whose Middle East coverage, past and present, provided great help in my research: Norman Kempster and Dan Fisher in Jerusalem; the late Joe Alex Morris, Doyle McManus, J. Michael Kennedy and Charles Wallace in Beirut; and Don Schanche and Michael Ross in Cairo.

Mike Kennedy, the *Times*'s Beirut bureau chief during the 1982 war, was among those I will long remember, for no two journalists ever got along better as a team than he and I during that scary summer. Somehow the war never sapped his courage or his sense of humor, and Mike and his wife, Becky Trounson, provided a constant source of support and inspiration. I will also hold dear the friendships made with journalists from other papers who covered the same terrain as I. Our profession told us we were competitors, but our instincts made us comrades first and foremost, sharing information and adventures, asking for nothing in return except the knowledge that a hand would be extended in time of need.

Finally, thanks to my friend Kent Gibson of Los Angeles, who helped me overcome the mysteries of the computer age and guided me through the transition from typewriter to word processor; to my editor at Random House, Peter Osnos, whose own extensive experience as a foreign correspondent made my task so much easier; to my agent, Carl D. Brandt, who shepherded this project from start to finish; to Bryce Nelson, director of the School of Journalism at the University of Southern California, who opened the doors of academia to me during the year it took to write The Arabs.

And to the countless people who offered hospitality and enlightenment in the Arab world and Israel, I would also like to say thank you. I hope one day we all will take the time to get to know one another better.

Arab American Almanac. 3rd ed. Edited by Joseph R. Haiek. Glendale, Calif.: News Circle Publishing Co., 1984.

Aramco and Its World. Edited by Ismail I. Nawwab, Peter C. Speer, and Paul Hoye. Washington, D.C.: Arabian American Oil Co., 1980.

Barakat, Halim. *Lebanon in Strife.* Austin: University of Texas Press, 1977.

Bianco, Mirella. *Gadafi, Voice from the Desert.* London: Longman Group, Ltd., 1975.

Cairo, A Practical Guide. 4th ed. Edited by Deborah Cowley and Aleya Serour, revised by Arunkumar Pabari. Cairo: American University in Cairo Press, 1983.

Collins, Larry, and Lapierre, Dominique. *O Jerusalem!* New York: Simon & Schuster, 1972.

Ernie's War: The Best of Ernie Pyle's World War II Dispatches. Edited by David Nichols. New York: Random House, 1986.

Fahmy, Ismail. *Negotiating for Peace in the Middle East.* Cairo: American University in Cairo Press, 1983.

First, Ruth. *Libya.* Middlesex: Penguin Books, 1974.

Fodor's North Africa. New York: Fodor's Modern Guides, 1981.

Forbis, William H. *Fall of the Peacock Throne: The Story of Iran.* New York: Harper & Row, 1980.

Goldschmidt, Arthur, Jr. *A Concise History of the Middle East.* Boulder, Colo.: Westview Press, 1983.

Gordon, David C. *The Republic of Lebanon, Nation in Jeopardy.* Boulder, Colo.: Westview Press, 1983.

The Government and Politics of the Middle East and North Africa. Edited by David E. Long and Bernard Reich. Boulder, Colo.: Westview Press, 1980.

Graham, Robert. *Iran, the Illusion of Power.* London: Croom Helm, 1978.

Guerrillas for Palestine. Edited by Riad N. el Rayyes and Dunia Nahas. Beirut: An-Nahar Press, 1974.

Gunther, John. *Inside Asia.* New York: Harper & Brothers, 1939.

Heikal, Mohamed. *Nasser, The Cairo Documents.* London: New English Library, 1972.

Herzog, Chaim. *The Arab-Israeli Wars.* New York: Random House, 1982.

Hirst, David, and Beeson, Irene. *Sadat.* London: Faber & Faber, 1981.

Kamil, Jill. *The Ancient Egyptians.* Cairo: American University Press in Cairo, 1984.

——. *Upper Egypt, Historical Guide and Descriptive Guide to the Ancient Sites.* London: Longman Group Ltd., 1983.

Keirnan, Thomas. *The Arabs, Their History, Aims and Challenge to the Industrialized World.* London: Abacus, 1978.

Khalidi, Rashid. *Under Siege: P.L.O. Decisionmaking during the 1982 War.* New York: Columbia Press, 1985.

Koran, The. Translation by Henry Mercier. London: Luzac & Co., 1975.

Lamb, David. *The Africans.* New York: Random House, 1982.

Lane, Edward William. *Manners and Customs of the Modern Egyptians.* London: East-West Publications, 1978. (First published in 1836.)

Lippman, Thomas W. *Understanding Islam.* New York: New American Library, 1982.

Majid, Khadduri. *Arab Personalities in Politics.* Washington, D.C.: Middle East Institute, 1981.

Matar, Fuad. *Saddam Hussein, the Man, the Cause and the Future.* London: Third World Center for Research and Publishing, 1981.

The Military Balance, 1984–85. London: International Institute for Strategic Studies, 1984.

Moorehead, Alan. *The Blue Nile.* London: New English Library, 1962.

——. *The White Nile.* New York: Dell Publishing Co., 1960.

Mortimer, Edward. *Faith and Power, the Politics of Islam.* New York: Vintage Books, 1982.

Naipaul, V.S. *Among the Believers.* Middlesex: Penguin Books, 1981.

Neff, Donald. *Warriors at Suez.* New York: Linden Press, 1981.

——. *Warriors for Jerusalem.* New York: Linden Press, 1984.

Political Elites and Political Development in the Middle East. Edited by Frank Tachau. Cambridge: Scheukman Publishing Co., 1975.

Political Handbook of the World, 1984–85. Edited by Arthur S. Banks. Binghamton, N.Y.: CSA Publications, 1985.

Polk, William R. *The Arab World.* Cambridge, Mass.: Harvard University Press, 1980.

Qadafi, Muammar. *The Green Book.* Tripoli: Ministry of Guidance, 1979.

Quandt, William B. *Decade of Decisions.* Los Angeles: University of California Press, 1977.

———. *Saudi Arabia in the 1980s.* Washington, D.C.: Brookings Institution, 1981.

Raban, Jonathan. *Arabia, A Journey Through the Labyrinth.* New York: Simon & Schuster, 1979.

Randal, Jonathan C. *Going All the Way.* New York: Vintage Books, 1982.

Roberts, D. S. *Islam, A Westerner's Guide.* Middlesex: Hamlyn Paperbacks, 1981.

Rugh, William A. *The Arab Press.* Syracuse, N.Y.: Syracuse University Press, 1979.

Sachar, Howard M. *A History of Israel.* New York: Alfred A. Knopf, 1981.

Sadat, Anwar al-. *In Search of Identity.* New York: Harper & Row, 1977.

Salibi, Kamal S. *Cross Roads to Civil War, Lebanon 1958–1976.* New York: Caravan, 1976.

Shaheen, Jack G. *The TV Arab.* Bowling Green, Ohio: Bowling Green State University Popular Press, 1984.

Showker, Kay. *Fodor's Egypt 1984.* London: Hodder and Stoughton, 1983.

Thomas, Lowell. *With Lawrence in Arabia,* Garden City, N.Y.: Garden City Publishing Co., 1924.

Walz, Jay. *The Middle East.* New York: New York Times Co., 1971.

Wright, Robin. *Sacred Rage.* New York: Linden Press, 1985.

Wynn, Wilton. *Nasser of Egypt: The Search for Dignity.* Cambridge: Arlington Books, 1959.